New Perspectives
on Jacksonian
Parties and Politics

EDWARD PESSEN

Professor of History,
Staten Island Community College
of the City University of New York
ALSO *Professor of History,*
Doctoral Faculty in History,
Graduate Center of the City
University of New York

New Perspectives on Jacksonian Parties and Politics

ALLYN AND BACON, Inc.   Boston

*TO THE MEMORY
OF MY MOTHER
AND FATHER*

Contents
〰〰〰〰〰〰〰

INTRODUCTION

Part I   The New Politics of the Jacksonian Era

Richard P. McCormick   THE NEW STRUCTURE OF POLITICS   11

Robert V. Remini   THE TRIUMPH OF THE POLITICIAN   21

Lynn L. Marshall   OPPOSING DEMOCRATIC AND WHIG
CONCEPTS OF PARTY ORGANIZATION   38

Part II   The Major Parties

Lee Benson   WHO LED THE DEMOCRATS AND THE WHIGS?   69

Frank Otto Gatell   THE ANTI-JACKSONIAN ANIMUS OF
RICH MEN   91

Charles G. Sellers, Jr.   WHO WERE THE SOUTHERN WHIGS?   109

Grady McWhiney   THE SIMILAR CLASS STATUS OF ALABAMA'S
PARTY LEADERS   124

Glyndon G. Van Deusen   MAJOR PARTY THOUGHT AND
THEORY   138

Major L. Wilson   DISSIMILARITIES IN MAJOR PARTY
THOUGHT   159

Part III   . . . and the Minor

Edward Pessen   THE WORKING MEN'S PARTY REVISITED   191

Carl N. Degler   THE LESS THAN RADICAL LOCOFOCOS   216

Part IV   Party Contests and Issues

Sidney H. Aronson   JACKSON'S POLITICAL APPOINTMENTS   233

Mary E. Young   INDIAN REMOVAL AND JACKSONIAN JUSTICE   240

Jean Alexander Wilburn   BIDDLE'S NOT SO UNPOPULAR BANK   258

Richard H. Brown   THE JACKSONIAN PRO-SLAVERY PARTY   272

A BIBLIOGRAPHICAL NOTE   290

*New Perspectives
on Jacksonian
Parties and Politics*

Introduction

THE JACKSONIAN ERA has long been known as the age of the common man. When candidates for office invoke the name and reputation of the seventh president, as they regularly do, they indicate that—both to them and their constituents—Andrew Jackson continues to be regarded as the leader of the political movement that brought democracy to this country.

According to popular belief, his Democratic party was the party of commoners and the poor while the National Republican and Whig parties—the main political rivals of the Jacksonian Democrats—were the parties of wealth and privilege. The victory of the Jacksonians was allegedly made possible by a democratic revolution in American politics that, among other things, gave the vote to the common man and replaced the oligarchic caucus with the democratically elected nominating convention. Tom, Dick and Harry, once enthroned, proceeded to reward their stalwart champion. And once in power, Old Hickory and his party demonstrated their affinity for the masses by waging bitter political warfare against the forces of conservatism.

In what I shall call the "traditional view," Jackson's war on Nicholas Biddle's second Bank of the United States was a struggle against a hated financial monopoly. Even some of the unlovelier aspects of the Old General's administration were regarded as evidence of Jacksonian Democracy's common touch. Thus reliance on the "Kitchen Cabinet" showed a preference for plebeian over aristocratic types. The "Spoils System" may have turned office over to political hacks, but since the Democratic party faithful were supposedly men of humble station, it seemed clear that the controversy

1

over Jackson's appointments was largely due to the fury of the elite at their displacement by commoners.

Every student of the Jacksonian era knows that most of these notions are no longer tenable. Scholars of varied persuasion have recently produced either new data or new interpretations that leave the traditional version of Jacksonian politics in tatters. But old ideas die hard. A rule of "scholarly lag" assures that obsolete views will continue to command wide acceptance decades after they have been demolished by scholarship. Men do not like to give up comfortable beliefs. And how many people read scholarly works as they roll off the university presses or are published in academic journals?

Not that the traditional view has been totally deserted. For Jacksonian as for other historical topics, disagreement among the scholarly authorities happily continues to be the rule. Revisionism or iconoclasm in turn inspire defense and restatement of conventional views. For all the sophistication of his approach, Lynn L. Marshall finds the men of the Jacksonian party more common than their opponents. Charles G. Sellers places Southern Whigs in a different economic location than did Ulrich B. Phillips and Arthur C. Cole a half century ago, when they formulated what was to become the *orthodox* view. Yet Sellers' Whigs continue to be men of inordinate wealth, most unlike the yeomen who comprised the rank and file of the Democracy in the South. Frank Otto Gatell suggests that rich men overwhelmingly opposed the Jacksonians after all. Major L. Wilson discerns a clear difference between the major parties in their views of time and space.

Clearly, modern scholars, like their predecessors, find important distinctions between the Democrats and their opponents. Yet even in substantiating the belief that the major parties differed, contemporary historians manifest the unique traits of their era. They ask new questions and rely on new methods in searching for answers. Gone is the former preoccupation with socioeconomic factors, as well as the old assumption that Whigs and Jacksonians were clearly identified with opposing class interests. A new intellectual atmosphere is demonstrated as conclusively by the recent works that agree with Arthur M. Schlesinger, Jr.'s *The Age of Jackson* as by those that refute it.

Schlesinger's *tour de force*, published in 1945, was by far the most influential statement of the traditional view. In addition to its literary flair, it drew attention to the role of urban elements in the Jacksonian coalition and of ideological radicals in formulating the Democratic program. The conflicts it dramatized were not so much between geographical sections as they were between haves and have nots. It depicted Andrew Jackson as the charismatic hero of a popular struggle for human rights against property rights. It found amazing similarities between the Jacksonian Democracy and the New Deal.

According to Schlesinger, both movements combined high idealism, dedication to social justice, political knowhow and a pragmatism that earned them the enmity of big property, on the right, and doctrinaire ideologues, on the left. It is a high tribute indeed to a work by a young scholar not yet thirty to note that the modern Jacksonian controversy was initiated by it and has centered primarily on the questions Schlesinger raised.

In an age of relativism, which cheerfully admits that all interpretations are both subjective and ephemeral, attributing *influence* to a book may appear to be the highest praise that one can bestow on it. For to call it right or to agree with its judgments is only to reveal sympathy for its biases. Work done a quarter of a century ago is passé only in that it reflects, unavoidably, the interests and mood of a forever bygone time. It is superseded not because it is wrong but because it is old. The frame of reference which inspired and guided it has been replaced by a new one, which in its turn will give way to a yet different frame of reference at some future date, certain itself to evoke still newer—and possibly a return to older—historical interpretations.

There is no doubt that many of the modern refutations of *The Age of Jackson* were motivated by their authors' subjective distaste for Schlesinger's assumptions and his political philosophy. What has been called our own age of consensus no doubt explains to a large extent the tendency of some contemporary historians to blur the distinctions between the parties of the Jackson era, to devalue the radical rhetoric spoken by Democratic leaders, to mute the clamor of conflicting interests. A bland age may be said to produce a bland historiography.

And yet after we pay our respects to the undoubted influence the intellectual atmosphere of a given era has on its thought, the fact remains that historical judgments or interpretations must be evaluated on their intrinsic merits. Granted that no interpretation can be definitive; it can nevertheless be tested for its good sense, and above all for the quality of the evidence on which it rests. It appears to me that a number of the refutations of the traditional picture of Jacksonian parties and politics are not simply *au courant* but superior. They are based on massive research that is quantitatively more impressive and qualitatively more sophisticated than the accounts they set aside. Let any student compare the varied criteria closely examined by Lee Benson recently with the simplistic methodology employed a half-century ago by Dixon Ryan Fox [*Decline of Aristocracy in the Politics of New York, 1801-1840*, New York, 1918] in their studies of New York State voting behavior during that era. A similar gulf separates the performance of Sidney H. Aronson, painstakingly researching the social status and origins of Jacksonian civil service appointees, from earlier commentators whose impressionistic conclusions owed more to intuition than to research.

One of the least controversial findings of modern scholarship is the amazing complexity of life it discloses. Human affairs partake of this complexity. Not the least of the distinctions of the modern scholarship on Jacksonian politics is precisely the greater complexity revealed in its version of the era. It may be that scholars who deal in nuances and subtle shadings do so for emotional reasons of their own. But it would hardly matter. The scholarship of different eras is best compared not in terms of the psyches or inner motives of its practitioners but in terms of the relative quality of their work and their conclusions.

When judged by the latter standard much of the modern work is impressive indeed. Richard P. McCormick's *The Second American Party System: Party Formation in the Jacksonian Era*, itself drawing from dozens of studies of state politics, demonstrates that the democratization of the nation's political machinery early in the era in fact created new forms of politics that were as easily dominated by small cliques as were the less democratic devices they replaced. He shows that, on the state level throughout the nation, new parties were fashioned in the Jackson era not by idealists seeking the realization of their social or political dreams but by astute opportunists seeking influence and power. Robert V. Remini's account of the almost sordid realism of the men who created the national Jacksonian organization is all the more convincing in view of its author's sympathy for much of the Schlesinger thesis.

The many modern studies of Whigs and Democrats on the state as well as on the national level cast grave doubt on the traditional accounts of parties. Of course contemporary historians are in disagreement, but the burden of their argument is clear. The national Jacksonian party leaned toward laissez faire and a strong executive, the Whigs toward legislative dominance and relatively vigorous government. The major parties also differed in their styles of oratory and campaigning. Democratic spokesmen, more effectively than their opponents, professed their own humble origins and their love of the people, and proved far more adept in the art of building the strong party structure necessary to assure successful campaigns. In many states the Democratic constituency seemed particularly fond of strong liquor, a craving that Jacksonian party managers spent lavishly to satisfy.

A few studies have disclosed marked differences between the voters attracted by the great parties, but the dissimilarities have little in common with those emphasized in the older view. Instead of being determined by class and wealth, the party preferences of voters seemed to relate more to their religious denominations, ethnic identification, place of birth or general life style. At least this is what Lee Benson found in New York and his able student, Ronald P. Formisano, found in Michigan ["The Social Bases of American Voting Behavior, Wayne County, Michigan, 1837-1852, As a Test Case," Wayne State University Doctoral Dissertation, 1966]. In Kentucky footloose persons evidently were drawn to the Democracy, although in Michigan they voted Whig. Detailed suffrage studies disclose that when the electorate is examined in terms of its wealth or socioeconomic status, the loyalties of the poor and the middling groups in American life were more or less equally divided among Whigs and Democrats. American voters, as McCormick has established for New York and North Carolina, did not vote by class.

On the other hand, the wealthy seem to have been heavily anti-Democratic. In Gatell's phrase, the rich men of New York City thought that the "Whig Party ... better served their interests and better calmed their fears than did the Democracy." Of course the overwhelming preference of rich men for the one party, even if proven true outside New York, would hardly make Jacobins of the other party. As Glyndon G. Van Deusen reminds us, not only were Whigs and Democrats more alike than unlike in their fundamental convictions about society, but many contemporaries—including leaders of the two parties—were aware of that fact. Certainly the thousands of leaders of the two major parties were of roughly equal social and economic status, unusually successful men of affairs, whether in New York, New Jersey, Pennsylvania, Michigan, Tennessee, Mississippi, Florida or Alabama.

In view of the unrelenting realism and opportunism of leaders of both parties in most of the states, it is hard to disagree with Van Deusen that "the political conflicts of the Jacksonian period were fought more often with a view to gaining control of the government than out of devotion to diametrically opposed political and social ideals." Such third parties as the Antimasons [early in their career], the Working Men and the Liberty party were the closest thing to ideological parties during the era, focusing on principles above vote-getting. That they achieved little electoral success testified both to the unideological bent of American voters and to the astuteness of Jacksonians and Whigs alike in understanding this central truth of American politics.

Jacksonians, of course, strained to give the impression that their stand on the great national issues was somehow inimical to the interests of great wealth. That they sometimes succeeded in fixing this impression proves not that they meant what they said so much as it suggests the power of demagogy to sway voters. It also points up the lack of astuteness of Whig propagandists who, in branding the Jacksonians as "revolutionists," strengthened the popular belief in Democratic radicalism. The fairminded Mr. Gatell is among those scholars who have shown that wealthy Democratic bankers were delighted at Jackson's war on "Biddle's Bank," not least because of the speculative opportunities that opened up for the state "pet banks" that replaced the BUS as repository of federal funds. It is very hard to detect radicalism or sympathy for have nots in Jacksonian Indian policy, pro-slavery, expansionism and foreign policy. That bluster in international discourse may have been out of keeping with the traditional norms is no sign of either egalitarianism or opposition to "aristocracy."

＊   ＊   ＊   ＊   ＊

A brilliant Jacksonian scholar has asked me whether, in view of the flux in Jackson historiography, the time is ripe for a balanced statement. If American historians retain their iconoclasm—and there are no signs that they will not—flux is likely to remain the situation for the foreseeable future. For even if the majority of experts agree that a new scholarly consensus has been reached, some ornery revisionist is certain to argue that it should be overturned. If he does not appear, then we will have real cause for concern.

The essays that follow are only a small fragment of the recent volume of excellent studies on the parties and politics of the Jackson era. They illustrate the tenor and some of the leading themes in the recent discussion. They offer the reader an opportunity to bridge the gulf between outmoded ideas and contemporary scholarship.

Considerations of space have made it impossible to touch on all important aspects of the topic. Footnotes have been included for the most part, despite the problem of space. Some of the authors have insisted—quite rightly—that this be done. The worth of a number of the essays depends heavily on the research underlying them; the notes, without interfering with narrative continuity, indicate the nature of the research. It is also useful, in my judgment, for the student reader to see the work in its original form. Insights and brilliant intuitive stabs are vital to scholarship. But the hard work of digging out the data remains indispensable.

PART I

THE NEW POLITICS OF THE JACKSONIAN ERA

RICHARD P. McCORMICK*

The New Structure of Politics

A new two-party system emerged in the United States during the Jacksonian era. McCormick demonstrates the interrelationship between the character and style of the great new political organizations and the changes that were democratizing the machinery of American politics. In McCormick's assessment, neither the more democratic method of nominating candidates nor the new popular tone of campaigning detracted from the control of politics by small cliques. Rival politicos were organized in opposing parties for reasons that had little to do with principle. Instead, "between 1824 and 1840, the 'presidential question,' rather than doctrinal disputes was the axis around which politics revolved." Elsewhere Professor McCormick has shown that voters did not vote by social and economic class. Here he indicates that the major parties and their leaders were not divided by ideological factors.

XXXXXXXXXXXXXXXXXXXXXXXXXXXXXXXXXXXXXXXXXXXXXXXXXXXXXXXXX

EARLY IN THE nineteenth century . . . there had been a great diversity of political practices. The manner in which variety gave way to uniformity can best be studied in terms of the devices

* From Richard P. McCormick, *The Second American Party System: Party Formation in the Jacksonian Era* (Chapel Hill: University of North Carolina Press, 1966), pp. 346-356.

11

employed, particularly at the state level, for making nominations and directing party affairs.

There were, before 1824, three generalized types of political management. In two states, New Jersey and Delaware, the delegate-convention system was firmly established. In most of the other states where the first party system had at one time flourished, the legislative caucus, or some variety of mixed legislative caucus, was used to make state-wide nominations and manage party matters. In New England and the Middle States conventions were commonly employed to make nominations for other than state-wide offices. In some of the southern states and in the newer states of the West the functions performed elsewhere by conventions or caucuses were often handled by informal, self-constituted juntos, made up of men possessed of considerable influence. In those states where at particular times there was no evident management of politics in a formal sense, there might be self-nominated candidates and individual leaders who could command wide allegiance.

The adoption of the convention system proceeded gradually from region to region. After 1824 the state convention was an established feature of party organization in the Middle States, except in Maryland, where it first appeared in 1827. It was generally adopted in New England between 1828 and 1832, although it did not entirely replace the mixed caucus in Massachusetts and New Hampshire until much later. Rhode Island, of course, had its own peculiar mixed conventions. The state convention was slow in winning acceptance in the South. It was introduced into Kentucky in 1827, but elsewhere it was rarely employed before 1839. Although there were numerous conventions in Virginia after 1828, the Democrats continued to rely on a mixed caucus-convention even after 1840. Practices varied widely in the West. There were conventions in Indiana as early as 1824, and in Ohio, Mississippi, Louisiana, and Missouri by 1828, but they did not become regular features of party machinery generally until 1835 or later.

No adequate study has been made of the transition from the caucus to the convention. To the degree that the caucus represented an interior type of control, much might be made of the significance of the change. At the very least, the shift implies a considerable loss in the political authority of the legislatures. Whether it also implies the "democratization" of the parties is open to serious question.

The immediate reason for the substitution of the state convention for the legislative caucus in most states was a highly practical one. Where old party lines were blurred or violently shattered by the circumstances associated with the contests for the presidency, the old caucus arrangements broke down, both in Congress and in the states. Conditions varied from state to state. In New England, for example, where the Jacksonians initially had few representatives in the legislature, they turned to the convention as the only device that could give some kind of sanction to their nominations. In some states the Antimasons successfully adopted the convention for similar reasons. The convention also proved to be a convenient device for the "People's party" in New York in 1824, and for the Pennsylvania factions that endorsed Jackson in the same year. When the device had been adopted by one party, the opposing party—or parties— usually felt obliged to follow suit, for there was no doubt that the convention had the appearance of being more "open," and more "popular," than the caucus.

Having first demonstrated its efficacy in most of the northeastern states, the convention was widely copied elsewhere. Its sudden, full-blown emergence in Kentucky in 1827 suggests that some careful study had been made of the eastern models. In Illinois it seems quite clear that Stephen A. Douglas zealously promoted the convention system, presumably drawing upon his knowledge of party machinery in New York. No particular party can be credited with special partiality for the convention. The Jacksonians and the Antimasons were the chief innovators in New England, but in the South it was often the Whigs who displayed the greater initiative.

Where the caucus system had long held sway, the convention was generally hailed as a desirable alternative. But in those states where party organization of any kind had been lacking, there was frequently resistance to its introduction. To use Kentucky again as an example, both parties there in 1827 felt it necessary to justify their plans to hold conventions on the grounds that the opposition was engaged in similar projects. In Mississippi the Whigs denounced the Democrats for using the convention to "dictate" nominations. Especially notable was the controversy in Illinois, where the convention system met stubborn resistance from a segment of the Democratic party as well as from the Whigs. Despite these instances of hostility, the convention had become by 1840 the standard device for making party decisions.

In addition to the immediate circumstances that prompted the change from the caucus to the convention, there were other considerations involved. The caucus system had long been the object of popular suspicion in many states, and the operations of the Republican congressional caucus in 1816, as well as in 1824, had further weakened respect for the device. Perhaps the curtailment of the elective functions of the legislature—evidenced by the trend toward the popular choice of electors, governors, and other state officials—reflected a general loss of confidence in that branch of government, which found expression in attacks on the caucus.

The fact that delegate conventions had long been in operation at the levels of the county, senatorial district, or congressional district in several states where the caucus was also established meant that opponents of the caucus did not have to look far for an alternative. Certainly improvements in transportation facilities removed one of the major obstacles to the holding of conventions, especially in the larger states. Once the convention had acquired popularity in the eastern states, and especially after it had come into use for national nominations in 1832, its general acceptance was facilitated.

Probably the strongest argument in favor of the convention system was that it provided a means whereby party members, through elected delegates, could participate in the direction of party affairs at all levels. It was this consideration that gave such an authoritative sanction to convention nominations and thereby strengthened party discipline. But a full investigation might disclose that the conventions did not have precisely the functions that they appeared to have. Ostensibly they were decision-making bodies. In actuality they seem to have had a cosmetic function. That is, they gave the appearance of representing party sentiment whereas in fact they usually did little more than follow the dictates of party leaders. Made up in large measure of office-holders and party activists, they were readily susceptible to manipulation and control.

The convention system can also be viewed as the most conspicuous feature of the highly elaborated organization developed by parties in this era. Political tasks that had previously been carried out informally or by small, semi-secret committees now seemingly necessitated the involvement of enormous numbers of party activists. In addition to nominating conventions in all electoral units, there were central committees, poll committees, and various auxiliary organizations. Given the inordinately complicated nature of the American system of elections, it became evident that if politics was to be conducted on a party basis, an extraordinary amount of manpower was required. As competitive parties formed from state to state, therefore, the same process of elaboration of party organization took place. In general, parties in the Middle States were the most highly organized of all, with the lower South at the other extreme.

The second American party system also brought into vogue a new campaign style. Its ingredients can scarcely be described with precision, but they included an emphasis on dramatic spectacles— such as the mass rally, the procession, and the employment of banners, emblems, songs, and theatrical devices—and on club-like associations, colorful personalities, and emotionally charged appeals to party loyalty. Politics in this era took on a dramatic function. It enabled voters throughout the nation to experience the thrill of participating in what amounted to a great democratic festival that seemed to perceptive foreign observers to be remarkably akin to the religious festivals of Catholic Europe.

In their exciting election campaigns, the Americans of that generation found a satisfying form of cultural expression. Perhaps because there were so few emotional outlets available to them of equal effectiveness, they gave themselves up enthusiastically to the vast drama of the election contest. They eagerly assumed the identity of partisans, perhaps for much the same reason that their descendants were to become Dodger fans, Shriners, or rock-and-roll addicts. In this guise, at least, campaigns had little to do with government or public policy, or even with the choice of officials. For the party leaders, of course, the purpose of the campaign was to stimulate the faithful and, if possible, convert the wayward in order to produce victory at the polls.

The dramatic quality of the campaigns together with the intense efforts put forth by the elaborate party apparatus and the close balance of the parties produced measurable results in terms of increased voter participation. It is true that under the "old style" politics, in states as various as New Hampshire, Delaware, and Tennessee, as many as 80 per cent of the eligible voters had participated in elections. But in most states this high level was rarely approached, and presidential elections attracted relatively small turnouts.

The revival of the contest for the presidency did not have the immediate effect of stimulating maximum voter participation. In terms of national averages, only about a quarter of the eligibles voted in 1824, and in the three succeeding elections somewhat more than half went to the polls. Much more significant than the national average, however, are the rates of participation for particular states and regions. These reveal an obvious correlation between the degree of voter participation and the closeness of the party contest.

In general, those states where parties were most evenly balanced achieved the highest voter turnout. The most spectacular increases in voter participation in 1828, for example, occurred in Maine, New Hampshire, the Middle States, Kentucky, and Ohio. These were all states in which competitive parties had been formed to contest the election. Voter participation soared remarkably between 1832 and 1836 in states like Georgia, Tennessee, Alabama, and Mississippi for similar reasons. By 1840, when party formation had taken place in every state and when the two national parties were fully mobilized to engage in a spectacular campaign, voter participation surged upwards to new levels in every state. Throughout the nation nearly four-fifths of the eligibles voted.

There were some interesting regional differences in voter participation. The New England states tended consistently to rank well below the national averages, especially after 1840. Moreover, it was common in that region for voter participation to be somewhat higher in state elections than in presidential elections, except in Connecticut. In the new states of the West, on the other hand, participation was higher in presidential elections than in state elections, except in Missouri and Mississippi. It is difficult to single out any one region as leading the way in voter participation, so high was the general level of voting outside of New England, but in the 1840's the three states with the most impressive records were Georgia, Mississippi, and Tennessee. Whether the election returns may be accepted as accurate measurements of voter participation is, of course, open to some question, for there was undoubtedly considerable fraud in many states.

Among the influences that shaped the second party system, none is more difficult to evaluate than leadership. Parties did not "emerge," neither did they "form," rather, they were formed by astute and energetic politicians. When the process of party formation is examined from state to state, it can be seen that at some appropriate opportunity rival leaders, or groups of leaders, took the initiative in creating parties.

It is, then, to men like Isaac Hill of New Hampshire, J. M. Niles of Connecticut, Thurlow Weed of New York, John M. Clayton of Delaware, Romulus Saunders of North Carolina, John M. Berrien of Georgia, Amos Kendall of Kentucky, Moses Dawson of Ohio, and Stephen A. Douglas of Illinois, and their counterparts elsewhere, that the new party system owed its existence. It was they who marked out the lines of battle, determined the strategy, built the organizations, and directed the campaigns. Aiding them were a corps of lieutenants and a vast army of those best described as party workers, or activists. Finally, of course, there were the voters who became identified with the party and the elected and appointed officials who owed their positions to the party.

It was in the early stages of party formation that the leaders played their most conspicuous roles and registered their most impressive achievements. The suddenness with which the politics of a state could be transformed by their efforts—when the proper circumstances prevailed—was nothing less than amazing. Almost invariably it was the "presidential question" on which they first based their drive to form a party, but the parties that they formed and led were soon engaged in contesting elections at all levels of government.

A full consideration of party leadership is beyond the scope of this study, although the subject is certainly one that merits far more attention than it has received. We should know who these men were, what motivated them, how they operated, and what rewards they received. Although they had their predecessors in the era of the first party system, they were essentially a new category of men, performing highly specialized functions in a new political environment.

The second American party system must be understood in terms of the conditions that stimulated its formation. It was formed, essentially, for the purpose of contesting for the presidency. It assumed the character that it did because political leaders in every state related their actions closely to the presidential contests. Between 1824 and 1840, the "presidential question," rather than doctrinal disputes was the axis around which politics revolved.

It is paradoxical that although the parties were initially shaped by strongly sectionalized attitudes toward particular candidates, the ultimate effect of the several contests was to produce two parties that were truly national in their dimensions. In a very particular sense it could be said that the parties of the 1840's were "artificial," in that they seemingly existed in defiance of the real sectional antagonisms that were present at the time.

The relatively brief duration of this party system can be explained in terms of its "artificiality." It could survive only so long as explicitly sectional issues could be avoided. This party system could expend great energy on presidential contests, usually involving generals of more or less heroic stature, and it could engage in interminable debates on the sectionally innocuous issue of fiscal policy. But it could scarcely cope with the tariff or internal improvements issues, and, of course, it foundered completely when it could no longer ignore territorial expansion and slavery.

Matters of doctrine, as well as sectional feeling, had been extremely influential in molding the first party system, and the first parties evidenced a strong sectional bias. After the disruption of the second party system, another reorganization of parties took place. The occasion for the upheaval of the 1850's was not the "presidential question" but rather the set of issues that focused on the status of slavery in the territories but, more broadly, reflected the forces of sectionalism. The new, or third, party system was highly sectionalized, and remained so into the twentieth century.

Although it foundered disastrously, the second American party system left an impressive inheritance to succeeding political generations. The national two-party system, with its continuing great absorption in the drama of the presidential contest, had become traditional. The marvellously intricate and elaborate exterior type of party apparatus, with the delegate convention as its distinctive feature, was to survive until modified by the direct primary system. Popular-style campaign techniques, so expressive of our folk culture, have endured even into the age of Madison Avenue and television. The highly professional party manager, with his army of workers, continues to be needed to operate the exceedingly vast and complex party machinery. Perhaps the voter had changed. At least he no longer responds as loyally, or as numerously, as he once did to the call of his party.

Most of all, a new institution, with its own vested interests, had been added to the political scene. The institutionalized political party was to be not merely a "mirror" of opinion nor a "medium" through which pressures were transmitted. It was to exert its own active influence in furtherance of its own special interests. Its leaders, activists, and those who held office in its name were to act on what are termed "partisan considerations." Decisions had to be made with the welfare of the party in mind, as well as the presumed welfare of those whom the party purportedly represented. Moreover, those who identified strongly with the party were influenced in their behavior by virtue of having assumed such an identity. They were no longer free to calculate objectively their own course of political action; as identifiers they reacted as partisans.

Here, in essence, was the difference between the unstructured, individualistic politics that had prevailed in most states before 1790 and in some as late as the 1830's. Politicians formerly consulted their own individual interest, or perhaps that of the junto or faction with which they were associated. Voters, in turn, acted on the basis of personal identification with the candidates, or of attachment to locality or social group. The establishment of institutionalized political parties, however, added a new ingredient to the forces that influenced political behavior.

The mature political parties were to bulk extremely large in the American political process, perform a variety of functions, and meet a number of obvious needs. But they were incapable of performing the one function most commonly associated with the idea of party. They could not govern.

Two related obstacles prevented the parties from realizing fully their potential. One was the constitutional structure of both the federal and state governments. The other was the ambivalent attitude of the American people toward parties; they came to accept them as necessary features of the political system but at the same time remained suspicious of them as agencies of power.

The manner in which American constitutions frustrate party government needs little explanation, but it does require emphasis. If one thing is clear about the intentions of those who framed the federal Constitution, from which few state constitutions have departed, it is that they consciously sought to make it extremely difficult for any section, class, numerical majority, or party to control the government. Among the more obvious devices instituted for this purpose were the establishment of three co-ordinate branches of government; the election of the two houses of the federal Congress by different constituencies and for different terms; the election of a president by indirect means for a term different from that of either body of Congress; and the division of sovereign powers between the states and the federal government.

It could be argued that after 1790 numerous detailed constitutional changes and revisions of election procedures diminished the possibilities of party government. The popular election of presidential electors, United States senators, and governors; the election of congressmen from districts, rather than from the state at large; the general extension of the principle of popular election of officials at all levels; and the direct primary system have all had the effect of adding to the frustrations of parties. They have greatly complicated the electoral tasks undertaken by parties and have resulted in the fragmentation of political authority.

The point is not that these constitutional impediments to party government were unwise or that party government is an ideal to be sought at any cost. It is, rather, that the functions performed by

American political parties must be studied and appraised in the light of the constitutional environment in which they must operate. It would be fallacious to assume that the only function of parties was that of providing a government or an opposition to the government. American parties have flourished because they have had other functions.

ROBERT V. REMINI*

The Triumph of the Politician

Robert V. Remini is a close student of Andrew Jackson and his party who very much admires Old Hickory's contributions to statecraft. As the following selection from Remini's study of the election of 1828 indicates, he is a critical scholar who is well aware of the part played by pragmatic and realistic considerations in the success enjoyed by Jacksonian Democracy.

⚙⚙⚙

THERE WAS ALSO a touch of craft and guile in the old General. No sooner did Calhoun and Van Buren draw close to him than Jackson began repeating that he was much too old and ill to serve *two* terms as President. (He was sixty in 1827, the same age as John Quincy Adams.) Four years as chief executive was all he wanted; then he would turn the reins of government over to younger men. His protestations of feebleness had Calhoun quivering with anticipation, to say nothing of Martin Van Buren. Perhaps the Hero meant what he said; but whether he did or not, his words were perfectly cal-

---

* From "Structuring a National Party" of *The Election of Andrew Jackson* by Robert V. Remini. Copyright © 1963 by Robert V. Remini. Published by J. B. Lippincott Company. Reprinted without footnotes by permission of the author.

21

culated to swell the loyalties of several important and ambitious men in Washington.

Jackson always insisted that he would not electioneer for the presidency, but every letter he wrote, every delegation of visitors he entertained at the Hermitage, every politician he sent off on an assignment in different sections of the nation, was part of a careful campaign to wrest the presidency from John Quincy Adams. His trip to New Orleans in January 1828 to celebrate his victory over the British was electioneering in the grand manner. Ostensibly non-partisan, the celebration happily combined national pride in a great historical event with the political ambitions of the man who was responsible for that event.

Around this popular and politically wise old gentleman other men were now constructing a new national party; yet as long as he lived Andrew Jackson remained its head and vital force.

IV

As Van Buren had promised earlier, once re-elected to the Senate in February 1827 he really got down to the work of forging a "new political combination." Characteristically, he began his task by calling a series of conferences among Jacksonian Congressmen, where, according to one opposition report, "schemes [were] devised, questions debated & the minority was ruled by the majority." It was said that the conferees agreed to commence their "labors" to elect Jackson on July 4, 1827, "in every part of the Union at once." There may have been no such agreement as reported, but conferences were held and the formal canvass did begin on the assigned date. "Little squads in the North and East, West and South," in recognition of Independence Day, "made toasts of egregious length" to the election of Old Hickory and to the restoration of liberty.

Present at Van Buren's conferences were representatives from most of the large states, including Calhoun; Senators Benton, Eaton, Dickerson of New Jersey, Johnson of Kentucky, and McLane of Delaware; and Representatives Buchanan, Moore, Ingham, and Houston. Reportedly, they met several times a week, although that sounds a bit excessive even for such a caucus-minded politician as Van Buren. Whatever the frequency, the meetings were extremely fruitful in initiating plans for the "substantial reorganization of the old Republican party."

As soon as the congressional conferences were under way, new lines of communication were opened between Washington and the Nashville Central Committee, principally through the good offices of Alfred Balch. The letters that Balch received from Van Buren, Benton, and others kept the Central Committee abreast of breaking developments on Capitol Hill. Not a few times a select group of Jacksonians held private conversations in Washington to improve campaign strategy, the essentials of which were forwarded to Nashville through Balch. "I have talked with V. B. & others," read one of Benton's communiqués, "[and] they think as I do" about the Central Committee's issuing policy statements. If a "friend," he hypothesized, should ask the Committee about Jackson's views on internal improvements, that "friend" should be made to realize that "there is no necessity for any public answer." If an "enemy" should ask, and do so in such a "respectable" way as to make an answer "indispensable, we think it ought to be given rather by a *general* reference to the votes given by J ——— in the Senate than by a *particular* confession of faith." Of course, Benton, Van Buren, and the other Congressmen admitted that the public had a right to know the "political sentiments of a public man," but the "delicacy" of "declaring those sentiments on the eve of an election might be stated," advised Benton. In any event, put them off by referring them to Jackson's record in the Senate; and never forget, he concluded, that newspaper questions deserve only "newspaper answers."

In addition to these congressional conferences and caucus sessions, a Central Committee of twenty-four men was formed in Washington early in the campaign as a clearinghouse for much of the propaganda emanating from the House and the Senate. The Committee's meetings were usually held at Williamson's or Carusi's Assembly Rooms, with only eight men necessary for a quorum. The chairman was the president of the Bank of the Metropolis in Washington, General John P. Van Ness. Van Ness originally came from Van Buren's home town of Kinderhook, New York; his brother had been one of the Magician's law tutors as well as Aaron Burr's second in the duel with Alexander Hamilton; and he himself had contributed financially to Van Buren's legal training. His own family always regarded Van Ness as something of a ne'er-do-well destined for a tragic end; but he fooled them: he married a Washington fortune and returned to Kinderhook in high feather. Later, he settled in the District, built a magnificent house designed by Benjamin Latrobe, and helped in the organization of the Jackson party by backing the 3,000-dollar note for the *Telegraph* signed by Senator

Eaton. However, the most important member of this Committee was not Van Ness but General Duff Green, that rough-writing editor who stomped and bit and abused the President so fiercely. Green was ordinarily a jovial sort, a capital storyteller and a pleasant host; but, despite his many "noble qualities," especially as an editor and party organizer, he was overly vain and opinionated and later (after the election) liked to give the impression "that he is the ruler of the nation." Other members of the Committee included Thomas Corcoran, a dry-goods merchant and former mayor of Georgetown; Dr. Thomas Sim, the Committee's secretary; Richard Mason; General Steward; and Colonel Ashton. On the whole, these men performed yeoman service in keeping the state organizations stocked with propaganda pamphlets published in the capital; but their real day of glory came later, when they organized a tradition-shattering demonstration of popular enthusiasm for Jackson at the Hero's inauguration.

While Green, Van Ness, and company at times looked and acted as though they comprised a National Committee, it was really the Jacksonian Congressmen in caucus who served that function. Not only did these Congressmen work closely with the Nashville managers, but they also raised money, founded and subsidized newspapers, and distributed campaign literature under their personal frank. Most important of all, however, they forged the essential political "combinations for electing Gen. Jackson"—so said Representative John Floyd of Virginia, who participated in the forging. And, by the spring of 1827, he advised his Virginia cronies that those "combinations" were "nearly complete."

Partly by design and partly by accident, Floyd's words leaked to the Administration newspapers, and a horrendous cry went up about the "unnatural alliances" being concluded in Washington "under the standard of a new cabalistic party organization." "Combinations—and among whom?" they asked. "The People? No—but the Members of Congress." Despite the leak, Floyd neither denied nor retracted the statement attributed to him. Instead, he boasted of it. At a public dinner given in his honor at Richmond a few weeks later, he proclaimed "a great political revolution in progress" which would be consummated in the election of Andrew Jackson.

Floyd's use of the word "combination" gave the Administration newspapers a needed name for the Jackson-Calhoun-Van Buren alliance. The Adams press used it extensively during the campaign in the hope it would connote something sinister or undemocratic, but they were not too successful in this and the name never really caught on. Most often the factions allied against the Coalition were called simply "Jacksonians" or the "Opposition." Once in a while there were references to the "Democratic" Republican party as distinct from the Adams-Clay "National" Republican party. However, not until two or three years later did the designation "Democratic party" acquire universal usage. By that time it referred to the triumphant organization structured around President Andrew Jackson.

V

Now that the Adams newspapers were privy to the so-called "combinations," they demanded to know on what terms the agreement had been arranged, apparently without realizing that the sole condition required by some men was certainty over Jackson's ability to win the election. These editors jumped to the conclusion, of course, that Van Buren was the only politician slick enough to unite so many disparate groups. "The masterspirit with his magic wand," they said, "cast a spell over the heterogeneous mass, and the wolves and kids mingled together in peace and love!" But how long would this love-spell last? Can Senator Dickerson, the advocate of protection, cooperate with his Southern colleagues, asked the *National Journal?* Can John Randolph and Littleton W. Tazewell unite with the men whose opinions on improvements collide with their own? "Can the Tennessee and Kentucky and Virginia Hotspurs long coalesce with their new allies who desire to oust the present Administration because of alleged hostility to federal men and federal measures?" Surely such excellent men as McLane, Ingham, Buchanan, Houston, Drayton, and Macon, continued these editors, owed it to the public to "announce the terms and conditions of the agreement that has been made."

There were indeed many differences of opinion dividing the Jackson men, both in and out of Congress. The problem of settling on terms and conditions was complicated by the necessity of creating a national voting majority out of a patchwork of conflicting interest groups, classes, and factions. These groups ranged from farmers and mechanics to planters, businessmen, and bankers. They included Republicans and Federalists, nationalists and states' righters, conservatives and liberals. Some Jacksonians in Pennsylvania, New York, Ohio, Indiana, and Kentucky called for a protective tariff, a system of national roads and improvements, and the continued support of the Second National Bank; others, often from the same states, objected to these proposals and urged a freer capitalistic system, unhampered by governmental controls.

Undoubtedly, if these Congressmen had attempted a settlement on national issues, the alliances would have been stillborn. Because they represented a wide range of diverse interests among coalescing Jacksonians, no basic statement of purpose and direction seemed wise or feasible. Their first objective was to win the election, nothing more. What the Administration editors by their questions were really trying to do, therefore, was prove to the public that the Democrats were irresponsible opportunists bound together by little else than a will to oust Adams, even if that meant supporting an incompetent and illiterate military chieftain.

The problem of the Jacksonian Congressmen was, to a degree, solved by the General himself. When asked specifically about certain issues, he responded by following one of several alternatives: either he took Benton's advice and referred to his voting record in the Senate, or he refused a direct answer on the ground that it might be interpreted as electioneering (and no gentleman would ever electioneer for the presidency), or he wrote long, highly ambiguous replies that could be interpreted several ways, or he ignored the question and simply struck a pose as the Hero of New Orleans cheated of the presidency in 1825.

Yet for all his double talk and concern for his public image, Jackson did subscribe to a national program, one he vaguely alluded to during the campaign (very vaguely) but one he later outlined in detail to Amos Kendall, editor of the Kentucky *Argus of the West.* As he subsequently defined it, his program was neo-Jeffersonian and conservative, leaning toward states' rights and the economics of laissez-faire, but so bland and inoffensive that those previously disposed to follow him could not seriously object to a single point.

In the first place, Jackson told Kendall, he intended to reduce the patronage of the federal government. (By interpreting his words as loosely as the rules of language allow, this could mean a policy of economy, though the General did not say so specifically.) The Hero believed that Adams had used the patronage to pay off the men responsible for "stealing" the presidency in 1825, a belief documented to his entire satisfaction by the report on executive appointments submitted to the Senate by Thomas Hart Benton. Hence, Jackson saw as his first duty the wholesale removal of these Coalitionists, along with anyone else who campaigned for Adams' re-election. "All men in office," he assured Kendall, "who are known to have interfered in the election as committee men, electioneers or otherwise . . . will be unceremoniously removed. So also will all men who have been appointed from political considerations or against the will of the people, and all who are incompetent." Throughout the campaign this issue became a favorite theme with Jacksonian editors and politicians, who assured the people that the removals were necessary in order to "purify the Departments" and "reform the Government." "Let the cry be JACKSON and RE-FORM," they thundered. But obviously the word "reform" was hardly more than a euphemism for political head-chopping.

Next, Jackson informed Kendall that he favored a "middle and just course" with respect to the tariff question. As he had stated several years before in a letter to Littleton H. Coleman, he thought the rates of protection should be "judicious," a remark that prompted Henry Clay to declare his preference for an "*injudicious*" tariff. In an Albany speech Martin Van Buren seconded Jackson's position by calling for a tariff that would be "wise" and "just" and "salutary." One man in the audience cheered the speech and then turned to his neighbor and asked: "On which side of the Tariff question was it?"

Jackson may have preferred the "middle course"—wherever that was—but his friends frequently reshaped his preference to conform to local prejudice. In "protection-mad" Pennsylvania, Samuel D. Ingham assured his people that Old Hickory would "raise the tariff everytime he touched it." Yet in the South the Richmond *Enquirer* and the Raleigh *Register,* among others, expressed amazement that anyone could claim Jackson as a friend of protection. He favored a tariff, they wrote, only as a source of revenue and a means of strengthening the national defense and liquidating the national debt. Any other interpretation was unjustified. To clarify the matter the Indiana legislature pressed Jackson during the campaign for a more precise declaration, but the General refused to be drawn out. "Not, sir, that I would wish to conceal my opinions from the people upon any political, or national subject," the foxy Hero replied, "but as they were in various ways promulgated in 1824, I am apprehensive that my appearance before the public, at this time, may be attributed, as has been the case, to improper motives." The Hoosiers were delighted with his clarification and expressed their complete satisfaction with it. One report insisted that it even converted three Adams committees within the state!

The General did not double-talk all the issues, however. Regarding federally sponsored public works, he straightforwardly admitted his opposition. Then he modified his statement slightly by proposing to distribute surplus revenues to the states to permit them to undertake their own improvements. After all, the issue was important to the people of Kentucky, Ohio, Indiana, and Illinois, and it was necessary to relieve their minds about his intentions without antagonizing, at the same time, the people of New York and Virginia. Once again his attitude about the question was reshaped to accord with varying sectional opinions. In Pennsylvania, Jackson's partisans went so far as to declare that "His triumph will give expansion to the 'American System.'"

The final point in his program was the most startling of all. He actually told Kendall he was looking for "plain, business men" to assist him in running his administration. Presumably, these hard-headed realists would help restore the government to fiscal and ethical soundness. No Cabinet officer, he concluded, could be a candidate for President, and all members must concur in his "policies."

One additional policy might be added to this list, though Jackson did not include it himself. It concerned the Indians and their removal to the West, an issue that developed when Georgia renewed her efforts to despoil the Creek Nation. When President Adams negotiated a treaty with the Creeks by which the Indians were to cede their land in Georgia except for a strip west of the Chattahoochee River, Governor George M. Throup of Georgia objected. He wanted all the land. Defying both the President and the Secretary of War, he threatened to use his militia if they attempted to carry out the terms of the treaty. Adams responded to the verbal cannonade by vowing to employ "all means under his control to maintain the faith of the nation."

Jackson, whose affection for the Indian about equaled his affection for Henry Clay, unreservedly endorsed the policy of total removal. "Say to them [the Indians]," he once wrote, "their Father, the President will lay off a country of equal extent, transfer them to it . . . and give them a free [sic] simple title to the land." But, as the General's friends in Georgia understood only too well, it was less important to tell the Indians anything than it was to assure the electorate of the Hero's commitment to removal.

Meanwhile the Jacksonian-controlled Senate appointed a committee, headed by Thomas Hart Benton, to investigate the Administration's trouble with Governor Throup. As expected, Benton's final report faulted the government for its unwarranted interference in the internal affairs of Georgia and justified everything the governor had been "compelled" to do to protect the interests of his state. But long before Benton's report was published, Adams was "politically dead" in Georgia, and the stench arising from the corpse permeated the entire Southwest. In the Georgia 1828 race, both sets of electors pledged themselves to Jackson.

These policies, as Jackson liked to call them, revealed his excellence as a politician of compromise and accommodation; they explain in part why so many discordant groups could unite behind him in his campaign for the presidency, why the wolves and kids could mingle together in peace and love. For some people, of course, the issues had nothing to do with their decision to join the General's party. Far more important than a meaningless program was the energy, leadership, and exciting personality they felt Jackson could bring to the presidency—qualities that make history, not simply wait upon it. Others had an even more basic reason for supporting the Hero. He "is the man," commented one politician, "that alone can be run with success."

VI

Perhaps the single most important accomplishment of the Democrats in Congress and in the states was the creation of a vast, nation-wide newspaper system. The initiative and drive for this enterprise came from Congressmen, but the work was aided by governors, state legislators, county leaders, and politicians of every rank. Together, they strove to paper the country with enough propaganda to wrap the Coalitionists in defeat.

In one of their earliest sessions, Democratic Congressmen in caucus reportedly agreed to establish "a chain of newspaper posts, from the New England States to Louisiana, and branching off through Lexington to the Western States." While the report was exaggerated, if not invented, it is nonetheless true that an enormous number of new journals did appear in virtually every state— certainly in every section. North Carolina politicians, for instance, started nine new Jackson sheets by the summer of 1827, and in Ohio eighteen were added to the five that existed in 1824. During a single six-month period three papers were founded in Indiana and several were organized in Pennsylvania, Massachusetts, New Jersey, and Illinois. Even Mississippi came up with another organ, only to have it slip out of existence within a few weeks despite the pleas for financial help mailed to other states under the frank of Jacksonian Congressmen.

"We have at considerable expense," boasted Senator Levi Woodbury, "established another newspaper in the northern part of the state of New Hampshire. We have organized our fences in every quarter and have begun & shall continue without ceasing to pour into every doubtful region all kinds of useful information." Several other Congressmen either powered new publications into life or sustained those in danger of faltering. A Virginia Representative, for example, circulated a prospectus to party organizers in eastern Tennessee asking them to obtain subscribers for a journal in Lynchburg; at the same time Senator John Eaton poured 1,500 dollars into the tottering *Columbia Observer* in Philadelphia to keep it yapping at the President's heels. Most other Democratic Congressmen contributed or solicited funds, wrote articles under a favorite disguise, or supplied news and information to help the newspapers mount a driving campaign.

Snapping with irritation, established prints complained of the "mushroom rapidity" with which these new journals suddenly popped up, and the choking cost of maintaining them. By 1828 there were an estimated 600 newspapers in the United States, 50 of them dailies, 150 semi-weeklies, and 400 weeklies. The cost of publication for all these papers, approximating 1,000 copies of each, was placed at a half-million dollars per annum. Still they poured out. Each month a raft of publications flooded the reading market in all forms: newspapers, books, pamphlets, addresses, biographies, and throwaways. "I had a meeting of 12 or 15 friends ... at my house last night," bragged one politician to a crony in Congress, "& arrangements were made to publish and distribute extensively some of the best things that have appeared against the administration and in favour of Genl. Jackson."

The willingness of the Jacksonians to assist in the creation and distribution of these newspapers—especially the assistance they gave to journals outside their districts and states—was persuasive evidence of their concern for the national character of their party. When Duff Green admitted printing 40,000 weekly copies of the *Telegraph* (including the "Extra" that started publication on March 1, 1828), he said he relied "upon the Committees of Vigilance and Correspondence, appointed to promote the election of General Jackson ... to obtain subscribers." Isaac Hill, the short, lame, and cadaverous-looking editor of the New Hampshire *Patriot*, sent his brother into Vermont with instructions to establish a hard-hitting newspaper around which the Jackson party could rally. Impressed by the technique, John C. Calhoun asked North Carolinians for their assistance when the first Southern magazine was established in Charleston. "It would be gratifying," he wrote, ". . . to see it receive a due share of its patronage from your state, both in circulation of its contents and the contribution of its pages."

The task of filling the columns of this enormous press taxed the energies of all Jacksonians. Without the willing cooperation of party men from every section of the nation, the publication problems would have been insurmountable. In New England, for example, one Massachusetts politician sent down materials to New York with the comment, "You have the same authority with this, as with the others—change—expunge, add or withhold entirely at your discretion. I need not repeat that as to political writings I have none of the vanity of an author, and consult only the good of the cause and the party." In North Carolina a worker reported that the "Central Jackson Committee have in *press* a publication of 'Military Documents' accompanied with a pretty *spicey* introduction of 15 or 16 pages." And in Kentucky, Congressman T. P. Moore requested his colleagues from Virginia, Pennsylvania, North Carolina, and New York to keep him supplied with publishable materials. "I *beg* you to let me hear from you weekly throughout the summer," he added.

While this "mushroom" growth of the Jackson press was the work of an army of party organizers, a few nationally prominent men rendered outstanding service. In the *Telegraph,* Samuel D. Ingham contributed some of the most delectable slanders to appear in print against the President. Thomas Hart Benton was another powerful writer. His style was simple and direct and usually laced with invective. John C. Calhoun proposed valuable techniques for raising money to pay for all these newspapers, and Van Buren bought out journals and solicited articles from several gifted writers. On the Senate floor the New Yorker chided the government printers (they were editors of Administration newspapers) for their "improper" reporting of the proceedings of Congress. Manifestly, his only objective in making the complaint was the removal of the Adams men as printers and their replacement by Jacksonians. The *National Intelligencer* returned the fire by accusing him of maneuvering the presidential election "within the control of a Central Junto in Washington" and of establishing "machinery" to regulate "the popular election by means of organized clubs in the States, and organized presses everywhere." One of the purposes of his Southern tour, the editors charged, was "buying up or crushing all refractory newspapers which will not join the cry against the coalition."

As though to prove this accusation, two newspaper publishers in Delaware issued a sworn statement that Van Buren and his henchmen had attempted to blackmail them. They said that they were advised to turn over editorial control of the "American Watchman Newspaper Establishment" to the Democrats, or else suffer economic boycott. When they refused to be intimidated, 300 subscriptions were promptly canceled at a net loss of 1,200 dollars a year.

In the long "chain" of newspapers extending from New England to the South and "branching" off through Lexington to the West, several were authoritative and influenced wide areas of public opinion. These included: Green's *Telegraph* (unquestionably the most important), Ritchie's *Enquirer,* Edwin Croswell's Albany *Argus,* Hill's *Patriot,* Amos Kendall's *Argus of the West,* Nathaniel Greene's Boston *Statesman,* the New York *Courier, Inquirer,* and *Evening Post,* the Nashville *Republican,* the Baltimore *Republican,* the Philadelphia *Palladium,* and the Charleston *Mercury.* Besides turning out daily or weekly propaganda, these editors often exercised a more direct form of political power. Ritchie and Croswell operated through the Junto and Regency respectively; Duff Green belonged to Jackson's team of political strategists and had much to say in congressional circles; Isaac Hill, another former Radical, ran a well-oiled machine in New Hampshire, where it was said "he is determined to revolutionize the state by the next Presidential election." Finally there was Amos Kendall who was without doubt the biggest political noise heard in Kentucky since the arrival of Henry Clay.

As this newspaper "conspiracy" spread across the country, propagandizing the people about Jackson and his party and instructing the masses on the proper use of their franchise, the Adams editors groaned their fears for the safety of the Republic. "Why are *affiliated* presses erected throughout the Union, created by a common fund from the contributions of the opposition leaders, and maintained by their aid?" asked one. There was a hidden "identity of purpose" to subvert the democratic institutions of the nation, pontificated Joseph Gales, co-editor of the Washington *National Intelligencer.* Nonsense, snapped the Albany *Argus* in reply. "Professing a common political faith—members of the same great national party —and mutually seeking to promote its welfare, such 'an identity of purpose' was not only natural, but, we are free to say for ourselves, desirable."

The final word, however, came from Duff Green. "Mr. Gales knows," he wrote, "that an attempt is now making to organize new parties in the country."

VII

The establishment of this enormous press was one of the first important results of the alliances concluded in Washington among the Jacksonian Congressmen. Yet equally important was their attempt to raise money to subsidize this press, along with all the other costs with which presidential elections are encumbered. Setting an example for party members in future elections, the Democrats pleaded poverty right up to the day of the inauguration. "We are poor devils in purse," wailed Senator Levi Woodbury, "our opponents are . . . wealthy and cunning." Still, with all their difficulties, it was truly amazing how much hard cash they managed to raise.

At an early Democratic caucus, Vice President Calhoun offered a possible solution to their money problem by suggesting that the Senators and Representatives assume financial responsibility for the "Extra" *Telegraphs* to be sent into their counties and districts. They would then be at liberty to devise the best means of distributing this cost among the local leaders. Calhoun also proposed that they advance money to their poorer colleagues and accept a promise of future repayment. Apparently the suggestions were adopted, for Representative T. P. Moore of Kentucky later acknowledged a debt for the "money due Green for Extras sent to Indiana &c &c," but he complained of his difficulty in obtaining reimbursement. "Mr. Calhoun originated the idea," he wrote, "[and] I have cheerfully paid my portion, & performed all the labor & recd all the abuse. If the amt cannot be raised—be it so, I must & will pay it." And this was for "Extras" sent outside his own state!

It is also likely that Calhoun asked the Jackson Congressmen to accept responsibility for copies of the regular *Telegraph* sent to nonsubscribers, though Green repeatedly denied support from "secret service money" and insisted that his costs were met by public subscriptions. (For a subscriber the daily *Telegraph* cost ten dollars a year, while the weekly cost four dollars.) The editor was finally obliged to go to Boston in the summer of 1828 and secure additional loans. Still denying assistance from a contingent fund, he nevertheless accepted 11,000 dollars from the Massachusetts Jacksonians. Later he billed individual Congressmen for the papers sent into their districts, prompting one Westerner to complain of a ghastly misunderstanding when the bill came to several hundred dollars.

One of the most interesting and persistent rumors in the campaign was the report that the Democratic Congressmen created a special fund for the purpose of establishing "presses in the several states." It was also reported that the money amounted to 30,000 or 50,000 dollars and that Van Buren administered it. Furthermore, it was claimed that the fund was tapped for 25,000 dollars to underwrite the publication of the *Telegraph* and permit its distribution to every voting ward in the country.

Despite these rumors it is most unlikely that Van Buren controlled a 50,000-dollar bankroll. But he was a party treasurer of sorts. Amos Kendall, for instance, was sent to him with a letter of introduction from Senator Richard M. Johnson of Kentucky requesting a loan of 2,000 or 3,000 dollars. Kendall needed the money to repay a debt owed to Henry Clay, and he assured Van Buren that, should the money be advanced, "you will confer on me a favor which will never be forgotten." The editor was once the tutor of Clay's children but resigned to enter the newspaper business. Clay helped him: he loaned him 1,500 dollars and later offered him a job as a clerk in the State Department at a salary of 1,000 dollars. Kendall asked for 1,500 dollars, and evidently this financial haggle irritated Clay, who wrote back that he had no position to offer at that salary. When the arrangement fell through, Clay demanded repayment of the loan. Financially desperate, Kendall asked for and received an extension of time—at the usual rate of interest. When the editor again defaulted at the end of the grace period, Clay began legal proceedings. At this point Van Buren was invited to settle the difficulty with a loan, and the Democratic party bought itself a first-rate editor and politician.

The money given to Kendall by Van Buren, along with other sums disbursed by the Magician during the campaign, was probably raised in the New York-Philadelphia area—and raised under the Senator's own supervision. His Regency controlled the Mechanics and Farmers Bank in Albany, which in turn controlled most of the banks in the western counties of the state. The president of the Mechanics and Farmers, Benjamin F. Knower; the cashier, Thomas

W. Olcott; and several members of the board of directors, such as Benjamin F. Butler (Van Buren's former law partner), Charles Dudley, and William L. Marcy (Knower's son-in-law), were all Regency lieutenants. The Magician repeatedly hounded them to step up their activity in obtaining campaign contributions. Nor did he forget the splendid resources in New York City. "Let me entreat you to give your invided attention to the subject of funds," he wrote one crony. "You must absolutely do more in New York than you promised."

Most of the money Van Buren obtained was spent on newspapers (there were approximately fifty Bucktail newspapers in his own state which had first claim on his treasury) and other forms of propaganda. In addition, he established several new journals in other states, one of them as far west as Illinois; and, to hear the Coalition tell it, he bribed a small army of publishers. According to one report he also accepted campaign contributions from "foreign interests." Documents discovered in 1828 (possibly forged) indicated money received from "*English* merchants in New York and some from Montreal." Presumably, the funds were given to influence the tariff question and to hold down duties on those manufactured goods that would compete with British and Canadian products. If New York Jacksonians did accept such money (and there is no proof of this), they obviously did not consider it a bribe but rather legitimate support for their continuing fight to lower the tariff.

As in most elections, the regular costs incurred in this campaign were absorbed by local organizations in the states. Large contributions, the lifeblood of the party, were again solicited; but because the creation of popular majorities proved fantastically expensive, new techniques were introduced to procure additional revenue. In many states, delegates to a convention or a county meeting were taxed a fixed amount to pay for the publication and distribution of their address to the people. One of the most efficient organizations in the nation, Hamilton County, Ohio, requested each ward to "appoint a fund committee . . . for the purpose of receiving . . . contributions . . . and that the same be paid over to the treasurer of the general committee of the county." Elsewhere, public dinners and banquets at an individual cost of five dollars were sponsored to fill the party's coffers; or an admission of fifty cents was charged at local meetings. Since the party now belonged to the masses, leaders in towns and school districts were instructed to go among their people and collect whatever they could get. They accepted any amount and from any source. Even the notorious Aaron Burr supposedly contributed to the Jackson organization in Virginia. In a detailed financial statement to Senator Levi Woodbury, Isaac Hill complained that his costs in printing New Hampshire's convention proceedings, five important pamphlets, his biography of Andrew Jackson, the Fourth of July orations, and various addresses greatly exceeded the amount of money received from party members. Since the state convention had "authorized" him to take necessary steps to obtain remuneration, he asked Woodbury for a "contribution for the purpose," along with a loan of 2,000 dollars.

While it is impossible to give anything like a complete accounting of costs for this election, it appears certain that the largest single expense, running into the hundreds of thousands, was ingeniously shifted to the United States Government through the franking privilege. Hezekiah Niles estimated that over 2,250,000 dollars a year were involved in the privilege, but this figure sounds exaggerated; nevertheless, the amount of money did run quite high. The delivery of franked newspapers alone cost the federal government 40,000 dollars each year in allowance to postmasters. Except when Congress was not in session, hundreds of newspapers circulated freely throughout the country. Representatives and Senators were hounded by confederates at home to mail every scrap of campaign literature that crossed their desks. Thomas Ritchie happily noted that many enterprising Jacksonians were also franking wrapping paper, which they then turned over to local committees in their states to be used as needed. One Kentucky Representative sent pamphlets, books, letters, handbills, and other educational materials to a *single* post office at a cost of 150 dollars to the government. Even buttons, banners, and insignias went through the mails under the frank. Something close to the entire bill for delivering campaign propaganda was ultimately borne by the American taxpayer. And, in this regard, the usually fastidious Radicals found nothing in their dogma to forbid government participation in party affairs.

The Democrats, in other words, tried to shift the main burden of their campaigning costs to the federal government. There were several ways to do this. Besides the frank, there was money to be had from printing the laws of the United States. Duff Green received several thousand dollars as initial compensation when he was appointed printer for the United States Senate in 1827. Other editors, not elected by Congress, held their lucrative printing posts at the pleasure of the executive, but if they became too conspicuously Jacksonian they ran the risk of removal by Henry Clay. Isaac

Hill lost his printing stipend in just this manner, whereupon his colleagues along the newspaper "chain" set up a howl that his dismissal was the "first movement of the same spirit which produced the *alien and sedition laws* and brought in the reign of terror in 1798."

Next, there was the state government on which to saddle election expenses. Wherever the Democrats controlled the legislature and executive branches of a particular state, they awarded the position of state printer to the editor of their official organs. To provide additional revenue, editors were sometimes given minor offices that did not consume much time or interfere with their primary responsibility of running a newspaper. The editor of the *Inquirer,* however, made the astounding request that he be appointed sheriff of New York City, assuring the Regency that the "avails ... goes in fact into the pockets of the party." It could be done, he told Van Buren, with just a few words to three or four persons "who will press the question upon the Committee & no doubt with success."

In time, the procedures employed by the national leaders to raise money in the campaign developed into a system, although it took many more elections to perfect all the techniques. To begin with, Jacksonians tapped the national and state governments for every penny they could shake loose. Then they obligated themselves for additional costs that were repayable by party treasurers of their state or county committees. In turn, these committees drew upon local fund-raising groups. Obviously, such efficiency was not manifested in all areas, and Congressmen were frequently obliged to petition their colleagues and others for assistance. Sometimes they made private arrangements, since their own elections were at stake; sometimes they went to bank-supported leaders like Van Buren; and sometimes they made public appeals. It cost a great deal of money to enter politics, even in 1828, depending on the level at which a man wished to enter. For example, to be elected from a Western state to a disputed seat in the House of Representatives cost about 3,000 dollars (exclusive of mailing expenses), two-thirds of which was spent on the publication of pamphlets, handbills, and newspapers. In the South the figure was much reduced, while in the Middle Atlantic states, particularly Pennsylvania and New York, it was higher by a thousand dollars or so.

Beginning with the election of 1828, the cost of presidential contests soared. Estimating roughly, and including the franking expenses in the estimate, it cost approximately 1,000,000 dollars to elect General Andrew Jackson the President of the United States.

LYNN L. MARSHALL*

Opposing Democratic and Whig Concepts of Party Organization

Lynn L. Marshall is one of the most original of the new generation of Jackson scholars. In this essay, he concludes that Whigs and Jacksonians were indeed different but the reasons he cites are novel. According to Marshall, the major parties were composed of unlike personality types who, among other things, had antithetical notions as to how to build a political party. The greater reliance on impersonal structure by the Democracy's faceless men accorded better with the spirit of the times and to a large extent accounted for their relative success.

爻爻

THE WHIG PARTY's peculiar birth cannot properly be understood with reference to politics only. In fact, its birth seems to have been integral to concurrent changes in American social organization in a very general sense. Let us entertain the hypothesis that the most significant developments in early nineteenth-century America involved not elevated political ideology (as, for example, states' rights versus national power and laissez faire versus state

---

* From Lynn L. Marshall, "The Strange Stillbirth of the Whig Party," *American Historical Review*, LXXII (January, 1967), pp. 445–468.

regulation), but rather changes in the ways Americans organized themselves to solve immediate problems of all sorts, whether public or private. Whig birth coincided with the crest of a ground swell of social change that would shortly reorganize American life around a proliferating series of specialized, large-scale organizations, flexible, functional, and impersonal.

The key element in the formation of the Whig party was party organization, not ideology. There seems sufficient reason to assume that Whig ideology, in early infancy at least, limited itself to opposition to "executive usurpation," the negative issue implied in its choice of name and the focus of its electioneering efforts throughout the mid-1830's.[1] One can hardly find another common ground between John C. Calhoun, prince of nullification, and nationalists like Henry Clay and Daniel Webster, all of whom joined to establish the party. This issue expressed a reaction to threatening changes in party organization and the role of political leadership. How did the Whig party, then, differ from the Jackson party in organizational structure? How did each relate to the structure of society at large? The conditions of Whig birth, seen in this light, may offer some enlightenment on that much-disputed entity, "Jacksonian Democracy."

Part of the obscurity concerning Whig origins has involved its precise date of birth. It has usually been placed somewhere in 1833 or 1834.[2] The name "Whig" was not used formally to designate the party until 1834. If, however, the alignment around the issue of executive usurpation is taken as the effective birth, it may be fixed with precision at a considerably earlier date. It came in July 1832, in direct and explicit reaction to Jackson's veto of the bill rechartering the national bank. Although the anti-Jackson party continued to call itself National Republican through the campaign of 1832, it abruptly and consciously became proto-Whig with the veto message.

---

[1] The Whig name of course had originated long before in the English parliamentary party opposing usurpations of the king. American colonists during the Revolution had borrowed the name to indicate a similar opposition to the usurpations of George III.

[2] See, e.g., Charles M. Wiltse, *John C. Calhoun: Nullifier, 1829–1839* (New York, 1949), 223; Charles G. Sellers, Jr., *James K. Polk: Jacksonian, 1795–1843* (Princeton, N. J., 1957), 212–13; Glyndon G. Van Deusen, *The Jacksonian Era, 1828–1848* (New York, 1959), 96. The traditional view has attempted to make sense of the Whig party while maintaining primary focus on formal, explicit, ideological main currents running through the full span of American experience, rather than on more explicit, functional ideology. For an example of this, see *id.*, "Some Aspects of Whig Thought and Theory in the Jacksonian Period," *American Historical Review*, LXIII (Jan. 1958), 305–22.

On July 11, 1832, Webster rose in the Senate to denounce the Bank veto at great length, with all the force of his inimitable voice and commanding presence. Only the day before Jackson had sent his veto message to the Senate, and at the first possible moment Webster sprang to the attack. Webster paid scant attention to the arguments put forth in the veto message. He simply disdained it. He ignored, furthermore, what was ostensibly the principal doctrine of his National Republican party: nationalism versus doctrinaire states' rights. At one point he even noted that the veto's main argument was "little compliment to State sovereignty"—as indeed it was, despite rhetorical flourishes to the contrary. Webster focused instead on "executive usurpation."

> According to the doctrines set forth by the President, although Congress may have passed a law, and although the Supreme Court may have pronounced it constitutional, yet it is, nevertheless, no law at all, if he, in his good pleasure, sees fit to deny it effect; in other words to repeal and annul it.[3]

With this veto, concluded Webster, Jackson had effectively proposed a "pure despotism," and announced, like Louis XIV, " 'I AM THE STATE.' " [4]

On the following day, Henry Clay, the National Republican presidential nominee, delivered similar expressions to his Senate colleagues.[5] This double-barreled display was the more impressive because Webster, Clay, and the other pro-Bank oratorical giants had participated sparingly in the long debate that preceded passage of the bill, knowing that they had sufficient votes to ensure passage. Now, however, they unleashed their full power. Their speeches, moreover, in length, polish, and fluency of delivery, suggested considerable preparation.

Up to that time Webster, Clay, and party had not agitated executive usurpation, but for the remainder of the 1832 campaign it became the main party issue. The *National Intelligencer,* their principal party newspaper, hammered away at it in long series of editorials, calling Jackson a "monarch," "KING OF KINGS," and even "DICTATOR." This campaign originated the "King Andrew"

---

[3] "Speech of Mr. Webster," Washington *National Intelligencer,* Sept. 22, 1832.

[4] *Ibid.*

[5] "Speech of Mr. Clay," *Niles' Weekly Register,* Aug. 11, 1832.

cartoon that would become the Whigs' stock in trade for the next few years. The Bank veto message, the *Intelligencer* warned, had frankly announced "downright Tory doctrines." [6]

By August the accession of Calhoun completed the basic Webster-Clay-Calhoun Whig alignment. Just three weeks after the Bank veto, the *United States Telegraph,* Calhoun's organ in Washington, suddenly began to say pleasant things about Clay. Soon the *Telegraph* printed Clay's Bank veto speech and joined the opposition cacophony about "Executive tyranny." [7] It was odd, on the face of it, that this organ of nullification and ostensible enemy of the Bank should thus abruptly espouse the great hero of tariff and Bank, and strange too that the Webster-Clay-Calhoun alignment would remain intact through the subsequent nullification crisis. A more compelling issue than simple states' rights was at work here.

Prior to July 1832 the National Republicans, an alignment of leaders with strong local identifications, like Clay's to Kentucky and Webster's to Massachusetts, had bent their efforts mainly to showing themselves "national." They had sought to identify themselves with the Bank, internal improvements, and especially the tariff. Executive usurpation had not concerned them. Clay had devoted his campaign efforts mainly to the tariff; he delivered a great tariff speech before the Senate in February, which the party promptly printed and broadcast over the country for political effect.[8] The National Republican "platform"—called the "Address of the National Republican Convention to the People of the United States" —had likewise stressed such "national" issues as the tariff. It too had failed to feature a theme of executive usurpation.[9]

When Webster initiated the charge of executive usurpation so suddenly at the time of the veto, he presented an obviously trumped-up case. The Constitution gave the President an absolute right to veto legislation, *whatever* his reasons or lack of them. The

---

[6] Washington *National Intelligencer,* Sept. 22, 1832; "Review of the Veto," *ibid.,* Oct. 4–18, 1832, in seven numbers; Frances Kemble, *Journal* (2 vols., Philadelphia, 1835), I, 141.

[7] Washington *United States Telegraph,* July 23, Aug. 2, 6, 1832. Calhoun could not bring himself to announce personal, public support of Clay, but the *Telegraph* made his position perfectly clear. Cf. Wiltse, *Calhoun: Nullifier,* 141.

[8] *Niles' Weekly Register,* Feb. 2, 3, 6, Mar. 3, 10, 1832; Clay to Francis Brooke, Mar. 17, 1832, *Works of Henry Clay: Comprising His Life, Correspondence and Speeches,* ed. Calvin Colton (10 vols., New York, 1904), IV, 329.

[9] *Niles' Weekly Register,* Dec. 24, 1831.

Bank veto message clearly differentiated between the President's legislative and executive functions, just as did the Constitution. Webster, however, advanced the entirely specious argument that Jackson repealed and annulled an established institution, not a mere bill. Jackson, of course, had sought neither to repeal the original charter of the Bank nor to touch the existing institution in any way. For a nationalist, Webster certainly took a novel position. From the outset nationalists had demanded a powerful executive, and, in fact, the plan of the Bank of the United States itself had originated, in 1791, in the executive department. Clearly, something other than the question of nationalism was involved here.

The proto-Whigs calculated and literally forced the issue of executive usurpation, emasculating their ideology in the process. The Jacksonians had struggled to prevent the Bank issue from coming up in that session of Congress. Because Jackson's re-election in 1832 was almost assured without the Bank issue, they would have preferred to avoid anything so potentially dangerous, for Jackson had made known his intent to veto a recharter that did not involve basic changes in the character of the Bank. ". . . If Jackson is to be believed," Clay snidely commented, "he will veto it." [10] The proto-Whigs had to force the veto in order that they might raise their trumped-up issue.[11] Why should they have done it? Webster and Clay were shrewd political leaders, not accustomed to raise weak or meaningless issues in the midst of presidential campaigns. There was something substantial behind their actions, although they avoided stating it explicitly, something important enough to throw a nationalist into the arms of a nullifier. The apparent peculiarities of the case indicated changes of a profound nature threatening the

---

[10] Clay to Brooke, June 29, 1832, *Works of Clay*, ed. Colton, IV, 340.

[11] The issue of executive usurpation was strongly voiced in the address of the New York Antimasonic party convention, also timed to coincide almost perfectly with the Bank veto. At that convention prominent National Republicans were placed on the Antimasonic party electoral slate, in spite of their support for the well-known Mason, Clay. The Antimasonic party, meanwhile, continued ostensibly pledged to their own presidential candidate, William Wirt. Wirt represented, incidentally, a classic proto-Whig stance. The Jackson administration, he said, was a "millennium of minnows." Following the Bank veto he wrote: "According to General Jackson's principles, our government is a despotism. His veto doctrines, as illustrated by his practice, virtually annihilate both Congress and the Supreme Court." (Wirt to Judge [Dabney] Carr, Oct. 25, 1832, John P. Kennedy, *Memoirs of the Life of William Wirt* [2 vols., Philadelphia, 1856], II, 328.)

customary role of the political leader and the structure of his national political organization. The Bank itself symbolized the type of social structure for which the proto-Whigs stood, and the Jacksonian attack on it a new and challenging alternative.

The following circumstances concerning the Bank veto and the proto-Whig response to it deserve special consideration. Veto and response differed drastically in content, structure, and orientation. The one was aimed directly at voters; the other appealed to members of the political establishment. The veto sought to rally public opinion directly; the replies appealed to the authority of constituted leaders. The Jackson party was immediately voter oriented, and the proto-Whigs, leader oriented. This distinction underlay Ralph Waldo Emerson's epigrammatic characterization of the two parties: "I should say that one has the best cause, and the other contains the best men." [12]

The Bank veto speeches of Webster and Clay addressed fellow political leaders, in fact and in intent. Their style, their choice of language, and the arguments they advanced were not designed for popular consumption. These proto-Whigs sought to show that Jackson had infringed upon the accustomed powers of established, locally based political leaders. They could and did give scant attention to the arguments in the veto message, and none at all to its gist —its rejection of the use of government power to support exclusive private profit-making ventures by a pre-existing social elite—because their chief objection to the veto was its short-circuiting of established political leaders in Congress and Court. They objected to the direct appeal of the veto message to the electorate. The message chose arguments and language with an eye to popular appeal, proposing explicitly that "a new Congress, elected in the midst of such discussion [of the dangerous and unconstitutional features of the Bank], ... will bear to the Capitol the verdict of public opinion...." [13] Webster replied to this appeal with unconcealed disdain, "[t]he message toils through all the commonplace topics of monopoly, the right of taxation, the suffering of the poor, the arrogance of the rich, with as much painful effort, as if one, or another, or all of them,

---

[12] Ralph Waldo Emerson, *Complete Works of Ralph Waldo Emerson*, ed. Edward Waldo Emerson (12 vols., Boston, 1903–1906), III, 209.

[13] *A Compilation of the Messages and Papers of the Presidents, 1789-1897*, ed. James D. Richardson (10 vols., Washington, D.C., 1899), II, 589.

had something to do with the constitutional questions." [14] The *Intelligencer* likewise coupled its usurpation argument with denunciation of the "infuriate mob" to which the message directed itself, and bitter observations on how very little faith could be put in the "virtue and intelligence" of the electorate at large.[15]

One of the most striking features of the veto message was indeed its direct orientation to the electorate. It spoke not to the Congress that had passed the bill, nor to the Court that had, years before in the *McCulloch* v *Maryland* case, ruled a national bank constitutional; it spoke in plain language to voters. And those voters in November would overwhelmingly re-elect Jackson.

Webster and the proto-Whigs all too clearly recognized that the veto message and its direct orientation to voters represented a new approach to politics and new roles for political leaders. It was precisely this that produced their carefully planned proto-Whig alignment. The message was the product, they knew, of that informal board of advisers and organizers whom the anti-Jackson press had begun calling the "Kitchen Cabinet." To Webster, this new brand of political leadership compared invidiously with the old. No one in the Senate supposed, he said, that Jackson had written the veto message himself. This was reprehensible enough, but "whoever may have drawn it up," the President ought at least to have required it to have "passed under the review of professional characters." The matter was one to be decided by elevated, educated, established political leaders. Constituted bodies of such men, the Congress, the Court, even the President's own cabinet, had already decided the matter. How dare "these miserable people" in the "Kitchen Cabinet" presume to argue constitutional doctrine? The proto-Whigs assumed that they need only name the member of the "Kitchen Cabinet" mainly responsible for the authorship of the message to refute the whole of it. The *Intelligencer* demanded simply: "Are the People . . . willing to have AMOS KENDALL to rule over them in the name of ANDREW JACKSON?" [16]

The "Kitchen Cabinet" served as an early version of what would become a national committee. It directed the establishment

---

[14] "Speech of Mr. Webster."

[15] Washington *National Intelligencer*, Aug. 3, 16, 1832.

[16] *Ibid.*, Sept. 4, 1832. Note Richard Longaker, "Was Jackson's Kitchen Cabinet a Cabinet?" *Mississippi Valley Historical Review*, XLIV (June 1957), 94–108, which concludes that the "Kitchen Cabinet" was not a cabinet. The author gives no proper consideration, however, to its participation in noncabinet functions.

of an efficient national party structure, beginning with local committees headed by a county superintendent, then district managers to report to state committees, which in turn reported to the central coordinating body in Washington. It built for specialized, functional ends, rather than for such generalized purposes as reinforcing the status system of society at large. It sought to construct out of functionaries recruited without primary regard to extraneous social criteria a faceless party cadre, with well-defined lines of communication and command, designed to perform the special functions of electioneering and channeling of votes. The whole structure was firmly cemented by award of federal offices, especially local postmasterships and local offices connected with the taking of the 1830 census.[17] Into this wide-ranging, efficient structure the organizers at Washington fed campaign materials calculated to appeal to the grass roots, and in the Bank veto message they provided a campaign circular par excellence. The proto-Whigs publicly noted that these circulars and the organization distributing them were novel and "a matured system of electioneering." [18]

The Washington *Globe,* the principal Jackson newspaper, had been founded in 1830 as a fundamental part of this new party organization, and as the head of a system of coordinated presses throughout the nation. It so far surpassed its contemporaries in spirit and readability that the proto-Whigs considered its style bad taste. Much of the argument and rhetoric of the veto message had long since appeared in the Jackson press.[19] The Jackson party organization saw to it that special electioneering *Globe* extras and copies of the veto message papered taverns and public places throughout the land. In the remotest counties of the West, voters

---

[17] See, e.g., Kendall to Francis P. Blair, Jan. 9, Mar. 10, May 24, 1829, Blair-Lee Papers, Princeton University Library. This plan for "an efficient and universal organization of our party" involved the permanent establishment of procedures used for the 1828 Jackson victory in Kentucky, of which Kendall and Blair had been chief architects. For evidence of the extensiveness of party organization on this model, and its uses, consider the remarkably efficient party reaction to the Calhoun defection in 1831. Calhoun's Washington *United States Telegraph* (Mar. 18, 25, 1831) discovered to its dismay that the Jackson party organization produced identical, simultaneous, and shrewdly construed reactions to Calhoun's movements, in such widely separated locations as Ohio, New Hampshire, Kentucky, Washington, D. C., and Tennessee; the unseen hand guiding this "active corps . . . extending from Maine to Missouri" was the "kitchen cabinet."

[18] "The Babbling Politician," *ibid.,* August 2, 1832.

[19] Kendall to Blair, Jan. 9, Mar. 10, May 24, 1829, Aug. 22, Oct. 2, 1830, Blair-Lee Papers. Cf. the anti-Bank editorial printed in the Washington *United*

who had never experienced the least contact with the Bank had begun pressing politicians with detailed inquiries about it.[20]

Some of the most important and innovative features in Jackson party organization were in the roles of its functionaries. It introduced new and lasting types of political leaders. The fact that the party organizer and the party candidate, as redefined in the Jacksonian era, have continued with little change down to the present suggests the long-range significance of these developments. Martin Van Buren, Jackson's chosen successor in the presidency, epitomized the new type of candidate, and Kendall, whom the opposition press called "chief cook and scullion" in the "Kitchen Cabinet," the organizer. Van Buren earned the sobriquet "Little Magician" for political know-how. Wordy, smooth in delivery, practiced in traditional political rhetoric, noncommittal if possible, wise in the ways of voters, Van Buren always kept his finger on the public pulse and studiously avoided wounding anyone's feelings unnecessarily. Although intelligent and successful, he yet suffered from feelings of inferiority because he had never attended college, and he certainly never began to produce any theory of government to match those of John Adams, Alexander Hamilton, or Thomas Jefferson.[21]

Kendall was a former Kentucky newspaper editor rewarded by Jackson with an office in the Treasury. A sallow, tubercular little fellow, painfully shy, he entirely lacked the figure and presence that could attract votes. He nevertheless had abilities. He possessed enormous industry, genius for practical administration, and a remarkable grasp of the principles of organizational efficiency. He could write, moreover, with clarity and effect. At every opportunity he counseled the Jacksonians: "Organize, organize." [22]

States Telegraph, Dec. 16, 1829, with the Bank veto message, paragraphs 4, 5, 17, 47, *Messages and Papers,* ed. Richardson, II, 576, 577, 581, 591. Cf. also Washington *Globe* editorials of Jan. 19 and Apr. 27, 1831, with paragraph 36 of the veto message *Messages and Papers,* ed. Richardson, II, 586–87.

[20] "Speech of Mr. Clay."

[21] In his *Autobiography* Van Buren was at pains to express his regret at having failed to gain access to what he called the "highest branches of learning." He had often felt his disadvantage "in my conflicts with able and better educated men." He repeatedly expressed this regret at lack of discipline in "mental habits." See *The Autobiography of Martin Van Buren,* ed. John C. Fitzpatrick, *Annual Report, American Historical Association, 1918* (2 vols., Washington, D. C., 1920), II, 12.

[22] Kendall to Blair, May 10, 1829, Blair-Lee Papers. Among many other productions, Kendall was responsible for the veto message almost in its entirety, although several others did editorial work on it. Historical scholars

How did this party organization differ from the American party previously most highly developed, the Republican party of Jefferson? That party had likewise possessed centralized control and extensive organization—"machinery" and "cadre" of a sort—as well as a coterie of party newspapers. But the national and state caucuses of elected representatives had dominated Jeffersonian party structure. Where the Jeffersonian party had been oriented primarily to established leaders, and only through and by them to popular support, the Jacksonian party went directly to the electorate. The faceless functionaries of the Jackson organization, from socially marginal "Kitchen Cabinet" members like Kendall or *Globe* editor Francis Preston Blair, down to lowly local postmasters and census takers laboring for the party, contrast sharply both with Jeffersonian behind-the-scenes organizers like John Beckley and with party mainstays like Aaron Burr, James Madison, and Alexander Dallas.[23]

---

have subsequently become dreadfully confused about the veto's authorship, but it was known in Washington, well before the message appeared, precisely who was composing it. For a detailed examination of the authorship of the message, see Lynn Marshall, "The Authorship of Jackson's Bank Veto Message," *Mississippi Valley Historical Review*, L (Dec. 1963), 466-77. Research subsequent to the publication of this article, incidentally, has turned up abundant corroborating evidence of Kendall's authorship. For evidence of Kendall's social status, see Alfred Balch to Nicholas Trist [Sept. 1831], Nicholas Trist Papers, Manuscript Division, Library of Congress. This genteel observer and loyal Jacksonian, having seen Kendall at a presidential dinner, thought his "watchfulness and awkwardness" contrasted poorly with "the polished conversation the graceful manner & high tone" of the real elite. "To me he does not look like a Gentleman and therefore I could not talk to him. . . ."

[23] An example of the Jackson party's efficient functionaries was a lowly groceryman in Frankfort, Kentucky. He served also as a very efficient postmaster. (Blair to Van Buren, July 10, 1838, Martin Van Buren Papers, Manuscript Division, Library of Congress.) Among several recently published, provocative studies of party organization in the period 1790-1815, those of Noble Cunningham, Jr., are perhaps the most suggestive: *The Jeffersonian Republicans: The Formation of Party Organization, 1789–1801* (Chapel Hill, N. C., 1957), and *The Jeffersonians in Power: Party Operations, 1801–1809* (Chapel Hill, N. C., 1963). See also William N. Chambers, *Political Parties in a New Nation: The American Experience, 1776–1809* (New York, 1963); Paul Goodman, *The Democratic-Republicans of Massachusetts: Politics in a Young Republic* (Cambridge, Mass., 1964); David H. Fischer, *The Revolution of American Conservatism: The Federalist Party in the Era of Jeffersonian Democracy* (New York, 1965). For the preparation of this paper, furthermore, James Banner made available his thought-provoking unpublished article, "The Federalist Party Organization in Massachusetts, 1800–1815." These studies have pioneered a significant new perspective for viewing American politics. It is the thesis of the present paper that this eminently useful perspective should now be broadened in scope, so as to view party organization in its further development through the Jacksonian era in the context of concurrent development in other large-scale organizations as well as in social structure generally.

Beckley, in contrast to the Jacksonian organizers, was a particular protégé and confidant of Virginia's leading gentlemen-politicians of Republican persuasion, Jefferson, Madison, and James Monroe. A polished alumnus of William and Mary, Beckley had been co-opted into politics originally by the local gentry of Henrico County, Virginia, at the age of seventeen and entered national politics by a similar process after his Virginia gentlemen friends had first made him clerk of the House of Burgesses and then clerk of the federal House of Representatives. National organization of the Republican party had begun in Congress, thereafter radiating out to local areas, and in this process Beckley was perfectly placed to play a leading role. The Republican party, first a faction of established leaders aligned around a common ideology, reached out through men like Beckley to other local gentlemen-leaders of similar persuasion. Beckley, Madison, and other Republican organizers, whether operating in Virginia, Pennsylvania, New York, or elsewhere, directed their attention primarily to what they variously described as "respectable persons," "prominent characters," "persons of influence," "suitable characters," or "gentlemen" with "influence among their neighbors." [24] The party operated "particularly by setting on foot expressions of the public mind in important counties, and under the auspices of respectable names." [25]

Contrast this Jeffersonian style of organization with the spirit of the following "Kitchen Cabinet" proposal made in January 1830,

---

[24] See, e.g., Dallas to Albert Gallatin, Jan. 16, 1805, in Henry Adams, *Life of Albert Gallatin* (Philadelphia, 1879), 327–28; Jefferson to Archibald Stuart, Feb. 13, 1799, *The Works of Thomas Jefferson,* ed. Paul L. Ford (12 vols., New York, 1904-1905), IX, 44; and other correspondence of Jefferson, Monroe, Madison, Burr, and Gallatin in this period. See also, for similar language, Beckley's correspondence with General William Irvine, a respectable gentleman-leader of the Republican party in central Pennsylvania, as extracted in Noble Cunningham, Jr., "John Beckley: An Early American Party Manager," *William and Mary Quarterly,* XIII (Jan. 1956), 40–52. About Beckley, Cunningham concludes: "It is of no little significance that Beckley's efforts were, to a large extent, directed toward winning the support of important citizens who could be counted upon to have influence on their neighbors." (Cunningham, *Jeffersonian Republicans,* 105.)

[25] Monroe to Madison, Oct. 9, 1792, *The Writings of James Monroe,* ed. Stanislaus M. Hamilton (7 vols., New York, 1898-1903), I, 243; Jefferson to Madison, Sept. 1, 1793, *Works of Jefferson,* ed. Ford, VIII, 14; Madison to John Taylor, Sept. 20, 1793, as quoted in Cunningham, *Jeffersonian Republicans,* 57; Madison to Jefferson, Aug. 27, Sept. 2, 1793, *The Writings of James Madison,* ed. Gaillard Hunt (9 vols., New York, 1900-10), VI, 179, 191–93; Madison to Archibald Stuart, Sept. 1, 1793, *ibid.,* 190; see also Cunningham, *Jeffersonian Republicans,* 57–60. Note, incidentally, that Jefferson used the name "Whig" for his new party at this time.

and seriously entertained, although seemingly never implemented. The party must organize, it was proposed, in such a way as to circumvent the political dominance of the local gentry established as leading county lawyers, justices in the local courts, and sheriffs. The mass of Jackson voters, "plain farmers and mechanics," should therefore meet in simultaneous local conventions, too numerous for the local establishment to attend all at once, and pass resolutions suggesting candidates for office. "By these means," it was hoped, "the people would take the government into their own hands... and an active class of politicians would spring up opposed to them [the local establishment]." [26]

Whence came the new Jacksonian mode of party organization? Sophisticated popularly based party structures, on a small scale, had developed in various states by the 1820's. Although scholarly studies of these parties have not, for the most part, treated organizational structure per se (preferring to emphasize ideology and colorful individual careers), it appears that several state parties, at least, developed in this period a Jacksonian type of impersonal structure by-passing established local elites. The most significant for the national organization of the Jackson party was the Kentucky Relief party, which coalesced out of general popular demand for relief laws for debtors following the panic of 1819. Here, men destined to become important in national Jackson party councils received apprenticeship in popular politics. *Globe* editor Blair and efficiency expert Kendall simply transferred Kentucky techniques of the 1820's directly to the national arena. [27] In New York, moreover, Antimasonic and Van Burenite organizations alike had developed centralized, specialized party apparatus. Antimasons built upon popular antipathy to a secret elitist group suspected of conspiring to obtain special privileges, just as the Jacksonians would in the Bank veto message. [28] The advent of Jackson as a presidential candidate, with his great

---

[26] Kendall to Blair, Jan. 28, 1830, Blair-Lee Papers. This too represented a continuation of efforts first begun by Kendall and Blair in Kentucky politics during the 1820's.

[27] Lynn Marshall, "The Genesis of Grass-Roots Democracy in Kentucky," *Mid-America*, XLVII (Oct. 1965), 269–87; Arndt M. Stickles, *Critical Court Struggle in Kentucky* (Bloomington, Ind., a.d.).

[28] Jabez D. Hammond, *History of Political Parties in the State of New York* (4th ed., 2 vols., Cooperstown, N.Y., 1846), II, 384–85; Lee Benson, *The Concept of Jacksonian Democracy: New York as a Test Case* (Princeton, N.J., 1961), 21–27. Although opportunistic Antimasonic leaders aligned New York Antimasonry against Jackson in 1832, this does not diminish the essentially "Jacksonian" character of the new mode of organization they represented.

appeal to ordinary voters throughout the nation, suggested the viability of political organization on this model at the national level.

The new approach to politics, however, was part of a general change in American society. It represented a new approach to social organization for the accomplishment of any sort of practical purpose. Jacksonian national party development related very closely to the Jackson administration's development of new organizational principles for the government's executive departments. These organizational principles, in turn, developed directly from practical administrative problems that the Jacksonians faced when they entered office, rather than from any preconceived ideology. When in the Spring of 1829 the Jacksonians swept in, bent on "reform" as announced in Jackson's inaugural address, they set forth no new principles of organization. After a few months in office, however, they proclaimed in Jackson's first message to Congress their principles of "rotation in office." [29]

It is significant that the Jacksonians did not propose merely to replace rascals in office with men of honor from their own party, as might well have been expected had they been interested in "spoils" only. They certainly rewarded friends and punished enemies about as much as they were able in the award of offices, following the custom in American politics dating from the inception of party contests. The opposition legitimately screamed "spoils," but the moralistic condemnations of the "spoils system" as something peculiarly Jacksonian, which have continued almost without pause ever since, have obscured profoundly important organizational innovations introduced by the Jacksonians. In so far as these innovations were concerned, the spoils question was entirely irrelevant.[30] The Jacksonians used the concept of rotation in office as a cloak for organizational changes that might otherwise have appeared revolutionary. By 1829 the idea of rotation in office was neither novel nor did it imply any social change, for it had been proposed on various occasions since the time of the American Revolution, and it was

---

[29] *Messages and Papers*, ed. Richardson, II, 438–49.

[30] Historians seem to have been so mesmerized by the moralistic fervor of the civil service reformers of the late nineteenth century that they continue tirelessly to repeat their righteous condemnations of the Jacksonian spoils system. Leonard D. White, in *The Jacksonians: A Study in Administrative History, 1829–1861* (New York, 1954), has pointed out that the Jacksonians initiated administrative reform. The present paper is not meant to imply that spoils are efficient, but only that there are other more significant issues with which to deal.

occasionally implemented. South Carolina, doubtless the most conservative and class-controlled state in the Union, provided the leading example of that doctrine in 1830.[31]

Under this cover the Jacksonians proposed to organize the executive department as a rationalized complex of offices, ordered by function, and defined by rules and regulations, so as to be free in so far as possible from irregular custom and individual personalities. In this system individuals could be placed or replaced without upsetting the integrity of the whole. Men were fitted to this system, not it to men.[32] It was the administrative counterpart of the interchangeability of machine parts. Jackson's rotation proposal explicitly denied that office should become "a species of property" or be used to support "the few at the expense of the many." "The duties of all public officers," the message announced, "are, or at least are capable of being made, so plain and simple that men of intelligence may readily qualify themselves for their performance...." In spite of much emphasis on equality of opportunity for all citizens, the Jacksonians justified this system mainly by the "efficiency of Government" that it might bring.[33] The signal organizational insight was this: efficiency lay primarily in the system (rules and regulations) rather than in men (character).

The Jacksonian proposal of rotation in office was never actually put into practice, and the administrative principles it masked were only falteringly applied to the organization of government departments. The post office reorganization of 1836 was its most important product.[34] In part this resulted from opposition to the new system in Congress, which had to provide the basic rules and regulations of

---

[31] Carl Russell Fish, *The Civil Service and the Patronage* (New York, 1905), 79–104. Jefferson himself had proposed that rotation be written into the Constitution of 1787. (Jefferson to Madison, Dec. 20, 1787, *Works of Jefferson*, ed. Ford, V, 372.)

[32] This is what the great historian and social analyst Max Weber has called "bureaucratization." See "Bureaucracy" in *From Max Weber: Essays in Sociology*, ed. H. H. Gerth and C. Wright Mills (New York, 1946), 196–244. American "bureaucracy" differed in very important respects from Weber's ideal, however, for Weber emphasized professionalization and life tenure in officeholders. He admired "the apparatus" of administration itself and placed great value on maintaining its integrity. The American variety of "bureaucratic" social organization, as hereafter sketched, essentially the organizational model for the modern industrial world, has defined itself rather differently.

[33] *Messages and Papers*, ed. Richardson, II, 449.

[34] 5 US Statutes at Large 80 (July 2, 1836).

office. In part it resulted from opposition within the Jackson party itself, which, after all, was still in a process of development. The new administrative system eventually had its greatest effect outside the realm of government altogether: in large-scale private business. In its "rotation" form, furthermore, the innovative principle of the system—the interchangeability of human parts—was overstated. In any absolute sense it could not work and was not so intended by its authors. Certain offices required expert skills. That did not make them, however, any the less definable by impersonal rules or less subject to later functional redefinition.

It was not that American government had never previously been organized according to rational and functional principles. The government departments had been originally set up on a plan derived from a venerable tradition of bureaucratic structure.[35] Alexander Hamilton, for example, had consciously modeled the new Treasury Department upon its English counterpart. The British Exchequer itself belonged to one of the rationalized bureaucracies long since established during the rise of monarchical national states in Europe. These bureaucracies, however, had established and maintained prestige largely by filling their ranks with careful attention to pre-existing social gradations. Thus it had been with Hamilton's system too. The government would gain in respectability, President Washington had agreed, in proportion to the respectability of the officers serving it. Hamilton had therefore chosen men of character and "standing in the community" to fulfill Washington's intent that officials "give dignity and lustre" to their offices.[36]

The application of such social criteria to officeholders rigidified the system and inhibited its efficiency. It was thought that a man once placed in office ought not properly to be removed, except for the grossest misconduct, nor the office changed. The character of the officeholder, once appointed, largely defined the office; his removal or any arbitrary change in his office reflected on his character and was damaging to the whole social system. Consider the case of Federalist Timothy Pickering's clerks in the State Department whose removal, after they had been discovered levying strictly illegal fees

---

[35] Ernest Barker, *The Development of Public Services in Western Europe, 1660–1930* (London, 1944), 1–12; Hans Rosenberg, *Bureaucracy, Aristocracy, and Autocracy: The Prussian Experience, 1660–1815* (Cambridge, Mass., 1958), 1–25, 227–28.

[36] Leonard D. White, *The Federalists: A Study in Administrative History* (New York, 1948), 118, 126, 257–58, and *The Jeffersonians: A Study in Administrative History, 1801–1829* (New York, 1951), 347–68.

from applicants for passports, Pickering greatly regretted because they had "sustained fair characters" in the community at large.[37] Jefferson had acted upon similar premises. Government administration was to him a matter primarily of "virtue and talents." "The whole art of government," he said, "consists in the art of being honest."[38] The Jacksonian alternative, masked in the proposal of rotation in office, offered to increase efficiency by ignoring pre-existing social criteria like "character" and "respectability" and defining office impersonally, entirely by rules and regulations.

The Jackson press explicated and justified in various ways the new system announced in the rotation proposal. Throughout 1830 and 1831, and almost down to the moment of the Bank veto, "reform" provided their main issue of party agitation. In paper after paper the Jackson organs ran elaborate computations of how much money their administrative reforms had saved the government.[39] These and a multitude of other articles on "reform" made no distinction between general improvements in the efficiency of the system and the money saved by eliminating corruption in office-holders. Any sort of efficiency, as measured by money saved, was equally moral, and any sort of inefficiency, corrupt or otherwise, was equally immoral. While the Jacksonians were exceedingly moralistic and personal in their condemnations of the old administration, they championed a new system to replace it that was remarkably impersonal and strictly regulation. This was to be the officeholder's creed: "I want no discretion. I wish to be able to turn to some law or lawful regulation for every allowance I am called upon to make." [40]

The Jackson press had devoted a considerable proportion of its columns to justifying removals from office. When the opposition shouted "spoils," the Jackson press promptly showed, with remarkable specificity, how the officeholder's books had been in arrears and his accounts carelessly and irregularly drawn, concluding with an exact calculation of the sum lost to the government thereby.

---

[37] *Id., Federalists,* 286–87.

[38] See Jefferson's "A Summary View of the Rights of British America," Aug. 1774, *Works of Jefferson,* ed. Ford, II, 88.

[39] See, e.g., "The Black List," Washington *United States Telegraph,* Aug. 14–Sept. 24, 1830. The Washington *Globe* reprinted the same series, in corrected and amended form, in June of the following year.

[40] Fourth Auditor's Report, Nov. 30, 1829, Washington *United States Telegraph,* Dec. 10, 1829.

The opposition customarily replied with an article ostensibly written by the officeholder himself, but really by some such proto-Whig leader as William Wirt, who condemned the charges as "egregious insolence" and "a pitiful attempt to dishonor the word of a gentleman" by citing "paltry little omissions" (in one case, "that paltry little sum of $3835"). To this the Jacksonians responded in simple, direct, and telling style. Let the regulations of office be strictly obeyed, they said. Books should reflect reality, not false or misleading entries based on customs and justifiable only by appeal to the officeholder's honorable position in the social system. Regulations, not the social status of the officeholder, defined the office. "Property in office," they said, provided the basis for "aristocratic" control of government.[41]

The proto-Whig tacticians faced in an entirely different direction. In the masterful plan of operations they worked out for the campaign of 1832 they sought to gather all respectable political leaders under the "executive usurpation" banner, with the tacit assumption that they would bring with them their local constituencies—precisely the system theretofore traditional in American politics. They forced the recharter bill through, obtained the President's veto, driving thereby a wedge between Jackson and many of his original party leaders, and skillfully developed the Webster-Clay-Calhoun alignment around the "executive usurpation" position, but they failed utterly to take their principal objective, the presidential election. These battle-proven leaders seemed so rigidly to follow their plan of operations, drawn up according to well-established principles of political warfare, that they failed to comprehend the irresistible power of the new weapon introduced by the Jacksonians. Or perhaps they understood too well, but remained so attached to traditional political modes that they could not give them up without first doing everything in their power to defend them. It is altogether remarkable how many respectable political leaders were split away from the Jackson party without apparently impairing its effectiveness at the polls: Samuel Ingham, John M. Berrien, John Branch, John C.

---

[41] See, e.g., the disputes over Miles King, the removed naval agent at Norfolk, Virginia, and Major William Barney, removed "Superintendent of Light Houses and Buoys." (Washington *United States Telegraph*, July 5, 8, 20, Aug. 24, Sept. 21, 1830; Mary Barney to Jackson, June 13, 1829, *Correspondence of Andrew Jackson*, ed. John Spencer Bassett [7 vols., Washington, D. C., 1926-35], IV, 48; Mary Lane to Mary Barney, Aug. 9, 1830, reprinted from the Laurenceburg *Indiana Palladium* in the Washington *United States Telegraph*, Sept. 21, 1830.)

Calhoun, John McLean, Louis McLane, Littleton Tazewell, John Tyler, John Eaton, Hugh L. White, to name a few. These men shared common characteristics—stuffiness, social pretension, and great concern for honor, dignity, and decorum. Thus, curiously, from the outset the proto-Whigs methodically maneuvered as if bent on self-destruction, reinforcing their own anachronism by publicly eschewing direct popular appeal and gathering into their ranks as many established leaders as possible, while forcing the Jackson party to increase its voter orientation.

This party distinction was not absolute, however, for at least some proto-Whigs were not above trying to organize in the Jacksonian style or applying what was condescendingly called *"ad captandum"* (pleasing to the crowd) techniques. In their own way they had always wooed the electorate anyway. Clay himself, for example, received the plaudits of several of his party cohorts for frankly *"ad captandum"* antiforeign remarks in his widely distributed tariff speech.[42] In his vicious and personal attack on the venerable free trader, Albert Gallatin, whose half century in America could not make him more to Clay than "still at heart an alien," Clay hissed, "Go home to your native Europe." [43]

The proto-Whig alignment, moreover, included the Antimasonic party, a relatively small but highly organized and distinctly voter-oriented party. Some of these proto-Whigs understood the sources of Jacksonian party strength well enough to see clearly the power of the veto message, refusing sometimes even to publicize Webster's speech for fear it would further alienate the electorate. Clay understood the import of the veto at least enough to stop Nicholas Biddle from printing and distributing it generally as a pro-Bank handbill, for that benighted representative of genteel Philadelphia erudition had thought the message so obviously inappropriate and reprehensible as to make it Bank propaganda. In the midst of the election campaign, furthermore, when proto-Whigs in Virginia seemed ready to give up in despair, Clay counseled fighting fire with fire. "Let our friends organize . . .," he said, proposing a "central committee" with local committees to "bring the voters to the polls." [44] Even this

---

[42] James Barbour to Clay, Mar. 7, 1832, *Works of Clay,* ed. Colton, IV, 328.

[43] Adams, *Gallatin,* 641–42.

[44] Clay to Biddle, Aug. 27, 1832, Nicholas Biddle Papers, Manuscript Division, Library of Congress; Clay to Francis Brooke, Aug. 5, 1832, *Works of Clay,* ed. Colton, IV, 341.

proposed elaboration of organization, however, retained the flavor of the older model of party structure, an organization of respectable "friends" who condescended to "bring" in the votes.

The Jackson party, on the other hand, offered no perfect voter orientation either. At Jackson's first inauguration in 1829, that party had offered an alignment of ideologically diverse leaders very similar to the proto-Whigs of 1832. The party arrived at its voter orientation, as expressed in the veto message, haltingly and stumblingly. The 1831 cabinet crisis, revolving around Peggy Eaton, the tavernkeeper's daughter who married the Secretary of War, culminated in an intraparty rash of threatened duels. Such preoccupation with honor and decorum was characteristic of a highly traditional role of leadership. The new 1831 cabinet followed the traditional model of political leadership once more, attempting to weld together a group of socially respectable leaders like Edward Livingston and Louis McLane. Unfortunately the sympathies of these respectables turned out, many times, to lie with the proto-Whigs. McLane, Secretary of the Treasury, offered the prime example of this, becoming a most annoying irritation on the Bank issue. The Jacksonians' attempt to play down that issue in the President's message of December 1831 likewise represented an essentially leader-oriented gambit. They had to be pushed by the opposition, finally, into the Bank issue and frank voter orientation.

Inconsistencies within both parties suggest that each was moving generally in the same direction, in transition from leader orientation to voter orientation, although the Jackson party had advanced further. The Bank issue, however, was perfectly calculated to accelerate the development of the Jackson party and decelerate the opposition, pushing the parties apart until they offered a striking contrast in orientation. The Whigs attempted to exploit their leader orientation to the fullest even after defeat in the election of 1832, achieving their greatest success in 1834 with the Senate censure of Jackson. Their failure in 1832 resulted, they supposed, from Jackson's great popularity as a military hero, not his party organization and electioneering techniques. The decisive defeat in 1830 by less than heroic Van Buren, however, proved without doubt the utility of Jacksonian party organization and techniques. By 1840 the Whigs had adopted these techniques. Even the eminent Webster would brag to voters about his father's log cabin, stumping for such Whig candidates as "Old Tippecanoe," pseudo hero William Henry Harrison.

The two party types represented two distinctly different views of society at large. When the Whigs agitated the question of "spoils," for example, they dealt not so much with technical government administration as with general social values. Government service, in their view, ought to be a function of private social status; it had traditionally been so considered. They looked back to a world in which a gentleman, once appointed to an office, private or public, expected to be continued therein, and the functions of his position fitted to his capabilities. Though not quite "property in office," as the Jacksonians called it, this view emphasized long tenure based on criteria non-functional to the operations of the organizations involved, be they government bureaus, private businesses, or even churches. The Whigs were not terribly concerned about "spoils" proper; they objected not to the reward of "friends," but to the social character of the friends rewarded.

The Whiggish view looked back to a society embodying the Lockean liberalism of the eighteenth century. In it, all affairs, political or otherwise, moved under the effective control of sagacious men, each within his own locality sufficiently pre-eminent economically, intellectually, and socially to transcend immediate popular control even if the franchise were widely distributed. Greatest emphasis was placed upon the liberty of the individual to express himself, if he were able and sufficiently educated, in great social theories and high ideals. American constitutions embodied such theories. Hamilton's plan for organization of the Treasury Department likewise exemplified a part of a liberal theory of this sort, as did Gallatin's 1808 scheme for a system of internal improvements, Jefferson's education scheme for Virginia, and the handsome proposals offered by John Quincy Adams in his 1825 inaugural address. Liberal partisans of Republican and Federalist political alignments entertained important ideological differences, but they shared basic assumptions about social structure.

The Jeffersonians envisioned a locally established intellectual elite handing down great humane theories from on high, a conception that differed from the Hamiltonian only in the assumption that the theories would, if worthy, necessarily receive ratification from an enlightened populace. Political parties were defined as like-thinking alignments of sociopolitical leaders; it was always hoped that leaders would reach, through rational discussion, such a consensus as to eliminate the need for parties of any sort. It was quite possible to be both nationalist in ideology, like the Federalists, and to derive social status and the claim to political leadership primarily from membership in a local social establishment.[45]

The Constitution of 1787 perfectly illustrated the proper role of political leadership according to the conception of the eighteenth-century liberal. The Constitution was par excellence a noble theory of government, composed in secret by a group of eminently respectable political leaders representing various local establishments, and handed down to the electorate for ratification. If a majority of the delegates in Philadelphia turned out eventually to be Federalists, a proportion of them became Republicans, including, of course, the most prominent of them all, Jefferson's hand-picked successor to the presidency, James Madison. Jefferson himself quite approved the process by which the Constitution was drawn up. If he entertained misgivings about some of its provisions, at least until the Bill of Rights was added, he fully approved the leadership role it embodied.[46] That leadership role, mutually respected by Federalists and Republicans, the proto-Whigs sought only to continue.[47]

---

[45] Cf. Sidney Aronson, *Status and Kinship in the Higher Civil Service: Standards of Selection in the Administrations of John Adams, Thomas Jefferson, and Andrew Jackson* (Cambridge, Mass., 1964). This study attempts to compare the higher echelons in the administrations of John Adams, Jefferson, and Jackson, assigning to the Jeffersonians the main responsibility for democratic change, while denying the Jacksonians anything more than a minor and subsidiary role. Although commendable for attempting rigorous quantitative analysis of this distant and difficult area, its results are rendered inconclusive by substantial technical shortcomings. To cite one of several similar weaknesses, the study compares the social status of officeholders in the Jackson administration with those of the Jefferson administration, which preceded it by twenty years, as if this were no different from comparing the Jefferson administration with the Adams administration immediately preceding it. See also another more solid quantitative study, Richard P. McCormick, "New Perspectives on Jacksonian Politics," *American Historical Review*, LXV (Jan. 1960), 288–301. McCormick, however, has concluded from a careful examination of the numbers of voters participating in elections that the advent of Jackson involved no " 'mighty democratic uprising.' " By arbitrarily defining democracy simply as proportion of possible voters participating, however, McCormick ignored the effective power of the electorate as influenced by party structure. See also *id., The Second American Party System: Party Formation in the Jacksonian Era* (Chapel Hill, N.C., 1966), for a view of party formation contrasting with that of the present paper.

[46] Jefferson to Madison, Dec. 20, 1787, *Works of Jefferson,* ed. Ford, V, 370–75. It is suggestive that Jefferson here expressed some doubt about the scope of power given the House of Representatives, the most democratically elected body in the proposed government. He approved the executive veto explicitly, moreover, and even suggested that a judicial veto be included as well. Jefferson and Adams, by settling down in their dotage to a long, warm correspondence, showed how akin they really were. "For I agree with you," wrote Jefferson, "that there is a natural aristocracy among men. The grounds of this are virtue

The proto-Whigs sought to emulate Hamilton and Jefferson and to produce great liberal theories. Clay's "American system" was but a pale reflection, perhaps, but it was nevertheless an effort in this direction. Calhoun's "concurrent majorities," if strained and self-serving, came closer to the mark. Clay's "Ashland" and Calhoun's "Fort Hill" aped "Monticello" and Mount Vernon in emphasizing local attachment to native state and gentry. The Jacksonian reorganization of politics threatened to destroy all this, and the proto-Whigs drew together in a last-ditch effort to defend it. That the two surviving members of the old Republican triumvirate, Madison and Gallatin, should align themselves automatically with the proto-Whigs in 1832 was hardly surprising. Gallatin had long distrusted what would come to be the Jacksonian party type. He had counseled Jefferson in 1801 that they ought greatly to fear "men whose political existence depends on . . . party." [48]

The proto-Whig party alignment ought properly to have been restricted along ideological lines either to like-thinking nationalists, or, alternatively, to states' righters. Under the dire threat offered by the Jacksonians, however, the party included all who stood for the traditional leadership role, whatever their ideology. Thus did

---

and talents . . . ." (Jefferson to Adams, Oct. 28, 1813, *The Adams-Jefferson Letters: The Complete Correspondence between Thomas Jefferson and Abigail and John Adams,* ed. Lester J. Cappon [2 vols., Chapel Hill, N. C., 1959], II, 387–92.)

[47] Cf. Chambers, *Political Parties,* 95–109. Chambers has identified a significant change from an elitist, "plebiscitarian," "party of notables" Federalist party, to a truly democratic Republican party, a "party of politicians." He has derived this conceptual framework from Max Weber's essay "Politics as a Vocation." (See *From Max Weber,* ed. Gerth and Mills, 77–128.) These typologies resemble the distinction drawn in the present paper between leader orientation and voter orientation, but Chambers has followed Weber's model too closely and has the full scope of the development too early. Chambers has also suggested the importance of party organization to Jacksonian political developments, in "Party Development and Party Action: The American Origins," *History and Theory,* III (No. 1, 1963), 93, n. 6. Both this and his above-cited book cogently urge the utility of conceptual framework in the study of American party development. On Jacksonian political organization, see also Moisei Ostrogorski, *Democracy and the Organization of Political Parties* (2 vols., New York, 1902), II, 39–79. Weber, in "Politics as a Vocation," evidently based his analysis of American parties on Ostrogorski, and Weber too became preoccupied with righteousness about spoils. Note, however, Weber's identification of "bureaucracy" with *"mass democracy"* specifically in American political party development. "In the United States, both parties since Jackson's administration have developed bureaucratically." (*From Max Weber,* ed. Gerth and Mills, 224–25.)

[48] Gallatin to Jefferson, Aug. 10, 1801, Adams, *Gallatin,* 278.

Calhoun embrace Webster and Clay even while leading the nullification fight. In so doing they looked back longingly to a heroic era
when leadership in politics was integral to leadership in society.
They reached the *reductio ad absurdum* of their anachronistic
localism when, in the 1836 campaign, they put several local presidential candidates into the field simultaneously, to be beaten en
masse by Van Buren. Thus was the Whig party born dead in July
1832 and continued in that condition until 1836. Thereafter,
however, a total transfusion of Jacksonian blood would miraculously
bring it to life.

Alexis de Tocqueville sensed in the United States of 1831–1832
the already half-realized sociopolitical changes against which the
proto-Whigs reacted. He saw in a possible "tyranny of the majority"
the subversion of the traditional type of locally based, socially
secure, political leadership with which he himself identified. Historians have much praised, condemned, or explicated Tocqueville's
thought on this point, but have failed to point out that his "tyranny
of the majority" was in many respects exactly equivalent to proto-
Whig "executive tyranny," including its primary leader orientation.
At the very crux of his discussion of the power exercised by the
majority over contrary opinions, he noted that, although an individual in the United States may be allowed perfect freedom of
expression within certain limits, he absolutely dare not go beyond
them. Not that his life would be endangered, but "his political
career is closed forever." "You may retain your civil rights," said he,
"but they will be useless to you, for you will never be chosen by your
fellow citizens if you solicit their votes. . . ." In this way the individual would be "deprived of the rights of mankind." [49]

The Bank of the United States embodied just this leadership
ideal championed by Tocqueville and the proto-Whigs. Without
denying the obvious economic utility of central control on banking,
consider the socially impacted structure of this particular institution.
Originally constructed in accordance with a segment of Hamilton's
brilliant theory, it represented a grand scheme with which men of
honor might reach out imaginatively to secure possibly great benefits for the whole of society. It represented, pre-eminently, government buttressing of private socioeconomic position. Its enormous

---

[49] Alexis de Tocqueville, *Democracy in America* (2 vols., New York, 1945),
I, 274–75. For development of related elements in Tocqueville's work, see
Seymour Drescher, *Tocqueville and England* (Cambridge, Mass., 1964), 74–
104, and "Tocqueville's Two *Democracies*," *Journal of the History of Ideas*,
XXV (Apr.-June 1964), 211–16.

economic power was only nominally limited by public opinion, and the only real limitation lay in the honor and intelligence of its essentially dilettante-banker executives. The Bank's structure conformed closely to local social establishments. Each of its many branches had its own board of directors drawn from the local gentry, planters, and merchants, who were generally politicians too, and dilettante bankers all. Only the cashier in each branch represented directly the central institution in a full-time capacity. Obvious social criteria were used in the selection of cashiers, just as they had been used in the selection of Biddle himself as president of the mother bank. For all the banking skill he acquired subsequently, Biddle had been invited into the Bank not on the basis of experience as a banker, in which he was woefully weak, but on his general character, his "virtue and intelligence." [50] The Bank issue in 1832, therefore, was perfectly calculated to point up fundamental social changes then in process.

If the Whiggish ideal seems strange and remote in many respects, the ideal implied in Jacksonian innovations seems familiar by contrast. If the one harked back to the past, the other offered a vision of the future—although usually represented by the Jacksonians themselves as an ideal deriving from a more perfect era in the American past. The Jackson party forever talked of states' rights and paraded Jeffersonian rhetoric, straining to appear traditional. Actually, of course, the Whigs more resembled the Jeffersonians than did the Jacksonians. The Jacksonian ideal, while couched in Jeffersonian shibboleths, involved no great concern for local protection of individual liberty.

Since at least the close of the War of 1812 Americans had been experimenting enthusiastically with new modes of social organization, for purposes spiritual, practical, or merely for amusement. These new alternatives rapidly eroded away the old social order, once so firmly established in New England's townships and Virginia's counties. The new modes of social organization developed directly out of recognition of specific problems and attempts to solve them, as efficiently as possible, in keeping with certain assumptions about the nature of man. It had become obvious to Americans by that date that many things could be done to increase both material and spiritual comforts, things that could never be done by individual efforts of independent yeomen farmers of the Jeffersonian

---

[50] Biddle to John McLean, Jan. 10, 11, 1829, Biddle Papers; Thomas P. Govan, *Nicholas Biddle* (Chicago, 1959), 83–84.

image however dutifully they followed the wise counsels of the rightful *aristoi*. Goods needed to be grown, manufactured, and shipped, messages sent, taxes collected, and souls saved on a grand scale. The situation seemed to demand social reorganization. The resulting American penchant for organization and reorganization, by all classes and for all purposes, startled a sensitive observer like Tocqueville. This period's efflorescence of different types of organizations has been much noted, but here again historians have not concerned themselves with organizational structure so much as with formal ideologies, just as in the case of political parties.

This era's enthusiastic activity in economic affairs—in finance, manufacturing, transportation, and merchandising—involved basic experimentation in modes of social organization as well as advance in economic productivity. These experiments ranged from the Boston Associates' highly successful work force of respectable unmarried farm girls, to Kentucky's ill-fated Lexington Manufacturing Company with its great imported steam engine and cadre of Yankee production "engineers." They ranged from the Erie Canal, to the West's myriad state-chartered banks, to New York City's far-flung new merchandising houses. Apparently not until the 1850's, however, did any really large-scale business organizations develop in the United States, excepting Biddle's Bank and John Jacob Astor's American Fur Company, both of which operated on an earlier organizational model. In the boom during the mid-1830's there were textile factories in the Philadelphia area employing more than two hundred operatives. Simultaneously, factory workers first organized themselves into large-scale labor unions. That the National Trades' Union crumbled in the panic of 1837, along with many burgeoning factories, detracts nothing from the social significance of such organizational attempts.[51]

The most profound experiments in novel modes of social organization involved affairs other than economic. It seems more than fortuitous, however, that important New York merchants like the Tappan brothers led in establishing a series of new religious-

---

[51] Alfred D. Chandler, *Strategy and Structure: Chapters in the History of Industrial Enterprise* (Cambridge, Mass., 1962), 19–22. For the Lexington Manufacturing Company, see Ebenezer Stedman's charming recollections, published under the title *Bluegrass Craftsman: Being the Reminiscences of Ebenezer Hiram Stedman, Papermaker, 1808–1885*, ed. Frances L. S. Dugan and Jacqueline P. Bull (Lexington, Ky., 1959), 14–25; see also William A. Sullivan, *The Industrial Worker in Pennsylvania, 1800–1840* (Harrisburg, Pa., 1955), 17–23, 99–118.

associated organizations for special purposes, broadly Protestant evangelical or moral. Many such groups sprouted in the 1820's. Organized by laymen, each extended over the entire nation. Inter-denominational, they were in structure entirely outside either local churches or denominational organizations. The American Sunday School Union, the American Society for Promoting Temperance, the American Home Missionary Society, and several other groups quickly established themselves and grew at a rapid rate. Each soon claimed functionaries numbering in the hundreds or even thousands, with annual budgets approaching $100,000.[52] Antislavery organization in the 1830's was but one more such effort.

In addition to such specialized organizations, there was an extraordinary variety of attempts at total social reorganization: the familiar communitarian experiments like New Harmony, Brook Farm, and the Mormon communities. These ranged in political structure from Mormon authoritarianism to transcendentalist freedom, from Shakerite celibacy in family relations to Oneidan free love, and, in modes of economic productivity, from foolish bucolic idyl to highly profitable manufacturing enterprise. The widespread expectation, furthermore, among various American Protestant groups during these years that the millenium was at hand seems related to recognition of the passing of accustomed social roles and social order. Jacksonian party development and administrative reform were just one more such experiment in social organization, but they were essentially the system that would ultimately triumph over all others.[53]

The Jacksonians discovered the key to efficiency in an egalitarian ethic, that national principle which Americans generally had come to take for granted in the half century since the Declaration of Independence. The overwhelming triumph of the political party of Jefferson had helped to establish it, and the newness of all social institutions in America had doubtless buttressed it at least as much as formal liberal ideology. This egalitarian ethic provided a necessary foundation for Jacksonian changes in social organization. That the Jacksonians connected their "rotation in office" doctrine with egalitarianism was not simply opportunistic. Their recognition that ad-

---

[52] William Warren Sweet, *Religion in the Development of American Culture, 1800–1840* (New York, 1952), 188, 262–71.

[53] For an account of one of the most organizationally experimental communitarian groups, see Fawn M. Brodie, *No Man Knows My History: The Life of Joseph Smith* (New York, 1945).

ministrative efficiency might be increased by establishing interchangeability of human "parts" required an egalitarian ethic; their
faceless, specialized party organization did as well.

By starting with an assumption that, for organizational purposes,
individuals could be considered as essentially equivalent, it then
became possible to define offices by functional regulations only
rather than by the personality or social status of the individuals
who occupied them. An organization on this model gained efficiency
by its flexibility. It could shift or replace personnel without impairing the integrity of the system as a whole. Offices themselves could
be easily redefined so as to perform ever more efficiently the particular organizational function. A national political party should
thus efficiently organize to manufacture public support for the
administration or channel votes to it. Its principles of organization
differed not at all from groups organized to administer the government or to perform economic and other private functions.

A year prior to the Bank veto message, the *Globe* explicitly
described this vision. "Government is *a business*. It should be managed by *men of business*." Furthermore, "It is not for *show;* but for
use." The function of government in society should not be "to make
a few men *great*." Therefore, political leaders or officeholders "should
not be raised by distinctive marks or unusual incomes, above their
fellow-citizens"; nor should they have any "extraordinary dignity . . .
attach to their stations." Government ought not to be considered
the most important segment of society. In the ideal society, concluded the *Globe*, "In all that belongs to pomp and parade the rich
citizen would excell the highest officer of government." Such a
government would strictly tend to its business, furthermore, and
not use its power to buttress social or economic establishments by
granting "monopolies or exclusive privileges," an obvious reference
to the Bank of the United States. "Under governments . . . administered by plain, industrious men who would as soon follow any other
honest business, how happy would man be!" [54] The Bank veto message alluded to the same vision when it pronounced, with the same
emphasis, "Banking . . . is *a business*. . . ." [55] While the proto-Whigs

---

[54] Washington *Globe*, July 14, 16, 19, 27, 1831. Cf. Weber: "The idea that
the bureau activities of the state are intrinsically different in character from
the management of private economic offices is a continental European notion
and, by way of contrast, is totally foreign to the American way." (*From Max
Weber*, ed. Gerth and Mills, 198.)

[55] *Messages and Papers*, ed. Richardson, II, 587. Jefferson had also used
the terms "system" and "men of business" in connection with party organiza-

looked back to the role of political leaders like Washington, Hamilton, and Jefferson, this Jacksonian vision anticipated such opportunistic, popularly oriented politicians as Abraham Lincoln as well as such plain business organizers as John D. Rockefeller and Henry Ford. Kendall, architect of Jacksonian administrative reform, performed the same function, following his retirement from politics, for the early telegraph industry. The Jacksonian ideal, in short, envisioned a society made up of just the sorts of flexible, pragmatic organizations that have since become perhaps the most typical products of American culture.

As a political leader Jackson was a transitional figure. No matter how he might try to emulate Washington, the polished military paragon, or Jefferson, the humane political sage, he could not succeed. Jackson developed no elevated rational theory; he reacted directly to events, trusting to his intuitive grasp of immediate practical expedients. Thus he recognized the utility of efficient organization when he saw some particular practical function to be performed. Jackson's character may perhaps best be measured by his choice of chief political lieutenants. In Van Buren and Kendall he demonstrated his taste for the practical, the shrewd, the opportunistic, and the efficient—even though socially obscure.

No change occurred instantaneously in July 1832. The social movement in this period had begun long before and would continue for several decades, but the Age of Jackson, and specifically the veto of the Bank of the United States, was pivotal. Around this point a colonial order made itself over into modern industrial America. Political parties and government departments, especially the post office, were then the largest organizations in the country; the Jacksonian reorganization of them gave the first practical test to innovative techniques of large-scale rational organization on a peculiarly American model. American society would, before long, reorganize itself generally into a series of these great, specialized, flexible, rationally ordered systems, made up of mobile interchangeable operatives. The efficiency and productivity of those devoted to economic affairs would become the envy of the world. There has perhaps been no more sweeping and fundamental change in all of American history. The Whig party in the 1830's recognized it for what it was and fought valiantly against it, until the utter hopelessness of the struggle became too apparent.

---

tion, but clearly meant something quite different by them. (See Jefferson to Caesar A. Rodney, Dec. 31, 1802, as quoted in Cunningham, *Jeffersonians in Power,* 75–76.)

PART II

THE MAJOR PARTIES

LEE BENSON*

Who Led the Democrats and the Whigs?

*Lee Benson's highly original study of New York State politics is one
of the most forceful refutations of the long popular idea that Jacksonians
and Whigs were mortal ideological enemies. Certainly it demonstrates
that voters—and entire communities—identified with one or the other
party for reasons that had little to do with class interest. In this chapter
he shows that top- and middle-grade leaders of the two major parties in
the Empire State were essentially of similar socioeconomic status.*

▨▨▨

DURING THE DECADE 1834 to 1844, the two major parties
in New York displayed striking similarities and profound differences.
This chapter will analyze the social composition of their leadership;
the next one will analyze their political doctrines; and the following
one will analyze the minor parties in order to highlight certain
characteristics of the major parties.

* From *The Concept of Jacksonian Democracy: New York As a Test Case*,
by Lee Benson (Princeton University Press, 1961): Chapter 4, "New York
Party Leadership, 1834–1844," pp. 64–84. Reprinted by permission of Princeton University Press.

A. Who Led the Democrats and Whigs?

If parties were characterized solely by the leaders they keep, it would be difficult to distinguish between the Democrats and Whigs. A composite account of their social and economic backgrounds reveals striking similarities. Perhaps their most significant difference is that several Democratic leaders claimed Dutch or German ancestry,[1] while the Whigs invariably claimed British ancestry (mostly by way of New England). And Democratic leaders tended to be more affluent than their Whig counterparts, or to have more affluent relatives who supported their political careers. Unless fine criteria are used, however, both parties can be said to have recruited their leaders from *the same social and economic strata.* That generalization seems warranted when we sketch the socioeconomic attributes of the half-dozen men who led each party.

Many important changes occurred in New York politics between 1827 and 1844, but major party leadership displayed remarkable continuity. Ranked somewhat arbitrarily, the top Democratic leaders were Martin Van Buren, Silas Wright, William Marcy, Edwin Croswell, Azariah Flagg, and John Dix. All were prominent members of the Albany Regency before 1834, and all maintained or improved their place in the hierarchy afterwards.[2] Their Whig counterparts were Thurlow Weed, William Seward, Horace Greeley, Francis Granger, Millard Fillmore, and Luther Bradish. All six had been Antimasons, a significant indicator of the dominant role of that faction in the new party.[3]

---

[1] In addition to Martin Van Buren who was of Dutch ancestry, William C. Bouck and Michael Hoffman were the leading representatives of the Schoharie and Mohawk Valley Germans in the Democratic Party.

[2] This rank order is based on the accounts of Jabez D. Hammond, *History of Political Parties in the State of New York,* 2: 157; Harriet A. Weed, ed., *Autobiography of Thurlow Weed,* 1: 103, 2: 36–37; De Alva S. Alexander, *Political History of the State of New York,* 1: 293–294, 2: 53; John A. Garraty, "Silas Wright and the Election of 1840 in New York State," *New York History* (July 1947), 28: 288–289; Robert V. Remini, "The Early Political Career of Martin Van Buren, 1782–1828," 318–342.

[3] The chain of command was not as distinct among the Whigs as among the Democrats. Moreover, since they did not win any statewide election before 1838, the Whigs had fewer prominent leaders. The rank order was arrived at on the basis of several criteria, including nomination for office and my estimate

1. **Top Democratic Leaders, 1834, 1844.** From the early 1820's to 1844, Martin Van Buren controlled the Albany Regency. His career might serve as the classic model for the self-made man in America. Though the Van Burens had settled on the Van Rensselaer Manor in the mid-seventeenth century, the Regency chief's father can best be described as a farmer and tavern-keeper of modest status and fortune. Despite his lower-class origin, and before he completed the course of study at Kinderhook Academy, Van Buren was articled to a leading lawyer of Columbia County. Once admitted to the bar, he rose rapidly in his profession and in politics. On his way up, he acquired polish and wealth. In 1829, when he assumed the governorship, he already had "a competence fairly earned, which his prudence and skill made grow into an ample fortune." Fulltime devotion to politics—Governor, Secretary of State, Ambassador to Great Britain, Vice-President, President—failed to diminish his fortune or lessen his financial skill. In 1837, when he assumed the presidency, the tavern-keeper's son was described as "a very rich man" whose understanding of business was "vastly better" than General Jackson's.[4]

Unlike the Regency's leader, Silas Wright came from Yankee stock, and his family ranked higher on the socioeconomic ladder than did Van Buren's. A moderately prosperous farmer, his father won election several times to the Vermont legislature. As befitted a "solid" citizen of Vermont, his son Silas attended Middlebury Academy and Middlebury College. Upon graduation, young Wright turned to the law for a career and had the good fortune to work in the office of a leading Regency politician. After his admission to the bar in 1819, with good political connections but little capital, he joined the Vermont trek to northern New York and opened a law office in Canton, St. Lawrence County.

[margin note: Van Buren]

[margin note: Silas Wright]

---

of their influence upon the party's program. For a lengthy list of "prominent men" in the Antimasonic and Whig parties see, Weed, *op.cit.*, 1: 336–337, 451–453; Alexander, *op.cit.*, 2: 18–20, 31–33, 78–81; Glyndon G. Van Deusen, *Thurlow Weed,* 74–76, 134–135; Van Deusen, *Horace Greeley* (Philadelphia, 1953), 13–14, 50–56, 96–98. Greeley had been too young to play a role in politics during the Antimasonic period, but "became deeply suspicious of the Masonic Order as a menace to democratic institutions." *Ibid.,* 13, and *New York Tribune* (w.), November 15, 1851, p. 3.

[4] Dennis T. Lynch, *An Epoch and A Man: Martin Van Buren And His Times* (New York, 1929), 15–48; Remini, *op.cit.*, 2–63, 319–326; B. Hammond, *Banks and Politics In America,* 331–332. The quotation is from Hammond.

Like many another young lawyer in New York, Wright polished up his politics while practicing law. He polished up his politics so successfully that from 1823 to 1846 he was never out of office. From the state senate he went to the House of Representatives, crossed over to the United States Senate, and wound up his career as governor of New York.

By the time he retired to private life, Wright was financially "comfortable." Compared to Van Buren and most Regency leaders, however, he had been uninterested in or had failed to take advantage of the many profitable opportunities open to politicians of note and power. In 1840, according to his own reckoning, he was "now worth about $8,000." His most recent biographer writes that, after losing his bid for re-election in 1846, "Silas undertook to become a fulltime farmer [in Canton]. His long career in politics had not made him rich, but he had accumulated a reasonable amount of property and a little money. His farm was run by several hired hands while he was away on political business at Washington or Albany, and he had interests in several local enterprises, such as grist-mills and saw-mills." [5]

William Marcy was born into a Massachusetts Federalist family, but grew up to become an ardent Jeffersonian whose views clashed sharply with those "of his family and . . . social class." He graduated from Brown University in 1808 and soon moved to the New England "colony" of Troy, New York. Like Van Buren and Wright, he practiced law and worked hard at politics. His devotion to Van Buren's Republican faction brought rich rewards. Appointed to an important state job in 1823, Marcy held a variety of offices during the next fifteen years. In succession, he served as state comptroller, judge of the state Supreme Court, United States senator, and governor. After Seward defeated him in 1838, he held important cabinet posts, including secretary of war and secretary of state.

Apart from his direct role in politics, Marcy's career symbolizes the intimate relationships enjoyed by the Democratic Party and the "business community." That he married the boss's daughter is not quite accurate, but by 1824 he had become the son-in-law and trusted associate of Benjamin Knower, a charter member of the Albany Regency and a wealthy, self-made entrepreneur. As Marcy's biog-

     [5] John A. Garraty, *Silas Wright* (New York, 1949), 11–23, 391; Franklin B. Hough, *History of St. Lawrence and Franklin Counties, New York* (Albany, 1853), 613–616; John Bigelow, *The Life of Samuel J. Tilden* (New York, 1895), 1: 102–103.

rapher puts it, a close bond developed between the two men, and "in a sense he had married not only Cornelia [Knower], but also father Benjamin as well." Knower, leaving his son-in-law to represent him in the Regency, "retired" from public life in 1824 and devoted himself to the job of expanding his business interests.

Knower had originally been a self-made man. Once on his way, he had ceased to depend solely upon his business acumen and is perhaps best described as a "political entrepreneur." Highly placed in Jacksonian ranks and president of the Albany Mechanics' and Farmers' Bank, he used his financial and political connections for grand-scale speculations in wool, real estate, water rights, and related enterprises. His "gambling proclivities" repeatedly landed him in financial hot water, however, and he "issued frequent calls for help and endeavored to warp Marcy's political course to suit his own business predilections." Marcy's intimate association with entrepreneurs on-the-make was not limited to his father-in-law, nor were his ties to the business community unusual. Among his "associates in the Democracy . . . ties with business were all too numerous." [6] With the Marcy-Knower connection in mind, this portion of the 1831 Antimasonic legislative *Address* takes on new significance: ". . . The political organization which controls this state is combined with a moneyed aristocracy . . . which owns the Mechanics' and Farmers' Bank. We find the officers and large stockholders of that institution, and their immediate connections, the most prominent leaders in the dominant party. . . . We find them embarking with the highest officers of the state, in speculations where the power of government, or the influence of its officers, can be brought to aid their projects of aggrandizement." [7]

Edwin Croswell was another Democratic leader who enjoyed close and profitable "ties with business." Born of Yankee stock in 1797 in Greene County, New York, he rose rapidly in the Regency hierarchy after his appointment as editor of the *Albany Argus* in 1823. When Van Buren picked him to run the party organ at the state capital, Croswell already had considerable experience as a Republican editor. His father had founded and edited the *Catskill Recorder* and had made him an apprentice by 1811, a partner by

---

[6] This sketch is based largely on, and the quotations are from, Ivor D. Spencer, "William L. Marcy Goes Conservative," *Mississippi Valley Historical Review*, 31: 205–224 (September 1944). See also Hammond, *Political Parties*, 2: 114, 289, 346–347, 423–488; Alexander, *op.cit.*, 1: 292–294.

[7] See pp. 48–49 above.

1818 or 1819. Apparently he was well educated, for he was respectfully referred to as "the cultured editor of the *Albany Argus*." Under his guidance, the *Argus* laid down the party line for the Van Buren press in New York and eventually became the most influential Democratic organ in the North.

One reward bestowed upon the editor of the *Argus* by a grateful party was the lucrative office of state printer. His long tenure from 1823 to 1840 proved so profitable, in fact, that a clutch of other Regency editors clamored for "rotation in office." Croswell later suffered serious financial reverses, but, while the Regency reigned, he found little difficulty in accumulating considerable wealth. Unlike Wright, he had a keen ear for opportunity knocking and "was up to his neck in the Canal Bank of Albany and other speculations."[8]

Azariah Flagg was another member of the Regency who started political life as a Republican editor. A Vermonter, he served his printer's apprenticeship with a relative and then "swarmed from the New England hive" to a Yankee colony in New York. Settling in Clinton County in 1811, he rapidly made the *Plattsburg Republican* his party's leading organ in northeastern New York. Skillful "politicking" and unrestrained attacks upon DeWitt Clinton brought him fame, Regency approval, and appointment as New York secretary of state. After 1826, his occupation is most accurately described as "government official." Seven years as secretary of state and ten years as comptroller established him as his party's expert on state finances and internal improvements.

Flagg was a leading member of the faction that later became known as "Radical Democrats," because they wanted to reverse the state's traditional policy of active intervention in the economy. He dedicated himself to strict construction, severely-limited government aid to enterprise, rigid economy, and the pay-as-you-go principle for internal improvements. True to the ascetic creed of the Radical Democrats, he was one of the few leaders of his party who "seem[s] to have stayed fairly aloof" from the "charter-mongering and meloncutting [which] were rife" at Albany during the Regency's reign.

(margin note: D.E. Yankee*)*

---

[8] The sketch of Croswell has been pieced together from a variety of sources. See Hammond, *Political Parties*, 2: 122–123, 524; Alexander, *op.cit.*, 1: 374–375, 2: 56–59; Herbert A. Donovan, *The Barnburners*, 20, 38–40; Beman Brockway, *Fifty Years In Journalism* (Watertown, N.Y., 1891), 15–18; Milton W. Hamilton, *The Country Printer* (New York, 1936), 105, n.42; Remini, 328–330; Spencer, in *MVHR*, 31: 214. (This last citation is the source of the quotation on Croswell's participation in speculative activities.)

Measured by the criteria of high political office or rich financial rewards, he apparently profited less than any other Jacksonian leader.[9]

John A. Dix completes our roster of the Regency inner circle. He belonged to the "gentlemanly" or, as critics dubbed it, "the *clean-shirt* party of the Democracy." His ancestors were "early New Englanders of English and Puritan stock. All were substantial though undistinguished citizens." New Hampshire born, Dix had been educated at Phillips Exeter, the College of Montreal, and St. Mary's College in Baltimore. An officer in the War of 1812, he had remained in the Army and been appointed aide-de-camp to the Commander of the Northern Military Department in 1819. Impressed with the prominent politicians he met during his tour of duty and having made an excellent impression upon them, Dix decided to become a lawyer. He was admitted to the bar in 1824. Two years later he married the daughter of John P. Morgan. Thanks to his father-in-law's generosity and his position as a prominent, wealthy Republican businessman and large landholder, "after his marriage ... Dix no longer depended upon the law or upon office for life's necessities."

In 1828 Dix resigned from the Army and moved to Cooperstown, New York. There he opened a law office, served as Morgan's land agent, and started to climb the Regency ladder. His father-in-law was a close friend and political ally of Martin Van Buren, which, coupled with Dix's own charm and talents, made his swift rise almost inevitable. Appointed state adjutant-general in 1830, he succeeded Flagg as secretary of state in 1833 and held that post until the Whig victory in 1838 brought the long Regency régime to an end.

Dix had been so valuable a member of the Regency that Van Buren and other leaders were disturbed by the prospect of his leaving Albany. As a result, President Van Buren wrote a letter to Dix's father-in-law and speedily relieved the anxieties of the Regency. According to Dix's biographer, "Both Dix and Mr. Morgan appreciated the need of retaining an important defender of the Administration in Albany ... [so] John stayed on with the aid and blessing of his father-in-law and his wife. The President quickly voiced his great satisfaction with the decision [to Morgan]." Though without government office for several years, Dix continued to labor in the Democratic vineyards and, in 1845, succeeded Silas Wright as

(margin note: N.E. Yankee)

[9] Remini, 330–331; Brockway, *op.cit.*, 44–45, 419; Donovan, *op.cit.*, 15–21; Hammond, *Political Parties*, 2: 214, 431; Spencer, *op.cit.*, 31: 214. (This last citation is the source of the information on Flagg's aloofness from speculation.)

United States senator. Whatever else may be said of the Regency under Van Buren's aegis, it always remained true to its first principle—to reward men for faithful service to the cause.[10]

2. The Top Whig Leaders, 1834–1844. Of the dozen men who led the two parties, Dix's family probably ranked close to highest on the socioeconomic scale; Thurlow Weed's family certainly ranked lowest. The future "dictator" of the Whig Party—like Edwin Croswell, his journalistic counterpart among Democrats—was born in 1797 and grew up in Catskill, New York. Again like Croswell, he was of New England stock and Republican heritage. There similarity stopped.

similar background

Croswell's father was owner of the village newspaper; Weed's father was a cartman frequently imprisoned for debt. "I remember with a shudder," Weed wrote in his *Autobiography*, "a sad and sleepless night occasioned by the incarceration of my own father, who though a poor man was known to be an honest one, and for that reason was enabled to give bonds that he would remain on the 'gaol liberties' until the debt (of something less than $20) was paid."

To know of the contrasting family backgrounds of their editors gives a new significance to the contrasting positions taken by the *Evening Journal* and the *Argus* on the bill abolishing imprisonment for debt. The family backgrounds also help to explain Weed's vitriolic, personal attack upon Croswell in connection with that bill. Many years later, in a letter to the editor of a Catskill paper, Weed recalled his father's imprisonment for debt and gave this account of his relationship with young Croswell: "Your correspondent [the author of an article on early Catskill days] kindly refers to the circumstance that Mr. Edwin Croswell and myself 'were boys together at Catskill.' Though of the same age, we were not intimate as boys. He had the advantage of me in position, education, etc." [11]

According to Weed's later recollections, which may exaggerate the humbleness of his birth but which are probably essentially correct, he enjoyed less than a year of formal schooling. At any rate, he was a self-educated and self-made man and whatever learning he acquired as a boy undoubtedly derived from his years of wandering as

---

[10] This sketch is largely based upon, and the quotations concerning Dix's father-in-law are from Martin Lichterman, "John Adams Dix" (Columbia University Ph.D., 1952), 3–44, 103–140. See also Alexander, 2:2–4; Spencer, 31: 207, n. 12.

[11] Weed, 1: 1–9, 379–380. The quotations are from pp. 8, 380.

a printer's apprentice and journeyman. By 1818 he had made up in experience what he lacked in schooling and Clintonian politicians set him up as a newspaper proprietor in Chenango County. Without financial resources and unable to make the paper pay, he sold out in 1820 and went to work as a journeyman printer. He knocked about for a couple of years and then settled in Rochester where he became the energetic but debt-ridden editor of an enthusiastically anti-Regency newspaper. By 1823, a local leader of the People's Party, Weed rose rapidly in politics. By 1828, he had become campaign manager of the Adams faction in western New York, Antimasonic leader, and editor of the Rochester *Anti-Masonic Enquirer.*

By 1828 Weed had worked his passage to political power but not to fortune. During his Rochester years he was poor and chronically in debt. When he moved to Albany in 1830 to edit the *Evening Journal,* however, his financial as well as political stock rose. While the 1835 to 1837 boom lasted, he dabbled modestly in real estate, railroads, and banks; he was aided in this by well-placed friends (Democrats and Whigs). During the Panic his campaign to get rich quick stalled temporarily, but started up again in high gear after the Whigs took power in 1839. By then he was firmly established in politics as "My Lord Thurlow," the "dictator" of the Whig Party. In addition to political power, he held the post of state printer, which his predecessor (Croswell) had estimated to be worth $30,000 a year. His actual income from the post can only be conjectured, but "it was enough so that after four years' possession Weed could bear witness that it had given him 'at least one man's fair proportion of this world's goods.'" Like Van Buren, his opposite number in the Regency, the humbly-born leader of the Whigs had not overlooked the possibility that the road to power could also become the road to riches.[12]

The middle man in the Whig triumvirate of "Weed, Seward, and Greeley" was born in Orange County, New York. He came of "good, plain" British stock who "stood well in the communities in which they lived." During the course of a many-sided career as physician, landowner, merchant, and county judge, his father had improved the family's fortune and prestige. He had done so well, in fact, that in addition to owning a few slaves, he had been able to found an academy, name it after himself, and endow it with $20,000—a sizeable sum in early nineteenth century rural New York.

Blessed with a father of such academic tastes and financial acu-

---

[12] This sketch is based primarily upon Van Deusen, *Weed,* 3–109. The quotation is from p. 108.

men, William H. Seward received an excellent education and was admitted to the bar shortly after graduating from Union College. He accepted the offer of a law partnership in Auburn, county seat of Cayuga County. Located in the midst of a fertile region recently settled by New Englanders, Auburn offered many opportunities to a well-educated man of Seward's background and talents.

Politics was traditionally the high road to fame and fortune of ambitious young New York lawyers; Seward was off and running hard soon after arriving in Auburn. Dr. Seward had been a staunch Jeffersonian who had passed his Republican faith on to his son, and, like many other Republicans in 1824, young Seward joined the anti-Regency faction. He was active in the People's Party campaign and during the next four years became firmly identified with the "friends of Adams" while working discreetly with the Antimasons in Cayuga County. After the 1828 election, which left the Adams Republican faction "practically dissolved and in ruins," Seward openly joined the Antimasons and continued to battle against the Regency and Jackson. In 1830, after having been a delegate to several Antimasonic state and national conventions, he won election to the state senate from a district once counted as a Regency stronghold. Not yet 30, Seward was already a "full-fledged politician."

Seward took full advantage of the four-year term in the senate to display his political talents and to help consolidate the Regency's opponents. As a result, despite Seward's youth, Weed succeeded in making his protégé the first Whig candidate for governor. Defeated in the 1834 campaign, Seward won in 1838 and again in 1840, but did not stand for re-election in 1842.

During the next few years, Seward worked hard to repair his badly-battered financial position. By the time he took office in 1839, he had accumulated about $50,000 or $60,000 from his law practice and from investments in Auburn real estate and other speculations. In addition, he owned a substantial interest in the firm that had bought part of the Holland Land Company's remaining holdings; eventually it yielded rich returns, but not until years after he retired to private life in 1843.

Not only had Seward failed to make the governorship pay, but his "moderate personal estate had nearly melted away" as a result of "the general financial crisis and his large expenditures when in office." He owed so much money, in fact, that some friends suggested bankruptcy proceedings as the only alternative to life-long indebtedness. Refusing to take that way out, he continued to be hard-pressed to meet obligations for several years. Clearly, their joint rise to political power had not brought Seward the financial rewards that had come to his more humbly-born mentor and friend, Thurlow Weed.[13]

Like the senior member of the Whig triumvirate, Horace Greeley was a poor journeyman printer who travelled the editorial road to political influence. But Greeley had a somewhat better start than Weed. His father at least held title to the farm near Amherst, New Hampshire where Greeley was born in 1811. He later described himself as the "son of a poor and hard-working farmer, struggling to pay off the debt he had incurred in buying his high-priced farm." [14] This self-description is consistent with a recent biographer's characterization of his mixed English and Scotch-Irish ancestors as "undistinguished, middle-class, small town and country folk, mostly farmers and blacksmiths." [15]

Although "middle-class" might describe Greeley's father, that term has a remarkably elastic range in the United States and is frequently misleading. Never prosperous, his father was hard-hit by the Panic of 1819. Like many other Yankees, he lost his farm and literally had to take to the Vermont woods to escape debtor's prison. After the farm was sold to satisfy creditors, and after a traumatic hand-to-mouth interval as a woodchopper—this experience left an indelible impression on his son Horace—he started to farm again in another section of New Hampshire. The miserable, hard-scrabble place was called, appropriately enough, "Flea Knoll."

Throughout most of Greeley's boyhood, the family experienced desperate poverty. In all, young Horace managed to get only 45 months of district schooling over a ten-year period. But formal education was an unnecessary luxury. A prodigy, he read remarkably well at the age of four. When he was thirteen, "an honest teacher confessed . . . that the boy knew more than he did and might as well stay home. This ended his formal schooling." Two years later he became a fulltime printer's apprentice.

Five years of hard work on a New Hampshire country weekly gave Greeley a trade. But at $40 a year the trade gave him little

---

[13] A modern biography of Seward is badly needed, but some of the requisite information is found in Frederic Bancroft, *The Life of William H. Seward* (New York, 1900), 1: 1–134, and Frederick W. Seward, ed., *William H. Seward: An Autobiography*, 1: 19–159. The financial information is compactly presented in Bancroft, 1: 131–134.

[14] Horace Greeley, *Recollections of a Busy Life* (New York, 1868), 38.

[15] Van Deusen, *Horace Greeley*, 5. The present capsule account is based largely upon *ibid.*, 5–128. It also draws upon Greeley's reminiscences of his trials and troubles in *Recollections*, 22–143.

chance to acquire much of the world's goods. Actually, most of his
scant wages went to help his family, who were then trying to make
a go of farming in Pennsylvania. After about another year as a
wandering journeyman printer, in 1831 young Greeley set out for
New York to find his fortune, "twenty-five dollars in his pocket and
his red-handkerchief bundle on his shoulder." He arrived there with
ten dollars.

Like most poor farmers in their section of New Hampshire (and
many other places) who were interested in politics, the Greeleys had
been ardent Federalists. Not surprisingly, the newspapers that
Greeley read as a boy and the one on which he served his apprenticeship were Federalist in tone. During his apprenticeship, though
not yet old enough to vote, he considered himself an Adams
Republican and strongly sympathized with the efforts of the People's
Party to overthrow the Albany Regency. That campaign to win
popular suffrage for presidential electors apparently instilled in him
a deep and abiding distrust of Van Buren; thereafter, he identified
himself with the anti-Jackson, anti-Regency political factions. In
turn, he was Adams Republican, Antimason, and Whig.

But in August 1831 when Greeley arrived in New York, he was
only a poor journeyman printer in search of a job. He worked on
various papers for a couple of years, formed a partnership in 1833
with another young journeyman, and scrounged around for jobwork.
Moderate prosperity spurred ambition. In 1834 the young printers
turned publishers and brought out the *New Yorker,* a literary
weekly. The partnership dissolved in 1836, however. As his share,
Greeley took sole ownership of the magazine. Then came the Panic
of 1837. Like many other enterprising men, he was on the verge
of bankruptcy. At this critical juncture in his career, the proverbial
good angel appeared in the guise of Thurlow Weed.

With Weed's assistance, Greeley became editor of a cheap political weekly which the Whigs founded to promote their cause in the
1838 campaign. Greeley, aided by two newly-acquired partners,
hung on to the *New Yorker* while he edited the *Jeffersonian* for the
Whigs. During the 1840 campaign, he edited the *Log Cabin,* a remarkably popular paper that replaced the *Jeffersonian.*

By the spring of 1841, Greeley enjoyed modest prosperity. Freedom from debt again spurred ambition. He abandoned both the *New
Yorker* and the *Log Cabin* to found a new kind of journal, a cheap
Whig daily in New York City. Together with a well-to-do partner
who supplied some capital and managed the business end, Greeley
rapidly established the *Tribune*—particularly its weekly edition—

as one of the country's great papers. His intellectual and political influence grew with the growth of the *Tribune's* circulation and prestige. By the mid-1840's, Greeley ranked as junior partner in the famous firm of "Weed, Seward and Greeley."

Though he had experienced desperate poverty, Greeley, unlike Weed and Van Buren, showed little interest and less ability in improving his fortune. To quote the foremost historian of American journalism: "Greeley was never a moneymaker.... None of his various enterprises thus far [prior to 1841] had been profitable; and even in later years, when the *Tribune* was showing large profits, he received little more than a salary—having allowed nine-tenths of his proprietary stock holdings to pass into other hands." [16]

According to family position, Francis Granger can be ranked as the Whig equivalent of John A. Dix. Actually, he ranked higher on the social scale than any other major party leader, and stands out as the only Whig leader who had important family connections. Significantly, they were Jeffersonian Republican family connections.

The first Granger in America arrived in Massachusetts from England in 1652 and moved to Connecticut in 1674. Granger's father was born there and was educated at Yale. A successful lawyer, he served as a distinguished member of the Jefferson and Madison cabinets. After thirteen years in the nation's capital, he retired and settled in western New York, "whither his reputation had preceded him, and where he was at once accorded the station to which his abilities entitled him." Elected to the state senate, he "became conspicuous in cooperation with Governor DeWitt Clinton in promoting the [state's] great system of internal improvements...."

With remarkable fidelity, Francis Granger followed the pattern of public service set by his father. Born in Connecticut, educated at Yale, trained as a lawyer, he practiced his profession in Canandaigua, which might well be called his family seat. In Weed's words, he was "a gentleman of accomplished manners, genial temperament, and fine presence, with fortune, leisure, and a taste for public life." Beginning in 1826, admiring constituents gratified that taste and for a number of terms elected him to the legislature.

As might have been expected, given his father's career, his residence in western New York, and his "taste for public life," Granger emerged as a high-ranking Adams Republican and a prominent Antimason. He was narrowly defeated for governor in 1830 and 1832 and had no better luck in 1836 as the Whig candidate for vice-

_____

[16] Frank L. Mott, *American Journalism* (New York, 1950, rev. ed.), 269.

president. Since he had been the party's standard-bearer during its years of adversity, Granger felt entitled to head the state ticket in 1838 when a Whig victory was almost certain. But "my lord Thurlow" used his persuasive arts, and Seward received the Whig nomination; Granger contented himself with a seat in Congress. Re-elected in 1840, he resigned to become postmaster-general in Harrison's administration.

But Harrison's death and Tyler's succession to the presidency disrupted the first Whig cabinet, and, together with most of its other members, Granger resigned. Faithful constituents re-elected him to Congress in November 1841. He served that term but never again held a major public office, although he remained an influential Whig leader and eventually headed the faction opposed to the Weed-Seward-Greeley wing of the party.[17]

Millard Fillmore celebrated the arrival of the nineteenth century by being born in a log cabin in Cayuga County, New York. His autobiography records, with apparent accuracy, that he came from New England stock and "humble origins." As was true of many other pioneers, Fillmore's father lost his property because of a faulty title. He then moved to another part of that county and took a perpetual lease on a small "farm," wholly uncleared and covered with heavy timber. Following the typical pattern of poor boys on the New York frontier, Fillmore spent his first fifteen years learning "to do all kinds of work which is usually done in clearing and cultivating a new farm." (Poor boys do not necessarily become "friends of the poor" when they grow up, but Fillmore's background may partly account for his introduction of the bill to abolish imprisonment for debt and his leadership of western New York debtor-farmers in their fight against the Holland Land Company.)

During childhood Fillmore received some intermittent instruction in village schools, but his education was as sketchy as his father's means were sparse. Misfortune having given the elder Fillmore a "great distaste" for farming, he earnestly wanted his sons to

(margin note: N.E. Yankee)

---

[17] George S. Conover, ed., *History of Ontario County, New York* (Syracuse, N.Y., 1893), 469–473; Weed, 1: 391–392; Alexander, 1: 358–377, 393–404; 2: 19–21, 47–51, 153–154; Seward, ed., Seward's *Autobiography*, 1: 171–172. No direct information is available concerning Granger's efforts or abilities to increase the family fortune. But if Seward's assessment in 1831 was accurate, it is highly likely that Granger had done so—or at least attempted to do so. Writing to his wife about Granger, Seward noted, "There is yet one quality of Granger's character which you do not dream of—he loves money almost as well as power." *Ibid.,* 1: 172.

take up some other occupation. "His means did not justify him or them in aspiring to any profession," however, "and therefore, he wished them to learn trades." In 1815 young Fillmore was apprenticed to a wool-carder on a part-time basis. From June to December he carded wool, "went to school some during the winters of 1816 and 1817, and worked on the farm during the spring."

Driven by the desire to rise above the station of a wool carder, Fillmore acquired additional schooling and, by the stroke of good fortune usually found in the careers of self-made men, became a lawyer's clerk. He intermittently taught school and clerked at law in Cayuga and Erie counties until he won admission to the Buffalo bar in 1823. "But not having sufficient confidence in myself to enter into competition with the older members of the [Buffalo] Bar . . . I opened an office at East Aurora, where I practiced till May, 1830; when I formed a partnership with Joseph Clary and removed to Buffalo, which has ever since been my place of residence [written sometime after 1858]."

Little detailed information is available about Fillmore's finances, but it seems likely that his law firm prospered as his political career advanced. The historian of Erie County, however, suggests that although Fillmore made the law "a stepping stone to public life," he was not greatly interested in making it "a direct route to the center of economic affairs."

After he met Weed at an Adams convention in Buffalo, in 1828, Fillmore's political career flourished. The young lawyer impressed Weed, who suggested his nomination for the state assembly. Fillmore was elected as an Antimason and represented Erie County for the next three years. Devotion to Antimasonry, support of bills to abolish imprisonment for debt, and political opposition to the Holland Land Company made Fillmore increasingly popular. Elected to Congress in 1832, he served four terms in the House of Representatives and by 1844 "was well known and at the height of his popularity."

Having been born in a log cabin and filling to perfection the role of the self-made American, the erstwhile wool carder's apprentice envisioned himself as the ideal Whig candidate for vice-president in 1844. For various reasons, his party chose to regard him as the most available Whig gubernatorial nominee, and in that year he was defeated for state rather than national office. In 1848, however, he was elected vice-president; when Taylor died in 1850, he succeeded to the presidency. More than Van Buren, perhaps even more than

Jackson, Fillmore demonstrates how every American boy can grow up to be president.[18]

The family status of Luther Bradish can be compared with that of William Marcy. He was born in a small town in Massachusetts, the son of Colonel John Bradish. His father's rank, his own graduation from Williams College in 1804, and his subsequent activities, suggest that he came from at least a moderately well-placed and well-to-do family. Moving to New York City after graduation, Bradish studied law and was admitted to the bar. Apparently his first identification with Franklin County, New York, came in 1815 when he and several partners purchased approximately 30,000 acres in the town of Moira. Bradish eventually took over his partners' interests and continued to buy and sell lands in Franklin and nearby counties until 1859, although he had disposed of most of his holdings for $54,000 in 1835.

Bradish actually took up residence in Franklin County in 1826, and, as befitted the local landed proprietor, his establishment at Moira was "a pretentious one." According to Franklin's historian, since he was "of imposing presence, courtly manners, gracious and benign consideration for others, entertaining in reminiscences of extensive travel and public affairs, erudite in politics and law, and a master among men, he became with his first appearance in the county a popular leader and exercised a commanding influence. Whether he should be regarded as the ablest man that this county has ever given to the public service, no adequate record remains to form a basis for judgment, but it probably may be safely claimed for him that he was at least the most accomplished, and that no one here surpassed him in personal popularity and in the public estimation which it is worth while to gain and hold."

The popular Bradish, elected to the assembly in 1827 as an Adams Republican, served two more terms before the Antimasons nominated him for Congress. Although defeated, he continued to lead the Antimasons in his section of the state, and in 1834 helped to organize the Whig Party. From 1836 to 1838 he represented Franklin County in the assembly and served as speaker during his last term.

---

[18] Fillmore's brief autobiographical account of his life until 1828 is printed in Frank H. Severance, ed., "Millard Fillmore Papers," Buffalo Historical Society *Publications*, 10: 3–15. See also *ibid.*, 10: v–xxxv, 17–26, 43–65, and *passim*. Other sources on which this sketch is based are John T. Horton, et al., *History of Northwestern New York*, 1: 88–90, 93–94, 108–109; Alexander, 1: 371–372, 379, 2: 38, 79–89; Van Deusen, *Weed*, 93, 98–104, 127, 132–136. (The quotation concerning Fillmore's attitude toward money-making is from Horton, *op.cit.*, 1: 109.)

Bradish attracted attention as "an unusually able speaker" whom the northern counties chose for Whig gubernatorial nominee in 1838. Like Granger, his political aspirations were frustrated when Weed artfully secured the prize for Seward. As consolation, Bradish was nominated for lieutenant-governor and served in that post from 1839 to 1842. In the latter year, he finally secured the gubernatorial nomination, only to be defeated by the Democratic resurgence.

The 1842 campaign represented Bradish's last bid for elective office, but he remained an influential figure in the Whig Party. Like Granger and Fillmore, he eventually identified himself with the Whig faction that opposed the Weed-Seward-Greeley triumvirate. And, though the appointment came several years after the time span covered by this chapter, it is worth noting that Bradish was named to the office of United States assistant treasurer for New York by "his early and much esteemed friend, President Fillmore." [19]

B. Middle-Grade Democratic and Whig Leaders: Who Were They?

To say that the major parties recruited their *top* leaders from essentially the same social strata only partially answers the question of who led the Democrats and Whigs. Partial answers frequently give rise to misleading or erroneous conclusions, and comprehensive analysis of the social structure of party leadership requires more than a collective socioeconomic biography of the one or five dozen men who formally fulfilled that role. Political leadership is exercised in ways other than formal public activity. Political power is no less potent for being indirect.[20]

On the crudest level, one question relevant to political leadership is: where did the "sinews of war" come from? Posed more comprehensively: upon which groups did the top party leaders depend for financial, intellectual and moral assistance and stimulus? Did men

---

[19] This account is largely based upon the material in Frederick J. Seaver, *Historical Sketches of Franklin County* (Albany, 1918), 696–704. See also Alexander, 2: 18–21, 51; Hammond, *Political Parties*, 2: 263, 293, 480–485; Van Deusen, *Weed*, 134.

[20] See Charles E. Merriam and Harold Foote Gosnell, *The American Party System* (New York, 1949, 4th ed.), 146–163; Heinz Eulau, et al., *Political Behavior* (Glencoe, Ill., 1956), 175–204.

of wealth strongly tend to give their resources, talents, and prestige to the Whigs rather than to the Democrats? Did a large proportion of the business community—however defined—adhere to the Whig faith? [21] Or, did a Whig orator describe the situation more accurately when, in 1844, he sarcastically rejected the Democratic charge that "the privileged orders," the "rich men," restricted their support to his party? "The rich men are divided;—*how* divided may be seen in the fact that the five largest landed proprietors of this State, each owning [or claiming] a large fraction of the counties in which they reside, are Loco-Foco—*ultra*-Loco-Foco [that is, Democrats]—and that a formidable number of the wealthy merchants of this city are Loco-Foco. *Many of the sons of rich men, ambitious of political preferment are Loco-Foco, though their fathers may be nominal, inactive Whigs* [italics added]." [22]

The last sentence is suggestive. By exploiting the clue it supplies, historians may be able to clear away the rhetorical rubbish and reveal the social structure of party leadership during the Age of Egalitarianism.

After Jackson's Bank veto message in 1832, and particularly after 1837, when Martin Van Buren awoke to the political possibilities of Locofocoism (discussed in Chapter V), Democratic rhetoric was designed to sound something like class war. One Whig response to that rhetoric was to portray the Democrats as "desperate and revolutionary enemies of Law and Order" who would impose "agrarian and destructive legislation" and bring about "popular demoralization, ruin and revolution. . . ." But class war rhetoric need not reflect reality. In fact, it has frequently been used to conceal rather than to reveal the socioeconomic status and the political objectives of those who use it. Moreover, it cannot be automatically assumed that class war rhetoric actually influenced political reality and changed the social structure of political leadership.

After long years of Antimasonic frenzy and Jacksonian counter-

---

[21] The thesis that they did seems to have received its first full statement in Dixon Ryan Fox, *The Decline of Aristocracy In The Politics of New York*, 285, 409–439, and *passim*. The evidence it adduces for dividing the parties along class lines is flimsy, where it is not erroneous. The basis for this conclusion will appear in Chapter VII through IX, where an analysis is made of 1844 group voting patterns. The fullest expression of the thesis that American political history has been an enduring struggle between the business community and "the other sections of society" is presented in Arthur M. Schlesinger, Jr., *The Age of Jackson*, 505, and *passim*.

[22] *New York Tribune* (w.), October 19, 1844, p. 1.

frenzy, who listened, and who believed? More precisely, who from 1834 to 1844 took the campaign claptrap literally? Had not partisan rhetoric come to be regarded as another form of American folklore, an oratorical indulgence to be enjoyed at regular intervals and ignored once the election was over and the country again "saved"? Granted that party loyalties were passionate and deeply rooted and that politics intensely concerned Americans in that decade. It does not follow that *all* aspects of the political process were regarded with equal seriousness and that campaign rhetoric was treated as Holy Writ.

The relative stability of New York voting patterns from 1832 to 1844 (discussed in Chapter VII) suggests that later historians have been more vulnerable to partisan claims than were contemporaries who experienced them directly. Populistic rhetoric had become so standard a feature of election campaigns that voters may well have developed immunity to it. (Do American voters take American politicians at face value today?) Moreover, the daily experiences of contemporaries gave them a real-life basis for assessing how reliable were partisan claims. In short, political rhetoric is not a reliable source for inferences about the social structure of American political leadership.

But an 1845 *Tribune* editorial made specific claims, which are subject to verification. "The Whigs are by no means all wealthy, nor are the wealthy all Whigs. A large proportion of the Capitalists, Landlords, Bankers, Brokers, etc., belong to the other party. For instance, of the manors of this State, we observe that far more than half the leased lands are owned by those who belong to what is called the Democratic party.—Most of the Banks of our City were chartered by that party, and a good many are still controlled by its members and officered from its ranks. The present Collector of Customs at this Port stepped out of a Bank Presidency into the Collectorship. *There are many members of the so-called 'Democratic' party in this city who are worth from $100,000 each to $1,000,000 or over.* [italics added]." [23]

The design of this study does not permit the research necessary to test all the claims made in the editorial quoted above. But testing one of them does provide a basis for assessing the *Tribune's* claims about party divisions among economic elite groups in New York.

---

[23] *Ibid.*, September 20, 1845, p. 3.

1. Ratification Meeting Officers Who Were "Wealthy Citizens."
In January 1845, the sixth edition of a fascinating social document
was published; the lengthy title suggests its contents: *Wealth and
Biography of the Wealthy Citizens of New York City, Comprising
An Alphabetical Arrangement of Persons Estimated To Be Worth
$100,000, And Upwards—With The Sums Appended To Each
Name. . . .* [24] If the *Tribune's* claims are verifiable, the men listed on
that roll-call should not have displayed heavily disproportionate
preference for the Whig Party. And for our purposes, the publication date could not have been better timed. If the much-advertised
Democratic conversion to Locofocoism in 1837 to 1838 had really
driven or frightened the "rich men" away, the purge should have
been complete by 1844, when the sixth edition was prepared.

In order to carry out this test, some sampling procedure must be
devised for an analysis of the register of approximately one thousand *Wealthy Citizens*. Since our aim here is to get at the social
structure of party leadership, not the sources of mass support, it is
desirable to find an objective basis for classifying as "middle-grade
party leaders" a limited number of "Wealthy Citizens." I believe
that the independent criteria used to draw up two separate lists
satisfy that requirement.

In New York City, during the 1844 campaign, both the Democrats and Whigs held their customary great public meetings to
"ratify" the nominees of their national conventions. Designed to
heal intraparty wounds and to rally the faithful against the enemy,
these meetings followed standard formats. Much the same considerations, we may assume, governed both parties in their choice of the
president and many vice-presidents who nominally controlled them.
Since the ratification meetings formed an important part of the campaign, in all likelihood politically active men, who can accurately be
classified as middle-grade party leaders, were selected for these positions. Although the *Wealthy Citizens* register cannot be considered
a comprehensive collective biography, we can learn from it how
many of the men who made the honor list at Democratic and Whig
ratification meetings also made its pages.[25]

Analysis of the register essentially supports the *Tribune's* claim

---

[24] That document (as well as several precursors) is conveniently repro-
duced in Henry Wysham Lanier, *A Century of Banking In New York: 1822–
1922* (New York, 1922), 151–184. It is alphabetically arranged.

[25] The Whig list is taken from the *New York Morning Express*, May 7,
1844, p. 2; the Democratic list from the *New York Morning News*, September

about party divisions among the "rich men" of New York City. Of the 54 Democrats honored by their party, the president and 13 vice-presidents, or 26 per cent, were "Wealthy Citizens." [26] Of the 35 Whigs honored by their party, 12 vice-presidents, or 34 per cent, belonged to the same class. [27] Not large enough to be significant in any case, the percentage difference disappears when *the same size sample is used.* Neither party list was alphabetical. Men's party status as well as their prestige in the community apparently determined their rank order position. Thus, of the first 10 names on each list, 60 per cent were "Wealthy Citizens." When we restrict analysis to the 35 highest ranking Democrats (the total number in the Whig sample), the proportion of Democratic rich men rises to 34 per cent. On this level of leadership, therefore, the Democrats and the Whigs had drawn upon rich men in the same proportion. Using another criterion to select a sample of rich, middle-grade party leaders, we get the same results.

2. **"Wealthy Citizens" identified as Party Leaders.** The *Wealthy Citizens* register provided widely varying information for each entry. It ranged from a bare listing of name and estimated worth ("McBrair James—100,000") to a lush, full-page biography celebrating John Jacob Astor's rise from furs to landed riches. But

---

17, 1844, p. 2. The Democratic meeting in September was used because Van Buren's defeat for the nomination at the party's national convention had aroused bitter resentment in New York. It took several months for important sections of the New York party leadership to become reconciled to the Polk and Dallas ticket. Thus the *News's* headline for its story on the September meeting read, "Old Tammany in A Blaze Of Glory/Tremendous Re-Union Of the Democracy of New York."

[26] John Targee, Stephen Allen, Preserved Fish, J. M. Bradhurst, Peter Cooper, Charles K. Ferris, Peter Smith, Walter Bowne, Abraham Van Ness, George Arcularis, Charles A. Clinton [DeWitt Clinton's son!], John B. Lasalla, Isaac L. Varian Beach, John Pettigrew. As printed, the list totaled 55 names, but one could not be identified positively. Several men who could have been "M. Burke" appear in contemporary directories and the widow of "M. R. Burke" was listed among the wealthy citizens in 1845. Abraham Van Ness's name was misprinted as "Abram Van Nest" in the *News,* but no such name appears in the city directories. From the description in the *Wealthy Citizens* register, it is clear that "Van Nest" was "Van Ness." See John Doggett, Jr., *The New-York City Directory for 1844–1845* (New York, 1844), 358. As was true of the top leaders, the Democratic list included more men of non-British stock than did the Whig list.

[27] Stephen Whitney, William Adee, William H. Aspinwall, Robert Hyslop, John Haggerty, Abraham R. Lawrence, John Drake, Peletiah Perit, Philip Hone, William Samuel Johnson, James W. Gerard, Gardiner G. Howland.

clearly, the compilers had not attempted systematically to ascertain or to list political affiliations. Only a small proportion of the entries contained such information and a number of well-known party leaders were not identified as such (for example, David Dudley Field, Samuel Ruggles, John Van Buren). Where political affiliations were noted, however, the descriptions suggest that they enjoyed at least some leadership status in their party. Typical characterizations read: "An influential man in the democratic ranks," "the democratic candidate for Mayor at the last election," "distinguished as a Whig politician," "the standing Whig candidate for Mayor."

Twenty five wealthy citizens were explicitly identified with the major parties: 13 Democrats (52 per cent) and 12 Whigs (48 per cent).[28] For all practical purposes, this finding parallels that obtained from analyzing ratification meeting officers. Because the two lists were based on independent criteria, it seems particularly noteworthy that they yielded the same results. (There was little overlapping; only five names appear on both lists.)

Aside from supporting the *Tribune's* claims, our analysis of party divisions among New York's wealthy citizens is also consonant with our findings about the top Democratic and Whig leaders. I do not claim to have "proved" that the men who led and controlled both major parties in New York belonged to the same socioeconomic strata. I do claim, however, that the above data make that hypothesis appear potentially verifiable.[29] If subsequent research does verify it, and if the same situation is found to have obtained elsewhere during the 1840's, American historians will be confronted by this interesting and difficult question: what, if anything, differentiated men who belonged to the same socioeconomic strata but who led parties that advocated different and directly conflicting theories of liberalism? For, as I shall now try to show, contrary to the concept of Jacksonian Democracy, party battles in New York cannot be viewed primarily as battles between "liberals" and "conservatives."

---

[28] The Democrats were David Banks, Henry Brevoort, Benjamin F. Butler, Johnathan I. Coddington, Charles G. Ferris, Preserved Fish, Eli Hart, William Paulding, John Pettigrew, John Targee, Johnathan Thompson, William W. Todd, James R. Whiting. The Whigs were Henry Andrew, R. M. Blatchford, Richard F. Carman, Edwin B. Clayton, Moses H. Grinnell, Oliver T. Hewlett, Philip Hone, William Samuel Johnson, Robert Jones, Gulian C. Verplanck, Caleb S. Woodhull.

[29] Additional support for the conclusions presented here is found in a study of New York party leadership during the 1850's. See an unusually thorough Master's Essay, Norman Dain, "The Social Composition of the Leadership of Tammany Hall in New York City: 1855–1865" (Columbia University, M.A., 1957), 94–99, and *passim.*

FRANK OTTO GATELL*†

The Anti-Jacksonian Animus of Rich Men

Frank Otto Gatell is the author of a number of penetrating essays on banking and politics in the Jacksonian era. On the one hand, he has exposed sordid aspects of the Jacksonian policy toward the "pet banks." On the other, he has effectively refuted Bray Hammond's thesis that the Bank War resulted from a desire to have Wall Street replace Chestnut Street as the nation's financial capitol. Clearly Professor Gatell is a scholar not easily categorized. In the following article he indicates that New York Ciy's rich men were overwhelmingly Whig in their political affiliations. He makes the important point that while the relatively small number of Democratic and Whig party leaders in New York State may have been of roughly similar wealth and social status, it does not follow that the Metropolis's many wealthy men were equally divided. His conclusions thus represent a significant challenge to the view that the two major parties of the Jackson era were basically similar.

XXXXXXXXXXXXXXXXXXXXXXXXXXXXXXXXXXXXXXXXXXXXXXXXXXXXXXXXXXXXXX

———————

* From Frank Otto Gatell, "Money and Party in Jacksonian America: A Quantitative Look at New York City's Men of Quality," *Political Science Quarterly*, LXXXII, No. 2 (June, 1967), pp. 235–252.

† Grateful acknowledgment is made to the American Philosophical Society, the American Council of Learned Societies, and the Academic Senate Committee on Research, University of California, for grants-in-aid which made possible the research for this article.

IN OLDEN TIMES, that is, a generation or more ago, American historians proceeded upon a basic assumption when discussing the Jacksonian period: the Democratic party was the party of the people, and the Whig party was the party of economic privilege. The Democrats included in their ranks the common man, the farmers, the artisans, and the mechanics, the poor but honest sinew of Jacksonian Democracy. Conversely, the Whigs were the rich merchants and the wealthy planters who made up a self-styled "better sort." They were thinly disguised Federalists, vainly striving to stem the populistic tide.[1]

This economic class interpretation of political divisions came under severe attack during the two decades following the Second World War. First the entrepreneurial or "Columbia" school argued that Jacksonians shared the capitalistic ethos of their Whig antagonists, and that they were merely demanding equal time at the feeding trough.[2] A short time later, the writers of the complementary consensus school went beyond the identity of outlook that supposedly existed between established Whig capitalists and nascent Jacksonian capitalists, and argued that agreement on fundamental issues has been the hallmark of American politics at all levels. They insisted that meaningful correlations between voting behavior and economic status were hard to come by, if not nonexistent.

In the latter category, the word of Lee Benson stands as an influential example. His study of voting behavior in New York State in 1844, *The Concept of Jacksonian Democracy*,[3] has in the few years since its publication in 1961 gone through several printings, including two paperback editions, and has become one of the most widely discussed volumes on Jacksonianism, even gaining the rare accolade of a session at a historical convention devoted entirely to its appraisal. Benson's book has not swept all before it—the con-

---

[1] See, for example, E. Malcolm Carroll, *Origins of the Whig Party* (Durham, No. Carolina, 1925), 189–220; George Rawlings Poage, *Henry Clay and the Whig Party* (Chapel Hill, 1936), 11–12; and, for New York, Dixon Ryan Fox, *The Decline of Aristocracy in the Politics of New York 1801–1840* (New York, 1919), 409–49.

[2] Charles Grier Sellers Jr., "Andrew Jackson versus the Historians," *Mississippi Valley Historical Review*, XLIV (1958), 627–30.

[3] Lee Benson, *The Concept of Jacksonian Democracy: New York as a Test Case* (Princeton, 1961). Benson does not write of an America without social conflicts, but he gives primacy to ethnic and religious factors as determinants for group behavior, discarding the haves-versus-the-have-nots basis of liberal historiography.

servatism of the historical profession is guarantee against such sweeping triumphs whatever the new viewpoint may be—but even critics have conceded that it made a breakthrough in methodology, a departure which afforded a fresh approach to the Age of Jackson, and perhaps to American politics in general.

Benson's methodology breathed academic modernity from every pore. He employed the rhetorical and structural paraphernalia of the social sciences. And particularly in those passages which demolished historiographical shibboleths, Benson ardently championed a marriage of historical dilletantism with the virile social sciences— an alliance meant to rescue history from old-maid antiquarianism.[4] Such a union will be solemnized before long, and the historical discipline will profit by it; so say most of the younger practitioners of the historian's craft. Thus Benson placed himself in the vanguard, and his methodological *tour de force* gave almost irresistible impetus to his thesis.

Benson was especially assiduous in attacking the older view that in the Jacksonian era parties divided along class lines. In a section on party leadership, he attempted to establish a sociological identity among New York State Democrats and Whigs at the top rank, and his analysis extended with similar results into "Middle-Grade Leaders."[5] But in the process, to borrow a figure from the politics of New York in the eighteen-forties, Benson may have turned Barnburner to get rid of a few rats. A closer inspection of a small but important part of the smoldering ashes than has previously been attempted is called for. The comments which follow are not offered as an assessment of Benson's book as a whole. His theory of voting cycles and his call for a multivariate analytical approach to voting behavior are stimulating, and they will doubtless receive careful appraisal and criticism as his hypotheses are tested.[6]

I

"Partial answers," Benson declared at the beginning of his section on party leadership, "frequently give rise to misleading or erro-

[4] See, for example, Lee Benson, "Research Problems in American Political Historiography," in Mirra Komarovsky (ed.), *Common Frontiers of the Social Sciences* (Glencoe, 1957), 113–83.

[5] Benson, *Jacksonian Democracy*, 64–85.

[6] Charles Sellers, "The Equilibrium Cycle in Two-Party Politics," *Public Opinion Quarterly*, XXIX (1965), 25, note; 32.

neous conclusions." [7] No one can fault that observation, but in practice Benson himself emerged with answers that were partial, misleading, and erroneous. The questions he posed in that section went beyond the stated initial problem of the social composition of middle grade political leadership. In addition, and much more significantly, he asked: "Did men of wealth strongly tend to give their resources, talents, and prestige to the Whigs rather than to the Democrats? Did a large proportion of the business community—however defined—adhere to the Whig faith?" [8] In arguing for the negative, Benson cited an unnamed Whig orator to the effect that New York's rich men were divided politically and that many Democrats were in fact wealthy. The orator did not contend, however, that the wealthy men were divided *evenly* between the parties. But, according to Benson, "by exploiting the clue" provided by the orator's imprecise claim, "historians may be able to clear away the rhetorical rubbish and reveal the social structure of party leadership during the Age of Egalitarianism." [9] Rhetorical rubbish, or the injection of something resembling class conflict into the Democratic-Whig struggle of the late eighteen-thirties, thus became the impediment. "Who from 1834 to 1844 took the [Democratic] campaign claptrap literally?" Benson asked derisively.[10] A fairer question might be: Who took the campaigning seriously? and the answer would be: A great many people. For, as is the case of twentieth-century advertising, which is also not to be taken literally, the effectiveness of rhetorical claptrap cannot be dismissed.

So much for rhetoric. What about verifiable data? Benson quoted from an editorial in Greeley's *Tribune* which tried to distribute part of the odium attached to the possession of wealth to the Democrats: "The Whigs are by no means all wealthy, nor are the wealthy all Whigs," etc., etc.[11] Some of Greeley's statements were themselves rhetorical claptrap. For example, Greeley "charged" that Democrats chartered most of New York City's banks. Since the Democratic Albany regency had controlled the legislature almost

---

[7] Benson, *Jacksonian Democracy*, 79.

[8] *Ibid.*, 80. Two questions (composition of middle-grade political leadership and voting behavior of wealthy citizens) run through the discussion on pages 79–85. I am concerned with the second.

[9] Benson, *Jacksonian Democracy*, 80.

[10] *Ibid.*, 81.

[11] *Ibid.*, 81–82.

continuously for a generation, the statement was a truism. But Greeley also specified that many New York City Democrats were worth $100,000 or more. Benson explained that "the design of this study does not permit the research necessary to test all the claims" Greeley made, but one assertion (the presence of $100,000-or-over Democrats) could be tested precisely to learn about "party division among economic groups in New York." [12]

Eventually, all discussions of New York City wealth in the eighteen-forties depend upon those exasperating, fascinating, incomplete, and indispensable compendia of the city's economic elite, *Wealth and Biography of the Wealthy Citizens of New York City* ..., published annually during most of the eighteen-forties and fifties by Moses Y. Beach, editor of the New York *Sun*.[13] Many historians have used them, Robert G. Albion wrote an article about them,[14] and Benson took samples from the sixth edition of 1845.

Beach's list of wealthy citizens for that year included about one thousand names. Benson chose not to analyze the list *in toto*, despite his stated intention to evaluate this specific Greeley claim. Therefore, "some sampling procedure must be devised." [15] He first matched the names of men who were officers of "ratification meetings" held in New York City in 1844 by both major parties with the names on the Wealthy Citizens list, and found that twelve Whig officers (or thirty-four per cent) qualified, as did thirteen (or twenty-six per cent) of the Democratic officers. Although Benson dismissed the percentage differential of eight per cent as "not large enough to be significant in any case," he nevertheless took the trouble to explain it away by the claim of "rank order position." [16] In other words, the importance of Middle Grade Leaders decreased as one read down from the top of this list. Thus if one took the first ten names, both parties supplied six (or sixty per cent) Wealthy Citizens. If one took only the first thirty-five names, the

[12] *Ibid.*, 82.

[13] [Moses Y. Beach,] *Wealth and Biography of the Wealthy Citizens of New York City, Comprising an Alphabetical Arrangement of Persons Estimated to be Worth $100,000, and Upwards. With the Sums Appended to Each Name: Being Useful to Banks, Merchants, and Others* (6th ed.; New York, 1845).

[14] Robert Greenhalgh Albion, "Commercial Fortunes in New York: A Study in the History of the Port of New York About 1850," *New York History,* XVI (1935), 158–68.

[15] Benson, *Jacksonian Democracy,* 82.

[16] *Ibid.*, 83.

Democrats supplied thirty-four per cent Wealthy Citizens to the Whigs' thirty-five per cent. This reduction procedure, although ingenious, was questionable to say the least. Benson nowhere established that the men were listed in order of social or political prominence. The Democrats may have been listed that way (although that is doubtful); the Whigs certainly were not. They appeared arranged not in "rank order," but by city wards. The eighth name among the many Whig vice-presidents, for example, was not that of the eighth most important New York City Whig, but that of the Whig sent to the city-wide party convention to represent the Eighth Ward.[17] And it should also be remembered that Benson's "ratification meeting sample" involved but twenty-five men out of the thousand Wealthy Citizens.

Benson's second sampling procedure was simpler but equally unsatisfactory. Taking the list at face value, he scanned Beach's biographical vignettes for political identifications and found information concerning the party affiliations of another twenty-five men, thirteen Democrats (fifty-two per cent) and twelve Whigs (forty-eight per cent).[18] Again, a consensus historian's dream. But the stumbling block here was the inaccuracy of the identifications. Beach, or his compilers, called two of the alleged Jacksonian Democrats, Jonathan Thompson and William W. Todd, "democrats." [19] Both men were in fact National Republicans who supported John Quincy Adams in 1828 and Whig candidates thereafter. Thompson was Adams' collector of the port, whom Jackson removed in 1829.[20] Corrected, the second sample then becomes fourteen Whigs (fifty-six per cent) and eleven Democrats (forty-four per cent). But the "sample" is not useful in any case. Beach's political identification of his Wealthy Citizens was arbitrary. Some men of political prominence were not identified by party (Benjamin F. Butler, for example), and some were identified incorrectly.

So, on the basis of these forty-five individuals (five were repeaters) out of one thousand (or 4.5 per cent of the total), Benson

---

[17] New York *Tribune,* May 7, 1844.

[18] Benson, *Jacksonian Democracy,* 84.

[19] [Beach,] *Wealthy Citizens,* 29.

[20] For Thompson see Henry Wysham Lanier, *A Century of Banking in New York 1822–1922* (New York, 1922), 136; James Grant Wilson and John Fiske (eds.), *Appletons' Cyclopaedia of American Biography* (New York, 1888–89), VI, 92–93; New York *Courier and Enquirer,* Nov. 2, 1832; New York *Tribune,* Sept. 27, 1844. For Todd see [Joseph A. Scoville,] *The Old Merchants of New York City* (New York, 1863–66), IV, 310–12; New York *National Advocate,* July 10, 1828; New York *Tribune,* Oct. 28, 1844.

asked us to believe that his "hypotheses appear potentially veri-fiable." [21] This is a very tall order for such scanty research to accom-plish, however tentative the claims. Obviously, the only construc-tive way to resolve the problem is to direct attention to the remain-ing ninety-five per cent and examine the Wealthy Citizens list in its entirety.

II

As already noted, the principal recommendation for the use of Beach's list is its availability. It contained no explanation of the selection procedure employed, but merely implied that *every* New Yorker of 1845 worth $100,000 or more could be found on the list. Nor was there any assurance of accuracy concerning the estimates of wealth (usually rounded off to the "nearest" $50,000).[22]

Striking omissions were plentiful. Take, for example, William E. Dodge of the important metals firm, Phelps, Dodge & Company. Dodge, aptly termed a "merchant prince" by his biographer, was already a very wealthy citizen[23] at the time of the Beach compila-tion. Even more perplexing is the fact that Dodge was omitted al-though the company's senior partner, Anson G. Phelps, was listed at one million dollars, and junior partners Anson G. Phelps Jr., and Daniel James (worth $400,000 each), were both included.[24] Simi-larly, Edwin D. Morgan, merchant and politician, did not receive a listing; nor did Marshall O. Roberts, a young capitalist worth $250,000 by 1847.[25] Dodge, Morgan, and Roberts were all Whigs,

---

[21] Benson, *Jacksonian Democracy,* 84.

[22] Albion, "Commercial Fortunes," 163, questions several estimates as too low; for a similar objection see Harry E. Resseguie, "A. T. Stewart's Marble Palace—the Cradle of the Department Store," *New-York Historical Society Quarterly,* XLVIII (1964), 136. On the other hand, Samuel B. Ruggles' biog-rapher thinks the estimate of his subject is high; D. G. Brinton Thompson, *Ruggles of New York* (New York, 1946), 31, note.

[23] Richard Lowitt, *A Merchant Prince of the Nineteenth Century: William E. Dodge* (New York, 1954), 20–22, 201–02.

[24] [Beach,] *Wealthy Citizens,* 15, 23.

[25] For Morgan see James A. Rawley, *Edwin D. Morgan, 1811–1883: Mer-chant in Politics* (New York, 1955), 7–8, 21; for Roberts see Allen Johnson and Dumas Malone (eds.), *Dictionary of American Biography,* 21 Vols. (New York, 1928–37), XVI, 11–12. Dodge and Roberts are listed in Beach's thirteenth edition of 1855.

but one can probably produce names of some prominent Democrats of means who did not gain inclusion. Obviously, Moses Beach was as capricious a practitioner of the art of "elite listing" as any of his predecessors or successors.

Theoretically, one might spurn Beach's offering and try to draw up a comprehensive and accurate list of New York City wealth in the eighteen-forties or any other decade of the period. But the task would involve a lifetime of research in the city directories and tax lists, among other sources. The scope of *this* inquiry does not permit such a luxuriance of preliminary investigation. I propose to limit myself to the one thousand individuals found in the Beach list of 1845.

The figure "one thousand" has cropped up several times. It is an approximation, since the precise number of "workable" names is actually 909. The elimination of some names was advisable for several reasons. Female wealthy citizens could not vote or participate politically, whatever their views. Men who died before 1828 (the first year of a meaningful pro- or anti-Jackson alignment) have been eliminated, as have those identified by a last name only. There were also a dozen names repeated on the list.

Among the remaining 909 names, problems of identification arose. In some cases, men shared the same name, sometimes with another man on the list and far more often with another citizen who was not listed. There are two wealthy citizens named David Banks, and two men named George Douglass. In these instances, separate identifications were possible, and each pair split politically. But significantly, perhaps, at least as far as this study is concerned, the two Whigs were wealthier than their namesakes. There was also the problem of identifying the politics of men with common given and family names. For example, many John Wards lived in New York City at the time, but businessmen (who made up the vast majority of those on the list) often signed their firms' names to political pronouncements, such as calls for ratification meetings, or patronage petitions. Thus the presence of "Prime, Ward & King" on a Whig call or petition provided the political stand of John Ward, as well as that of Edward Prime, Samuel Ward, and James G. King, his partners in that well known brokerage firm. Of course, not all the names were that "common." Happily for the investigator, there was only one Aquilla G. Stout in New York City in 1845, and, of course, only one Preserved Fish.

Whatever the deficiencies and difficulties, the list still beckons.

An intensive search in both primary and secondary sources, Whig and Democratic, produced the political identification of 642 men, or (70.6 per cent). The extent of political involvement varied widely. Thus, among the Whigs, the men ranged from Moses H. Grinnell, a Whig congressman, and Jonathan Goodhue, president of many an anti-Jacksonian New York City rally, to merchants such as George T. Trimble and Oliver T. Hewlett, who apparently were not lured into participating in political meetings but who publicly opposed Democratic policies, such as the removal of the deposits and the refusal to charter a new national bank. The Democratic minority showed a similar spread, from ex-cabinet member Benjamin F. Butler to Democratic merchants such as Reuel Smith, who voiced general approval of the Van Buren administration in 1840. In any case, of the 642 men identified politically, the overwhelming majority (541 or 84.3 per cent) were of the Whig persuasion. New York City money in 1845 was decidedly Whig.

Not only was New York City wealth Whiggish to the general extent of 84.3 per cent but big money showed an even more pronounced affinity for the party of "sound principles." If we divide the Wealthy Citizens into groups according to the size of their estates, at the highest levels the incidence of Democratic affiliation shrinks well below the already miniscule overall average of 15.7 per cent. All four men worth five million dollars or more were anti-Jacksonians. And at the next three levels, the Democrats averaged only 8.4 per cent of those identified. Thus among those worth $400,000 or more (with one hundred identified out of a total of 129), ninety-two men (ninety-two per cent) were Whigs. Demo-

Table 1
Party affiliation by amount of wealth

	Total No.	Identified No.	%	Whig No.	%	Dem. No.	%
$5,000,000 or more	4	4	(100%)	4	(100%)	0	(0%)
$1,000,000 to $4,999,000	18	13	(72.2%)	12	(92.3%)	1	(7.7%)
$500,000 to $999,000	80	59	(73.8%)	54	(91.5%)	5	(8.5%)
$400,000 to $499,000	27	25	(92.6%)	23	(92.0%)	2	(8.0%)
$300,000 to $399,000	101	67	(66.3%)	50	(74.6%)	17	(25.4%)
$250,000 to $299,000	63	47	(74.6%)	37	(78.7%)	10	(21.3%)
$200,000 to $249,000	162	110	(67.9%)	98	(89.1%)	12	(10.9%)
	455	325	(71.4%)	278	(85.5%)	47	(14.5%)

crats fared better in the categories $300,000 to $399,000 and $250,000 to $299,000, dropping off again sharply in the $200,000 to $249,000 class. But to revert to America's common yardstick for measuring great wealth, of the seventeen millionaires identified out of a total of twenty-two, sixteen (94.1 per cent) were Whigs.[26]

III

Benson could not have chosen a less suitable point in time than 1844-45 to seek validation for his thesis. In fact, his study of Jacksonian Democracy is curiously unhistorical in its neglect of chronology. True, he provided a summary of New York political history from 1815 to 1844 which set the Fox-Schlesinger accounts topsy-turvy, and he specifically chided political historians for their unhistorical use of isolated election returns,[27] but in essence his study concentrated upon voting behavior in 1844. With regard to a negative correlation between upper-class membership and party, 1828 would have served far better.

In 1828, a New York City businessman or professional might as easily have supported Jackson or Adams. Or with equal probability, he might have ignored the organized aspects of politics and done no more than cast his vote. This was no longer the case in 1844. In the intervening sixteen years, businessmen had soured on Jacksonism-Loco Focoism in a series of revolts which culminated in opposition to Van Buren's subtreasury proposal during the late eighteen-thirties and in the feverish enthusiasm of the election of 1840.[28] The defection process began in New York City as early as 1827, when several Tammany sachems supported Adams instead of Jackson.[29] Then during the Bank Veto campaign of 1832 several

---

[26] The only millionaire identified as a Democrat, Jacob Lorillard, died in 1838. Had he lived on into the forties he may well have become one of the many wealthy Democratic defectors to Whiggery.

[27] Benson, *Jacksonian Democracy*, Chaps. 1–3, p. 124.

[28] For a general account of these movements, see William Trimble, "Diverging Tendencies in the New York Democracy in the Period of the Locofocos," *American Historical Review*, XXIV (1919), 396–421. See also William G. Carleton, "Political Aspects of the Van Buren Era," *South Atlantic Quarterly*, L (1951), 167–85.

[29] Gustavus Myers, *The History of Tammany Hall* (New York, 1901), 86.

Democratic leaders bolted (among them Gulian Verplanck and
Moses Grinnell),[30] and a year later the crisis brought on by the removal of federal deposits from the Bank of the United States caused
further defections. The Panic of 1837 and the subtreasury proposal,
which ostensibly would have cut the ties between the national government and the bank credit system, produced the major party
split known as the conservative revolt, and created more recruits
for the Whig column. Most conservatives found their way back to
the Democratic party in time, but not all.

Among the Wealthy Citizens of 1845, many such defectors from
the Democracy can be found. Of the men identified as Whigs by
the eighteen-forties, fifty-two (or almost ten per cent) were former
Democrats. The total of men identified as having been Democrats
at one time or other was 153 (101 in good standing by 1845, and
fifty-two defectors). Thus fully one-third of the wealthy who had
originally been Democrats reacted violently to their party's policies in the eighteen-thirties and joined the enemy. One simply cannot dismiss the "Loco Focoizing" of the Democratic party in the
middle and late eighteen-thirties as rhetorical claptrap; something
caused a third of the wealthy Democrats to bolt. And there was no
corresponding reversal of the process. Not a single individual
among the 101 Democrats of 1845 had previously been an anti-
Jacksonian.

As important as were the defections, perhaps even more significant was the fact that the Democratic response to the Bank War and
Panic of 1837 temporarily solidified the New York City business
community into an anti-Democratic force. It may be difficult now
to comprehend what terrors the subtreasury scheme would have
imposed on the merchants, or to tremble at the Loco Foco oratory,
but the businessmen of that day did not have the balm of historical perspective to soothe them. Many believed that they were standing on the "ragged edge of anarchy," to employ a conservative pro-
nouncement of the latter part of the nineteenth century. In the late
eighteen-thirties, New York City businessmen displayed their col-
ors, many of them for the first time. A contemporary observer described a leading merchant financier's reaction:

> With very clear and decided notions on public subjects, Mr. Ward
> had yet kept himself—as was, indeed, until 1834, the case with very

[30] Robert W. July, *The Essential New Yorker: Gulian Crommelin Verplanck*
(Durham, No. Carolina, 1951), 172–79.

many of the leading and active commercial men in New York—free from party strife. . . . When, however, in 1834, that series of disastrous measures commenced, which, under the auspices of General Jackson and his successor, have caused such accumulated ruin and misery, Mr. Ward . . . entered the political arena.[31]

Merchants supporting the Whig ticket convened a meeting in September 1840 in front of the Merchants Exchange. Over two thousand firms signed the call for the meeting, a list which took up the entire front page of the Whig newspapers.[32] The Whig diarist Philip Hone was both exultant and accurate when he wrote:

> The great meeting of Whig merchants took place to-day. . . . The appearance of the mass of people was perfectly sublime. It was a field of heads, occupying a space about six times as large as the area of Washington hall, from which I calculated the number at fifteen thousand; all respectable and orderly merchants and traders. . . .[33]

The Democratic merchants also held a meeting. Its call, again in the form of company names tabulated in small print, consumed one-tenth the space in newspaper columns that the Whig call had used.[34] As Democrat Joseph A. Scoville (the "Old Merchant") put it, colorfully but not exultantly: "Very few merchants of the first class have been Democrats. . . . The Democratic merchants could have easily been stowed in a large Eighth avenue railroad car." [35]

Table 2 illuminates the intensification of political activity on the part of New York City businessmen following the initiation of the Bank War. In the period 1828–31 slightly less than ten per cent of the Wealthy Citizens could be identified politically and, of them, nearly half were Democrats. But in the next four-year period, 1832–35, a span which coincided with the Bank Veto and the Removal of Deposits, the number of Wealthy Citizens taking a political stand more than quadrupled, and the proportion of Democrats fell to 23.2 per cent. The Democratic percentages continued to dip in the late

---

[31] Charles King, "The Late Samuel Ward," *Hunt's Merchants' Magazine*, VIII (1843), 553.

[32] New York *Times and Evening Star*, Sept. 26, 1840.

[33] Bayard Tuckerman (ed.), *The Diary of Philip Hone 1828–1851* (New York 1889), II, 44.

[34] New York *Evening Post*, Sept. 16, 1840.

[35] [Scoville,] *Old Merchants*, I, 81.

Table 2
Party affiliation by time period

	Total No.*	Identified No.	%	Whig No.	%	Dem. No.	%
1828-31	909	90	(9.9%)	48	(53.4%)	42	(46.6%)
1832-35	909	379	(41.9%)	291	(76.8%)	88	(23.2%)
1836-39	905	298	(32.9%)	244	(81.9%)	54	(18.1%)
1840-43	900	324	(36.0%)	270	(83.4%)	54	(16.6%)
1844-47	892	190	(21.3%)	156	(82.2%)	34	(17.8%)
1848-51	880	134	(15.2%)	106	(79.2%)	28	(20.8%)

* Twenty-nine Wealthy Citizens died between 1828 and 1847.

eighteen-thirties and early forties. By the mid-forties the incidence of political identification declined as the fires of the Bank and currency questions died down, but by then the bond between the business community and the Whig party had been established. Of course, these figures are not a mirror of the political loyalties of all the Wealthy Citizens from 1828 to 1851, but they do reflect the willingness of the elite economic groups to make public their political preferences at certain times. We can reasonably assume that nearly all of the Wealthy Citizens voted in 1828, but the fact that only ten per cent were part of the visible political superstructure indicates a lack of mercantile hostility toward the Jacksonians before the coming of the Bank Wars.

IV

It is abundantly clear that by 1845 New York City wealth was allied to Whiggery, and that the process had taken place progressively during the preceding fifteen years. Were there other factors which might have produced this pattern of political allegiance? Religious and ethno-cultural variables as determinants of political behavior are being investigated more and more, and I shall follow the trend.

Not surprisingly, the denomination with by far the largest representation among the Wealthy Citizens was the Episcopalian. Presbyterians followed next, and then Quakers and Dutch Reformed. The striking thing about the political breakdown for these four dominant denominations is that the percentages of Whig affiliation ran close to the overall Whig average of eighty-four per cent. Thus eighty-four per cent of the Episcopalians were Whig; eighty-eight per cent of the Presbyterians; eighty-four per cent of the Dutch Reformed; and ninety-two per cent of the Quakers. Benson observed that Protestant denominationalism was of little use in pinpointing political alignment, and this seems to be true for the wealthy. What we can observe is such a well known phenomenon as denominational social climbing. Of twenty-three men who switched religions, twelve became Episcopalians and joined, if not the established church, then the church of the establishment.

The number of Wealthy Citizens in the remaining denominations was too small for generalizations. Unitarians were Democratic by sixty-six per cent, but only two men were involved. Congregationalists and Jews were one hundred per cent Whig—all four Congregationalists and all seven Jews. There were only eight Catholics, including a mathematician from Columbia College who converted as an adult, and the Delmonico brothers, the Italian-Swiss restaurateurs, but only one man from Ireland (a Democrat).

Table 3
Religious affiliation

	No.	Politics Known		Whigs		Democrats	
Baptists	8	7	(87.5)	5 [1]*	(71.4)	2	(28.6)
Catholics	8	4	(50.0)	2	(50.0)	2	(50.0)
Congregationalists	6	4	(66.7)	4	(100.0)	0	(0.0)
Dutch Reformed	33	25	(75.8)	21 [2]	(84.0)	4	(16.0)
Episcopalians	204	157	(78.0)	132 [13]	(84.0)	25	(16.0)
Jews	8	7	(87.5)	7	(100.0)	0	(0.0)
Methodists	9	8	(89.0)	7	(87.5)	1	(12.5)
Moravians	2	2	(100.0)	2	(100.0)	0	(0.0)
Presbyterians	118	99	(83.9)	87 [4]	(87.8)	12	(12.2)
Quakers	45	36	(80.0)	33 [1]	(91.7)	3	(8.3)
Unitarians	3	3	(100.0)	1	(33.3)	2	(66.7)
Fundamentalists	1	0	(0.0)	0	(0.0)	0	(0.0)
No Religion	2	1	(50.0)	1	(100.0)	0	(0.0)
	447	353	(79.0)	302 [21]	(85.5)	51	(14.5)

* Numbers in brackets indicate Democrats who defected.

On the ethnocultural front, I have followed the native-immigrant division (and sub-categorization) employed by Benson. He also provided rough estimates of political affiliation among the groups[36]—native Dutch, for example, he estimated to have been sixty per cent Democratic. Although the estimates are expressed in

---

[36] Benson, Jacksonian Democracy, 185, 342–43.

percentages, Benson requested that the figures not be taken "literally." Their precision cannot be verified, but precise or not, there is a pronounced dissimilarity between Benson's ethnocultural estimates for the New York electorate as a whole, and the ethnocultural breakdown of wealthy New Yorkers.

Among the natives, Benson estimated that the Old British and Dutch were both sixty per cent Democratic; but among the wealthy, the Old British were eighty per cent Whig, and the Dutch were eighty-three per cent Whig. These two categories were large, but the largest single native category was the "Yankees," or as Albion put it "the swarm of New Englanders who were seeking their fortunes in New York City, just as it was clinching its leadership over the rival American ports." [37] Benson estimated that New York Yankees as a whole voted Whig by fifty-five per cent; wealthy New Englanders in New York City voted Whig by ninety-two per cent. Two other native groups identified as Democratic by Benson, Germans (sixty per cent) and Penn-Jerseyites (fifty-five per cent), were also Whig by seventy-five per cent and seventy-two per cent respectively. There were a dozen native Southerners. Though they came from Jackson's banner region, they were eighty-three per cent Whig.

The immigrant categories reveal the same patterns. All but one group represented among the wealthy were Whig. There was only one Irish Catholic, no French Canadians, no Welsh, and no Negroes on the Wealthy Citizens list. Immigrant French, supposedly ninety per cent Democratic, were eighty-six per cent Whig (but that includes only seven men). The immigrant English, estimated at seventy-five per cent Whig, were one hundred per cent Whig (fourteen of fourteen). The Scots, estimated at ninety per cent Whig, were ninety-three per cent Whig. The lowest Whig percentage among immigrant groups (excluding the one Irish Catholic), was the German (fifty-four per cent), a group estimated at eighty per cent Democratic. Although the German percentage involves but a dozen men, it seems to demonstrate the tug of various factors operating on a man's political decision-making process. One can accept, almost axiomatically, the proposition that religious and ethnocultural background will influence his response to politics, but surely one need not have to argue excessively for considering the possession of great wealth as an important factor, perhaps the preponderant factor, in analyzing the American wealthy as political men.

[37] Robert G. Albion, "Thomas Tileston," *DAB*, XVIII, 541.

Table 4
Ethnocultural background

Natives	No.	Politics Identified	Whigs		Benson's Estimates for Whigs	Democrats
British	146	106 (72.6%)	85 [10]*	(80.2%)	40%	21 (19.8%)
Dutch	102	77 (75.5%)	64 [7]	(83.1%)	40%	13 (16.9%)
German	11	8 (72.8%)	6	(75.0%)	40%	2 (25.0%)
Huguenot	7	3 (42.8%)	2	(66.7%)	75%	1 (33.3%)
Penn-Jersey	26	21 (80.8%)	15 [3]	(71.5%)	45%	6 (28.5%)
Southern	13	12 (92.3%)	10	(83.3%)	–	2 (16.7%)
Yankee	147	122 (83.0%)	112 [3]	(91.8%)	55%	10 (8.2%)
Sub-totals	452	349 (78.0%)	294 [23]	(84.2%)		55 (15.8%)
Immigrants						
Dutch	4	4 (100.0%)	4 [1]	(100.0%)	–	0 (0.0%)
English	32	14 (43.7%)	14	(100.0%)	75%	0 (0.0%)
French	12	7 (58.4%)	6 [1]	(85.7%)	10%	1 (14.3%)
German	15	13 (86.6%)	7 [1]	(53.8%)	20%	6 (46.2%)
Cath.-Irish	1	1 (100.0%)	0	(0.0%)	5%	1 (100.0%)
Prot.-Irish	17	14 (82.4%)	10 [3]	(71.4%)	90%	4 (28.6%)
Scottish	31	29 (93.6%)	27 [2]	(93.1%)	90%	2 (6.9%)
Swiss	5	0 (0.0%)	0	(0.0%)	–	0 (0.0%)
West Indian	1	1 (100.0%)	1	(100.0%)	–	0 (0.0%)
Polish	1	0 (0.0%)	0	(0.0%)	–	0 (0.0%)
Sub-totals	119	83 (69.7%)	69 [8]	(83.2%)		14 (16.8%)
Totals	571	432 (75.7%)	363 [31]	(84.0%)		69 (16.0%)

* Numbers in brackets indicate Democrats who defected.

V

What do these data prove about the political alignment of America's wealthy classes in cities other than New York? Nothing. To what extent New York, City or State, represents the country at large, or to what extent it can usefully be called a "test case," remains to be determined, especially among non-commercial, rural elites. Several additional studies using other "Wealthy Citizens" lists (they exist for Boston and Philadelphia, for example) would be feasible and profitable. Even the absence of such lists does not close the door to counting the heads of the elite. There are directories for all major cities in the Jackson period, and in some cases they go beyond a mere alphabetical listing of heads of households to include classified business and professional directories. From these one might "do" the politics of, say, the importing merchants of Providence, or the lawyers of Pittsburgh, or the physicians of Charleston.

But it is important to begin with men of a non-political grouping and then proceed to their political identification. To start with vice-presidents of ratification meetings or with members of Congress from Tennessee in the antebellum period is to beg the question, since a sociological identity, or near-identity, is almost predictable in those instances. In the case of ratification-meeting vice-presidents we can expect that both parties, whatever their rhetoric, produced lists of solid men—that is, men of material substance—even though one party might have had a much smaller reservoir of "vice-presidential types" to draw upon.[38] It was not likely that the New York City Democracy, whatever its Loco Foco professions, would put a score of illiterate and inarticulate hod carriers on the Tammany Hall platform. In the second case cited, it was no surprise that the Tennessee congressmen were usually middle-aged lawyers of similar social background. The nature of the group chosen for investigation predetermined that result.[39] But what of the Tennessee professional and commercial classes, the upper crust of the state (and other states as well), taken as solid blocs? Only after such groups have been isolated and examined can we begin to speak with certainty about upper class and party in Jacksonian America.

Much of the previous debate has floundered upon the semantic difficulty of whether Whigs were wealthy. Once again, the terms are in reverse order; the question should read: Were wealthy Americans Whigs? If by "Whigs" we mean all who voted for that party, or even the party functionaries at all levels, it is obvious that the possession of great wealth was not a prerequisite to association with Whiggery. The party had to appeal to a mass electorate in an age of ballot-box egalitarianism. By definition, a man of wealth was one who owned more than the majority of his neighbors, and

---

[38] Yet even among the vice-presidents of ratification meetings who were Wealthy Citizens there was considerably more Whig money than Democratic. The thirteen Democrats were worth, collectively, 2.5 million dollars; the twelve Whigs were worth 13.4 million.

[39] Milton Henry, "Summary of Tennessee Representation in Congress from 1845 to 1861," *Tennessee Historical Quarterly*, X (1951), 140–48. The similarities between congressmen of both parties emerge clearly in the table on page 141, although the author concludes, contrary to the evidence he submits, that "Tennessee Democrats were dynamic and radical, while the Tennessee Whigs were generally conservative" (p. 148).

there were simply not enough of the "wealthy" available to achieve election-day victories without the creation of an exclusive, high-level electorate. One Democratic editor described the situation in 1840 in simple terms: "There was a meeting of Whig merchants in Wall Street, and a meeting of the people in the Park, both of which were very large, but the latter much the larger, for the very simple reason that there are more people—more mechanics and laborers—than there are merchants." [40] If we begin with the parties, and especially with the entire electorate, it is indeed difficult to find "any evidence that the party situation reflected basic economic or social cleavages in the population," as has recently been remarked of New Jersey.[41] But perhaps the judgment would be altered if one plotted the location of economic status groups in the New Jersey political spectrum, especially for the eighteen-forties.

In a viable two-party system, operating within the context of universal white manhood suffrage, the class nature of political alignment must be sought in areas other than a pristine partisan division of rich versus poor. The validity of projecting the New York City experience to points beyond has yet to be established, but I suspect that the monied men of New York City in the eighteen-forties were not out of step with their peers elsewhere in thinking that the Whig party of that decade better served their interests and better calmed their fears than did the Democracy.

---

[40] New York *Evening Post,* Sept. 29, 1840.

[41] Richard P. McCormick, "Party Formation in New Jersey in the Jackson Era," *Proceedings of the New Jersey Historical Society,* LXXXIII (1965), 173. McCormick was referring, however, to the decade 1824–34.

CHARLES G. SELLERS, JR.*

Who Were the Southern Whigs?

While Professor Sellers finds that Southern Whig leaders were distinctly wealthier than their Jacksonian counterparts, there is no mistaking the modernity of his study. It relies on quantitative data and—unlike the historiography of a half century ago—it denies that Southern Whiggery was controlled by planters whose chief ideology was states' rights. Sellers' Whigs were finance-minded capitalists who became increasingly nationalistic as the era progressed. Sellers' sympathy with the Schlesinger thesis is clearly expressed in the very last phrase of his article, which finds the Democratic administrations of the era "not conspicuously devoted to the interests of the propertied."

STUDENTS OF THE Old South have spent much of their time in recent years dispelling myths about that fabled land of moonlight and magnolias. Our understanding of the social, intellectual, and economic life of the ante-bellum South has been considerably revised and immeasurably widened by the work of a large number of able scholars.

---

* From Charles G. Sellers, Jr., "Who Were the Southern Whigs?" *American Historical Review*, LIX (January, 1954), pp. 335–345.

Political history, however, has been unfashionable, and one of the results has been the survival of a series of myths about the political life of the South in the 1830's and 1840's. The key myth may be called the myth of a monolithic South: a section unified as early as the 1820's in its devotion to state rights doctrines and its hostility to the nationalistic, antislavery, capitalistic North. The result of approaching ante-bellum history by way of Fort Sumter and Appomattox, this point of view found its classic statements in the apologias of Jefferson Davis[1] and Alexander H. Stephens,[2] but it was made respectable in the first generation of professional scholarship by such historians as Herman Von Holst[3] and John W. Burgess.[4] It colored such early monographs as U. B. Phillips' "Georgia and State Rights"[5] and H. M. Wagstaff's *States Rights and Political Parties in North Carolina, 1776–1861,*[6] and it is to be seen in most of the more recent works on the pre-Civil War South.[7] It has also given rise to the corollary myths that Calhoun was the representative spokesman and political leader of the South after about 1830, and that the Whig party in the South mainly reflected the state rights proclivities of the great planters.

---

[1] *The Rise and Fall of the Confederate Government,* 2 vols. (New York, 1881).

[2] *A Constitutional View of the Late War between the States,* 2 vols. (Philadelphia, 1868–70).

[3] *The Constitutional and Political History of the United States,* 8 vols. (Chicago, 1876–92).

[4] *The Middle Period, 1817–1858* (New York, 1905).

[5] *Annual Report of the American Historical Association,* 1901, II, 1–224.

[6] Johns Hopkins University Studies in Historical and Political Science, Series XXIV (1906), Nos. 7–8.

[7] See particularly Jesse T. Carpenter, *The South as a Conscious Minority, 1784–1861* (New York, 1930); Robert S. Cotterill, *The Old South* (Glendale, Calif., 1939); and Charles M. Wiltse, *John C. Calhoun,* 3 vols. (Indianapolis, 1944–51). Charles S. Sydnor, in what is, in many respects, the finest work on the ante-bellum South, presents a persuasive restatement of the traditional sectional-state rights interpretation. His chapter headings on politics from the Panic of 1819 to nullification describe a developing sectionalism: "From Economic Nationalism to Political Sectionalism," "End of the Virginia Dynasty," "The Lower South Adopts State Rights," and "Bold Acts and Bolder Thoughts." The 1830's and 1840's, however, present a paradox. Professor Sydnor finds a growing "Regionalism in Mind and Spirit," but a "decline of sectionalism in politics." This he explains as a result of the fact that "major Southern hopes and fears found no champion in either party," so that "party conflict south of the Potomac . . . had the hollow sound of a stage duel with tin swords." "The

These myths have been strengthened by Frederick Jackson Turner's sectional analysis of our early national history. Turner's approach has been extremely fruitful, but its sweeping application has tended to exaggerate differing sectional tendencies into absolute sectional differences. The application of geographic sectionalism to individual states, moreover, has fostered the further myth that political strife within the Old South was confined largely to struggles over intrastate sectional issues between upcountry and low country, hill country and "black belt." [8]

All of these myths have some basis in fact. They are, however, the product of a misplaced emphasis which has permeated nearly all of the studies of pre-Civil War southern politics. Sectionalism and state rights have been made the central themes of southern political history for almost the entire ante-bellum period. Southern opposition to nationalistic legislation by Congress has been over-emphasized. And the social, economic, and ideological lines of political cleavage within the slave states have been obscured. The early history of the Whig party below Mason and Dixon's line shows the character of these distortions.

It is too often forgotten that in the ante-bellum period the South had a vigorous two-party system, an asset it has never since enjoyed. Until at least the later 1840's, the voting southerner was much more interested in the success of his own party and its policies than in banding together with southerners of the opposite party to defend the Constitution and southern rights against invasion by the North. The parties were evenly matched, and elections were bitterly contested. It was rare for any southern state to be regarded as absolutely safe for either party. Of the 425,629 votes cast in the slave states at the election of 1836, the Whigs had a majority of only 243 popular votes. In this and the three succeeding presidential elec-

---

agrarian South felt little interest," writes Professor Sydnor, in that conflict between the "wealthier and more conservative segments of society" and the liberal, democratic elements "which formed a major issue between the Democratic and Whig parties" in the nation as a whole. *The Development of Southern Sectionalism, 1819–1848* (Baton Rouge, 1948), especially p. 316. Notable for their freedom from overemphasis on sectionalism are Thomas P. Abernethy, *From Frontier to Plantation in Tennessee: A Study in Frontier Democracy* (Chapel Hill, 1932); and Roger W. Shugg, *Origins of Class Struggle in Louisiana* (University, La., 1939).

[8] See especially William A. Schaper, "Sectionalism and Representation in South Carolina," *Annual Report of the American Historical Association*, 1900, I, 237–463; and Charles H. Ambler, *Sectionalism in Virginia from 1776 to 1861* (Chicago, 1910).

tions, a total of 2,745,171 votes were cast, but the over-all margin, again in favor of the Whigs, was only 66,295, or 2.4 per cent of the total votes. In these four elections the Whigs carried a total of twenty-seven southern states and the Democrats twenty-six.[9]

An equally close rivalry is evident in congressional representation. In the five congressional elections between 1832 and 1842, southern Democrats won an aggregate total of 234 seats, while their opponents captured 263. Whigs predominated among southern representatives in three of these five Congresses, and Democrats in two. In three of them the margin between the southern wings of the parties was five or less.[10] We have then a picture of keen political competition, with a vigorous Whig party maintaining a slight ascendancy.

What did this Whig party stand for? The pioneer account of the southern Whigs was the essay by U. B. Phillips which, significantly, appeared in the *Festschrift* to Frederick Jackson Turner.[11] This study shows Phillips' characteristic tendency to generalize about the entire South on the basis of conditions in his native Georgia. "The great central body of southern Whigs," he declares, "were the cotton producers, who were first state-rights men pure

---

[9] Edward Stanwood, *A History of the Presidency* (Boston, 1898), pp. 185–88, 203–204, 225, 243. *Cf.* Fletcher M. Green, "Democracy in the Old South," *Journal of Southern History*, XII (1946), 20–21.

[10] Party affiliations of members of Congress have been determined largely from election returns in *Niles' Register* up to 1837, and from the *Whig Almanac* for the subsequent years. These sources have been supplemented by information from: *A Biographical Congressional Directory* (Washington, 1913); Charles H. Ambler, "Virginia and the Presidential Succession, 1840–1844," in *Essays in American History Dedicated to Frederick Jackson Turner* (New York, 1910), pp. 165–202; Ambler, *Sectionalism in Virginia;* Henry H. Simms, *The Rise of the Whigs in Virginia, 1824–1840* (Richmond, 1929); J. G. de Roulhac Hamilton, *Party Politics in North Carolina, 1835–1860*, James Sprunt Historical Publications, XV (1916); Clifford C. Norton, *The Democratic Party in Ante-Bellum North Carolina, 1835–1861*, James Sprunt Historical Studies, XXI (1930); Phillips, "Georgia and State Rights," *loc. cit.;* Paul Murray, "The Whig Party in Georgia, 1825–1853," James Sprunt Studies in History and Political Science, XXIX (1948); Theodore H. Jack, *Sectionalism and Party Politics in Alabama, 1819–1842* (Menasha, Wis., 1919); Cleo Hearon, "Nullification in Mississippi," *Mississippi Historical Society Publications*, XII (1912), 39–71; James E. Winston, "The Mississippi Whigs and the Tariff, 1834–1844," *Mississippi Valley Historical Review*, XXII (1937), 505–24; James B. Ranck, *Alfred Gallatin Brown: Radical Southern Nationalist* (New York, 1937); Joseph G. Tregle, Jr., "Louisiana and the Tariff, 1816–1846," *Louisiana Historical Quarterly*, XXV (1942), 24–148; and Wendell H. Stephenson, *Alexander Porter: Whig Planter of Old Louisiana* (Baton Rouge, 1934).

[11] "The Southern Whigs, 1834–1854," *Essays in American History Dedicated to Frederick Jackson Turner*, pp. 203–29.

and simple and joined the Whigs from a sense of outrage at Jackson's threat of coercing South Carolina." [12]

Two years after Phillips' essay appeared, Arthur C. Cole published his exhaustive monograph on *The Whig Party in the South*.[13] Less than a third of the Cole volume is concerned with the period before 1844, when Whiggery was of greatest importance in the South, and he generally follows the Phillips interpretation of its origins. His account of the birth of the party devotes three pages to early National Republicanism in the South, twenty to the anti-Jackson sentiment aroused during the nullification crisis. and only four and a half to the fight over the national bank and financial policy.[14] "Various interests," he says, "linked in political alliance with the few southerners whose interests and inclinations led to the support of latitudinarian principles, a still larger faction made up of those who supported constitutional doctrines on the opposite extreme and whose logical interests seemed to point against such an affiliation." [15]

An analysis, however, of the record of the Twenty-second Congress (1831-1833) leads to somewhat different conclusions. It was this Congress which dealt with the tariff, nullification, and national bank questions, and it was during this Congress that the groundwork for the Whig party was laid. Of the ninety southerners in the House of Representatives, sixty-nine had been elected as supporters of Andrew Jackson, while twenty-one, nearly a fourth, were National Republicans. Of the sixty-nine Democrats, twenty-five were subsequently active in the Whig party. Eighteen of the latter were state rights Whigs, while seven were not identified with the state rights wing of the opposition. These twenty-five men then, together with the twenty-one National Republicans, may be regarded as representative of the groups which formed the Whig party in the South.[16]

---

[12] *Ibid.*, p. 209.

[13] Washington, 1913.

[14] Cole, pp. 2–30.

[15] *Ibid.*, p. 2. E. Malcolm Carroll, in his scholarly *Origins of the Whig Party* (Durham, N. C., 1925), pays almost no attention to the southern states and follows Cole where southern developments have to be mentioned. In his one general statement about the southern Whigs, he takes the position that they were men of property, who turned instinctively to an association with northerners of similarly conservative interests. *Ibid.*, pp. 190–91.

[16] See note 10 above.

These incipient Whigs voted twenty-four to twenty-one in favor of the tariff of 1832, a measure denounced by state rights men and nullified by South Carolina.[17] They also voted twenty-four to nineteen for the Force Bill, which was designed to throttle the nullifiers.[18] This backing of administration measures was hardly a portent of an opposition state rights party. The real harbinger of Whiggery was the vote on the national bank bill, which this group supported twenty-seven to seventeen.[19]

The Whig party actually took shape during the Twenty-third Congress (1833-1835), in which it gained the allegiance of fifty-two of the ninety-nine southern members of the House. They voted twenty-nine to sixteen in favor of rechartering the national bank[20] and unanimously in favor of restoring the government deposits to Biddle's institution.[21] By a closer vote of twenty-two to twenty they supported repairing and extending the Cumberland Road.[22] In the Twenty-fourth Congress (1835-1837) the forty-eight Whig Representatives from the South divided thirty-eight to three in favor of Clay's bill to distribute the proceeds from sales of public lands to the states.[23] Other votes showing similar tendencies might be cited, but enough has been said to suggest that, even in the beginning, a majority of southern anti-Jackson men were far from being state rights doctrinaires.

In the light of this record it is not surprising that only a handful of southern Whigs followed Calhoun when he marched his supporters back into the Democratic household during Van Buren's administration.[24] The record also prepares one for the increasing

---

[17] *House Journal,* 22 Congress, 1 session, pp. 1023–24.

[18] *House Journal,* 22 Cong., 2 sess., pp. 453–54.

[19] *Register of Debates,* 22 Cong., 1 sess., p. 3852.

[20] *House Journal,* 23 Cong., 1 sess., pp. 483–85.

[21] *Ibid.,* pp. 485–86.

[22] *Ibid.,* pp. 758–59.

[23] *House Journal,* 24 Cong., 1 sess., pp. 1023–24.

[24] Senator William C. Preston and Representative Waddy Thompson of South Carolina refused to leave the Whig party with Calhoun, and three other Representatives from the state took the Conservative, or anti-Subtreasury, position. Outside his own state Calhoun carried with him only seven members of Congress: Dixon H. Lewis of Alabama; Edward J. Black, Walter T. Colquitt, and Mark A. Cooper, of Georgia (in 1839-40); Samuel T. Sawyer and Charles Shepard of North Carolina; and Robert M. T. Hunter of Virginia (in 1839-41).

manifestations of nationalism among southern Whigs which Phillips and Cole found so difficult to explain.[25] The southern wing of the party backed Clay almost unanimously for the Presidential nomination in 1840.[26] Tyler's nomination for Vice President was more a sop to the disappointed Clay men, of whom Tyler was one, than a concession to the state rights proclivities of southern Whiggery, the reason usually given for his choice.[27]

The nature of southern Whiggery had its real test when Tyler challenged Clay for leadership of the party. Of the fifty-five southern Whigs in the lower house of the Twenty-seventh Congress (1841-1843), only three stuck by the Virginia President and his state rights principles, whereas Mangum of North Carolina presided over the caucus which read Tyler out of the party, and

---

The Georgia apostates were defeated for the next Congress by the regular Whigs, who made a clean sweep of the congressional elections under the general ticket system. In North Carolina Sawyer was displaced by a loyal Whig at the next election, and Shepard met the same fate two years later. In the Presidential election of 1840 the southern Whigs, far from being weakened, had a majority of 58,675, as compared with 243 four years earlier. See Murray, *Whig Party in Georgia*, pp. 90–95; Hamilton, *Party Politics in North Carolina*, pp. 55, 79; Stanwood, *History of the Presidency*, pp. 165–203.

[25] Phillips, "The Southern Whigs," *loc. cit.*, pp. 216–17; Cole, *Whig Party in the South*, pp. 65–89.

[26] Cole, pp. 53–54.

[27] George R. Poage, *Henry Clay and the Whig Party* (Chapel Hill, 1936), pp. 13, 34–35. Tyler's most recent biographer, Oliver P. Chitwood, maintains that "Tyler was given the second place on the ticket mainly because he was from the South and had been a strong advocate of States' rights," or, in another passage, that "he was put up partly to placate the Clay faction but mainly to satisfy the States' right element of the Whig party." Chitwood bases this position on the ground that it "is the explanation usually given." *John Tyler, Champion of the Old South* (New York, 1939), pp. 172, 194. In taking this position, Chitwood has to discount completely Henry A. Wise's story of an arrangement with Clay leaders in 1839, whereby Tyler was to withdraw as a competitor with W. C. Rives for the Senate but was to receive the Vice Presidential nomination. Chitwood is probably correct in denying that Tyler himself had any part in such an understanding, but he fails to explain why Tyler was expected to be Clay's running mate before the convention met and why the Clay men were so confident of their ability to control Tyler just after he succeeded Harrison. *Ibid.*, pp. 172–73, 210, 215. Chitwood also finds it necessary to try to disprove persistent reports that Tyler intimated during the campaign that he was friendly to a national bank. It cannot be denied that his campaign statements were highly equivocal. *Ibid.*, pp. 188–94, 171–77. On one occasion Tyler endorsed Harrison's contention that "There is not in the Constitution any express grant of power for such purpose [a national bank], and it could never be constitutional to exercise the power, save in the event the power granted to Congress could not be carried into effect without resorting to such an institution." *Ibid.*, p. 190.

southern Whig editors joined in castigating him unmercifully.[28] Southern Whigs supported Clay's legislative program—repeal of the Subtreasury, a national bank, distribution, and tariff—by large majorities.[29] Even the Georgians, Berrien, Toombs, and Stephens, defended the protective features of the tariff of 1842.[30]

Having said so much to the point that the Whig party in the South did not begin as and did not become a state rights party, it is necessary to add that neither was it consciously nationalistic. State rights versus nationalism simply was not the main issue in southern politics in this period. It is readily apparent from the newspapers and correspondence of the time that, except for Calhoun and his single-minded little band, politicians in the South were fighting over the same questions that were agitating the North—mainly questions of banking and financial policy.

It is hard to exaggerate the importance of the banking question. State and federal governments, by their policy in this sphere, could cause inflation or deflation, make capital easy or difficult to obtain, and facilitate or hinder the marketing of staple crops and commercial activity generally. And by chartering or refusing to charter banks, they could afford or deny to the capitalists of the day the most profitable field of activity the economy offered.

The banking issue is the key to an understanding of southern as well as northern Whiggery. Merchants and bankers were most directly concerned in financial policy, but their community of interest generally included the other business and professional men of the towns, especially the lawyers, who got most of their fees from merchants, and the newspaper editors, who were dependent on the merchants for advertising revenues. The crucial point for southern politics, however, is that the large staple producers were also closely identified economically with the urban commercial groups.[31] These were the principal elements which went into the Whig party.

---

[28] Cole, pp. 92–93.

[29] Southern Whigs in the House voted forty-four to four in favor of Clay's original bank bill. *House Journal*, 27 Cong., 1 sess., pp. 409–10. They supported the tariff of 1842 by a vote of twenty-nine to eleven. *House Journal*, 27 Cong., 2 sess., pp. 1440–41.

[30] Murray, *Whig Party in Georgia*, p. 109; Rudolph Von Abele, *Alexander H. Stephens* (New York, 1946), pp. 86–87.

[31] Ralph C. H. Catterall, *The Second Bank of the United States* (Chicago, 1903), pp. 140–44; Thomas P. Abernethy, "The Early Development of Com-

The Whigs generally defended the national bank until its doom was sealed, then advocated a liberal chartering of commercial banks by the states, and finally, after the Panic of 1837, demanded a new national bank. The Democrats fought Biddle's institution and either favored state-operated banks to provide small loans for farmers, as distinguished from commercial banks, or tried to regulate banking strictly or abolish it altogether.[32]

Much of the misunderstanding about the Whig party in the South may be traced to the technique of plotting election returns on maps. Such maps tell us much, but they may also mislead. They show, for example, that the "black belts" of the lower South were the great centers of Whig strength. This has led scholars to reason: (1) that the Whig party was a planters' party *par excellence,* (2) that planters were necessarily rigid state rights men, and (3) that the Whig party was, therefore, a state rights party. *Q.E.D.!*

What the maps do not illustrate, however, is the dynamics of the political situation—the elements of leadership, impetus, financing, and propaganda, which are the real sinews of a political organization. In the case of the Whig party, these elements were furnished mainly by the commercial groups of the cities and towns, with their allied lawyers and editors. Lawyers were the practicing politicians for both parties, but the greater incidence of lawyers among the Whigs is an indication of the commercial affiliations of the party. Seventy-four per cent of the southern Whigs who sat in Congress from 1833 to 1843 are identified as practicing attorneys, as compared with fifty-five per cent of the Democrats.[33] In the lower house of the Tennessee legislature of 1839, farmers predominated,

---

merce and Banking in Tennessee," *Mississippi Valley Historical Review,* XIV (1927), 316–19; Thomas P. Govan, "Banking and the Credit System in Georgia, 1810–1860," *Journal of Southern History,* IV (1938), 164, 178–84.

[32] Charles H. Ambler, *Thomas Ritchie: A Study in Virginia Politics* (Richmond, 1913), pp. 176–78; Ambler, *Sectionalism in Virginia,* pp. 237–39; George T. Starnes, *Sixty Years of Branch Banking in Virginia* (New York, 1931), pp. 71–103; William K. Boyd, *The Federal Period, 1783–1860,* Vol. II of *History of North Carolina* (Chicago, 1919), pp. 274–75; Norton, *Democratic Party in North Carolina,* pp. 54–59, 188–92; Hamilton, *Party Politics in North Carolina,* pp. 80, 88; Govan, "Banking in Georgia," *loc. cit.,* pp. 164–84; Jack, *Sectionalism in Alabama,* pp. 61–63; William O. Scroggs, "Pioneer Banking in Alabama," in *Facts and Factors in Economic History: Articles by Former Students of Edwin Francis Gay* (Cambridge, Mass., 1932), pp. 421–23; Abernethy, "Banking in Tennessee," *loc. cit.,* 321–24; Eugene I. McCormac, *James K. Polk: A Political Biography* (Berkeley, 1922), pp. 88, 169–70, 190; Shugg, *Class Struggle in Louisiana,* pp. 134–38.

[33] Based on vocational identification in *Biographical Congressional Directory.*

but a fourth of the Whigs were lawyers, as compared with only a tenth of the Democratic membership.[34]

The size and importance of the urban middle class in the Old South has yet to be fully appreciated. As early as 1831, Nashville, for example, contained twenty-two wholesale houses and seventy-seven retail stores, not to mention numerous other businesses, such as the sixty taverns and tippling houses.[35] Even the little county seat town of Gallatin, Tennessee, boasted in 1840 ten mercantile firms, a grocer, a merchant tailor, three hotels, five lawyers, five doctors, a paper and grist mill, and eighteen artisans' establishments of one kind or another.[36]

Businessmen dominated the towns socially, economically, and politically, and the towns dominated the countryside.[37] This was particularly true of the "black belts" of the lower South, since the great cotton capitalists of this region were especially dependent on commercial and credit facilities for financing and carrying on their extensive planting operations.[38] In recognition of the urban influence on politics, congressional districts were commonly known by the names of the principal towns in each—as, for example, the Huntsville, Florence, Tuscaloosa, Montgomery, and Mobile districts in Alabama.

Other evidence points in the same direction. A large majority of the stockholders in Virginia banks in 1837 lived in the areas of heaviest Whig voting. The principal commercial towns of the state

---

[34] Vocational identification from "List of Members of the House of Representatives of the Tennessee Legislature," broadside (Nashville, 1839). Party affiliations from a memorandum by James K. Polk in the Polk Papers (Library of Congress), First Series, placed at end of November, 1839.

[35] Nashville *Republican and State Gazette,* Oct. 20, 1831.

[36] Gallatin *Republican Sentinel,* Jan. 28, 1840.

[37] Lewis E. Atherton, *The Southern Country Store, 1800–1860* (Baton Rouge, 1949), especially pp. 191–92. This study is of great significance in indicating the importance of commercial interests and of even the smaller interior merchant in the life of the ante-bellum South. Atherton does not deal with the political activities of merchants in this volume, but in a similar study for Illinois, Missouri, and Iowa, he found the merchants active in politics. Seventy per cent of a sample for whom political affiliation could be determined were Whigs. *The Pioneer Merchant in Middle America,* University of Missouri Studies, XIV (1939), No. 2, pp. 23–26.

[38] Clanton W. Williams, "Early Ante-Bellum Montgomery: A Black-Belt Constituency," *Journal of Southern History,* VII (1941), 510–11, 515; Shugg, *Class Struggle in Louisiana,* p. 138; Stephenson, *Alexander Porter,* pp. 33–35; J. Carlyle Sitterson, "Financing and Marketing the Sugar Crop of the Old South," *Journal of Southern History,* X (1944), 188–99.

—Richmond, Petersburg, and Norfolk—gave unbroken Whig majorities throughout the period 1834-1840.[39] In North Carolina twenty of the twenty-one directors of the two principal banks in 1840 were Whigs.[40] The first Whig governor of North Carolina was a railroad president; the second was a lawyer, cotton manufacturer, and railroad president; and the third was one of the wealthiest lawyers in the state.[41]

Similar party leadership obtained elsewhere. In Virginia, younger men of the type of John Minor Botts of Richmond and Alexander H. H. Stuart of Staunton actually directed the party of which Tyler and Tazewell were nominal leaders. Senators George A. Waggaman and Judah P. Benjamin were typical of the New Orleans lawyers who guided Louisiana Whiggery. Poindexter and Prentiss in Mississippi were intimately associated both personally and financially with the bankers and businessmen of Natchez. The Tennessee Whigs were led by John Bell, Nashville lawyer and iron manufacturer, who had married into the state's leading mercantile and banking house; Ephraim H. Foster, bank director and Nashville's most prominent commercial lawyer; and Hugh Lawson White, Knoxville lawyer, judge, and bank president.[42]

This commercial bias of the Whig party did much to pave the way for the industrial development of the South after the Civil War. It was no accident that former Whigs provided a large part of the leadership for the business-minded Conservative-Democratic

---

[39] Simms, *Whigs in Virginia,* pp. 13, 167–92.

[40] Boyd, *Federal Period,* p. 274.

[41] Hamilton, *Party Politics in North Carolina,* pp. 36, 57, 92–94.

[42] Lawyers provided much of the leadership for the Democratic party also, but they tended to be from the smaller towns rather than the big commercial centers—as, for example, James K. Polk, Cave Johnson, and Aaron V. Brown, in Tennessee. There were also a goodly number of "Democrats by trade"— men like James K. Polk's merchant-banker-mail contractor brother-in-law, James Walker—who were active in Democratic politics for personal profit. The top Whig leadership, however, contained few men of the decidedly noncommercial backgrounds of such Democrats as Andrew Johnson, the Greenville tailor; Bedford Brown, the upcountry-small planter who inherited Nathaniel Macon's mantle in North Carolina; Richard M. Johnson, the ebullient Tecumseh-slayer, who continued to wait on customers in his Great Crossings inn while Vice President of the United States; David Hubbard, the self-educated carpenter who championed the poor whites of northern Alabama; Franklin E. Plummer, the picturesque loco-foco from the piney woods of eastern Mississippi; and General Solomon W. Downs, who led the "Red River Democracy" of northern Louisiana in the fights for suffrage extension and bank reform. Davy Crockett was, of course, the exception among the Whigs that proved the rule.

parties which "redeemed" the South from Republican rule and then proceeded to make the conquered section over in the image of the victorious North, often in the interest of northern capital.[43]

Commercial considerations and the banking question did not, of course, determine political alignments in the Old South by themselves. Pro-tariff sentiment made for Whiggery among the sugar planters of Louisiana, the hemp growers of Kentucky, and the salt and iron manufacturers of western Virginia and Maryland. The more liberal policy of the Whigs toward internal improvements by both the state and federal governments won them support in landlocked interior sections and along the routes of projected transportation projects. And the fact that the Democrats generally championed a broadened suffrage, apportionment of congressional and legislative seats on the basis of white population, and other measures for extending political democracy, inclined propertied and conservative men to rally to the Whig party as a bulwark against mobocracy.

These factors, however, merely reinforced the commercial nature of southern Whiggery. The business orientation of the Whigs and the relative unimportance of their state rights wing become quite apparent if the party is described as it actually developed in the various states, rather than on the basis of general assumptions about southern politics.

A state by state analysis would indicate that, in the four border slave states and Louisiana, Whiggery was simply National Republicanism continued under a new name. The National Republicans were also strong in Virginia, but here they were joined in opposition to the Democrats by a body of state rights men alienated from Jackson by his attitude toward nullification. The National Republican and commercial wing of the party, however, was the dominant one, especially after the business-minded Conservative Democrats joined the Whigs on the Subtreasury question.[44] In North Carolina and Tennessee, the Whig party was formed by the secession of pro-Bank men from the Democratic party, aided in Tennessee by the local popularity of Hugh Lawson White as a Presidential candidate in 1835-1836.[45]

---

[43] C. Vann Woodward, *Origins of the New South, 1877–1913* (Baton Rouge, 1951), pp. 1–50.

[44] Ambler, *Sectionalism in Virginia*, pp. 219–50, especially p. 222; Simms, *Whigs in Virginia, passim.*

[45] Boyd, *Federal Period*, pp. 181–84; Burton A. Konkle, *John Motley Morehead* (Philadelphia, 1922), p. 127; Lawrence F. London, "George Edmund

The state rights element was more conspicuous in the four remaining states of the lower South. But it was by no means the majority wing of the Whig party in all of them. Both Alabama and Mississippi had an original nucleus of pro-Clay, anti-Jackson men, and in both states the nullification episode caused a substantial defection from the Jackson ranks. In Mississippi, however, a greater defection followed the removal of government deposits from the national bank. The state rights men were clearly a minority of the opposition party, which elected an outspoken foe of nullification to the governorship in 1835 and sent the ardent Clay partisan, Seargent S. Prentiss, to Congress two years later.[46]

The state rights defection seems to have been more important in

---

Badger in the United States Senate, 1846–1849," *North Carolina Historical Review*, XV (1938), 2–3; Powell Moore, "The Political Background of the Revolt against Jackson in Tennessee," *East Tennessee Historical Society's Publications*, No. 4 (1932), 45–66; Thomas P. Abernethy, "The Origin of the Whig Party in Tennessee," *Mississippi Valley Historical Review*, XII (1927), 504–22; Joseph H. Parks, *John Bell* (Baton Rouge, 1950), pp. 58–133. The difficulty historians have had understanding why the North Carolina planters perversely remained in the Democratic party arises from the initial error of regarding the Whig party as primarily a planter group. The basic explanation is that the Old Republican planters of North Carolina, unlike the agricultural capitalists of the lower South, were antagonistic toward the commercial-financial group, rather than identified with it. With a smaller investment in land and slaves than his Mississippi counterpart, with little chance to make large profits by further investment, and relying less on a single cash crop, the average North Carolina planter was much less dependent on the town merchant and banker. For some years before the Jackson era, the planters had been resisting demands for banks and internal improvements, while simultaneously trying to stem the tide of democratic discontent with planter rule. It was the union of these two anti-planter forces, commercial and democratic, which produced the Whig party in 1833–1835. Businessmen controlled the new party, but they retained popular support by championing constitutional reform and by progressive legislation in the fields of internal improvements and public education. There is no adequate account of the North Carolina Whigs in print. The situation in Virginia was somewhat similar, in that a majority of the planters, Phillips and Cole to the contrary notwithstanding, remained Democrats. In the period 1833–1843, the twelve congressional districts of plantation Virginia, lying east of the Blue Ridge and south of the Rappahannock, were represented thirty-eight times by Democrats and twenty-two times by Whigs or Conservatives, with nine of the Whig elections being won in the commercial Norfolk, Richmond, and Fredericksburg districts. The Democratic party of Virginia differed from that of North Carolina, however, in having a much larger popular element.

[46] Hearon, "Nullification in Mississippi," *loc. cit.*, pp. 37–77; Winston, "Mississippi Whigs and the Tariff," *loc. cit.*, pp. 505–24; James E. Winston, "The Mississippi Whigs and the Annexation of Texas," *Southwestern Historical Quarterly*, XXIX (1926), pp. 161–80; Ranck, *Alfred G. Brown*, pp. 4–15; Dallas C. Dickey, *Seargent S. Prentiss: Whig Orator of the Old South* (Baton Rouge, 1945), pp. 45–266.

Alabama, where it was led by the able Dixon H. Lewis. The Lewis faction, however, maintained only a tenuous connection with the regular Whigs, and in 1837 Lewis and his supporters followed Calhoun back into the Democratic party. The significant fact is that in neither Alabama nor Mississippi were the Whigs greatly weakened by the departure of Calhoun's admirers.[47]

Only in South Carolina and Georgia did avowed state rights men make up the bulk of the anti-Jackson party. When the real nature of the new party alignments became apparent, the politicians of Calhoun's state gave proof of their sincerity (and of the Presidential aspirations of their chief) by moving back to the Democratic ranks at the first decent opportunity.

The principal Whig leader in Georgia was John M. Berrien, a Savannah lawyer and attorney for the United States Bank who had been forced out of Jackson's cabinet by the Peggy Eaton affair. At the time of the election of 1832, Jackson's Indian policy was so popular in Georgia that Berrien did not dare oppose the President openly. Instead, he went about stirring up anti-tariff and state rights sentiment, while secretly trying to prevent anti-Bank resolutions by the legislature. Immediately after Jackson's re-election, however, Berrien and his allies managed to reorganize the old Troup political faction as an openly anti-Jackson state rights party. In view of Berrien's pro-Bank attitude and his subsequent staunch support of Clay's policies, it seems probable that he was merely capitalizing on state rights sentiment to defeat Democratic measures which he opposed on other grounds. At any rate, the Georgia Whigs were soon arrayed against the Jackson financial program, and they held their lines nearly intact in the face of the desertion of state rights Whigs to the Democrats on the Subtreasury issue. By 1840 Berrien had brought his Georgia followers into close harmony with the national party.[48]

This summary sketch of southern Whiggery raises, of course, more questions than it could possibly answer definitively. It has attempted to suggest, however, that preoccupation with the origins and development of southern sectionalism has led to distortions of

---

[47] Jack, *Sectionalism in Alabama*, pp. 21–85.

[48] Thomas P. Govan, "John M. Berrien and the Administration of Andrew Jackson," *Journal of Southern History*, V (1939), pp. 447–67; Phillips, "Georgia and State Rights," *loc. cit.*, pp. 113–50; Murray, *Whig Party in Georgia, passim.* Despite the defection of three congressmen to the Democrats on the Subtreasury issue, the Georgia Whigs won the subsequent congressional election and carried the Presidential election of 1840 by three times their majority in 1836.

southern political history in the 1830's and 1840's. Specifically, it is suggested:

That only John C. Calhoun and a small group of allied southern leaders regarded state rights as the most important issue in politics in this period.

That the southern people divided politically in these years over much the same questions as northern voters, particularly questions of banking and financial policy.

That the Whig party in the South was built around a nucleus of National Republicans and state rights men, but received its greatest accession of strength from business-minded Democrats who deserted Jackson on the Bank issue.

That the Whig party in the South was controlled by urban commercial and banking interests, supported by a majority of the planters, who were economically dependent on banking and commercial facilities. And finally,

That this alliance of the propertied, far from being inherently particularistic, rapidly shook off its state rights adherents and by 1841 was almost solidly in support of the nationalistic policies of Henry Clay.

There is a great need for intensive restudy of southern politics in the 1830's and 1840's, and particularly for critical correlation of local and national developments. The story as it comes from the contemporary sources is full of the resounding clash of solid interests and opposing ideologies, hardly having "the hollow sound of a stage duel with tin swords" which one historian seems to detect.[49] And recent events should make the student wary of state rights banners, especially when raised by conservative men against national administrations not conspicuously devoted to the interests of the propertied.

---

[49] Sydnor, *Development of Southern Sectionalism*, p. 316.

GRADY McWHINEY[*]

The Similar Class Status of Alabama's Party Leaders

Grady McWhiney is one of a number of historians of southern politics who have challenged the belief that the Jacksonian party leadership south of the Mason and Dixon line was more plebeian than its Whig counterpart. He makes a most impressive quantitative case for the view that in Alabama, at least, "the Whigs were no more exclusively the 'silk stocking' party ... than the Democracy was exclusively the party of the 'common man.'"

※※

"THE WHIG PARTY in the South," writes Arthur C. Cole its most comprehensive examiner, "was from its origin, and continued to be throughout its history, the party of the planter and slaveholder." Led by aristocrats, its "members formed a broadcloth and

_____

[*] From Grady McWhiney, "Were the Whigs a Class Party in Alabama?" *Journal of Southern History*, XXIII (November, 1957), pp. 510–522. Copyright © 1957 by the Southern Historical Association. Reprinted by permission of the Managing Editor.

silk stocking party embracing a large part of the wealth, intelligence, and blue blood of the South." [1]

This concept of the Whigs as a class party has not only been incorporated into textbooks[2] but has been endorsed almost without exception by serious students of the period. As eminent a scholar as U. B. Phillips, for example, believed that the "southern people tended generally to be Democrats unless there were special considerations to the contrary" such as "the social class consciousness of the squires. . . . The squires almost with one accord joined the Whigs throughout the south," except in the Carolinas.[3] Following Cole and Phillips, students of the Whig party in various Southern states have generally reached similar conclusions.[4] Indeed, it has become almost a stereotype to characterize Southern Whigs as owners of "stately mansions, surrounded with almost every comfort of the day and with many luxuries"; as "men of culture and of broad interests"—"educated in the polished manners of their class" ("often they had received a college education in the North")—who

---

[1] Arthur C. Cole, *The Whig Party in the South* (Washington, 1913), 69, 71–72. The author wishes to acknowledge that much of the research for this article was made possible by a grant from the Southern Fellowships Fund.

[2] *Cf.* Harry J. Carman and Harold C. Syrett, *A History of the American People* (2 vols., New York, 1952), I, 385; John D. Hicks, *The Federal Union: A History of the United States to 1865* (Boston, 1948), 446–47; Samuel E. Morison and Henry S. Commager, *The Growth of the American Republic* (4th ed., 2 vols., New York, 1950), I, 555; Merle Curti and others, *An American History* (2 vols., New York, 1950), I, 464; and Robert S. Cotterill, *The Old South* (Glendale, Calif., 1936), 161.

[3] "The Southern Whigs, 1834–1854," in *Essays in American History Dedicated to Frederick Jackson Turner* (New York, 1910), 215.

[4] See, for example, Theodore H. Jack, *Sectionalism and Party Politics in Alabama, 1819–1842* (Menasha, Wis., 1919), 31; Henry H. Simms, *The Rise of the Whigs in Virginia, 1824–1840* (Richmond, 1929), 164–66; James E. Winston, "The Mississippi Whigs and the Tariff, 1834–1844," in *Mississippi Valley Historical Review* (Cedar Rapids, 1914–   ), XXII (December 1935), 506; and to a lesser extent Paul Murray, *The Whig Party in Georgia, 1825–1853* (Chapel Hill, 1948), 2–3. Murray finds many similarities between Whigs and Democrats in Georgia; and in Tennessee, according to Thomas B. Alexander, a "comparison of Whig with Democratic counties on the basis of geography, soil, slaveholding, urbanization, and concentration of capital or business and professional men reveals only imperfect correlations between the political map and the geographic or economic map . . . No simple dichotomy explains the political geography of Tennessee." "Thomas A. R. Nelson as an Example of Whig Conservatism in Tennessee," in *Tennessee Historical Quarterly* (Nashville, 1942–   ), XV (March 1956), 17.

earnestly believed "that their less fortunate neighbors were not fit to associate with them socially or politically." [5]

"Very early," writes Theodore H. Jack about Alabama, "the ultra democratic attitude of the Jackson men began to be distasteful to the developing aristocratic sentiment on the plantations." In those sections where "cotton was king and the large plantation was the predominant economic institution, it was natural for the Whig party to develop its greatest strength." Thus, in Alabama the Whig party "rapidly became the 'broadcloth' party, the party of the wealthier and more cultivated people." [6] Such distinguished scholars as Thomas P. Abernethy and Albert B. Moore have also stressed the strength of the Whigs in the Alabama Black Belt.[7] Abernethy points out, however, that the Whigs cannot be explained simply as the party of the planters. "The solidly Democratic vote in northern Alabama," he writes, "in spite of the large number of slaves in the Tennessee Valley, indicates that the rivalry between the two sections of the State had much to do with political alignments." [8] Moore

---

[5] Cole, *Whig Party*, 70. Writing a quarter of a century after Cole and Phillips, Charles S. Sydnor suggested that "one should not forget that ambitious politicians were calculating their chances of advancement and were throwing their influence to the party that held out the better prospects. The chief activity of Southern politicians in the 1830's and 1840's consisted in struggles for local place and power rather than in contests over any principles that differentiated the national parties." Sydnor nevertheless concluded that "the Whigs were strongest in the planting counties [except in North Carolina], and it is sometimes said that they owned three fourths of the slaves in the South." *The Development of Southern Sectionalism, 1819–1848* (Baton Rouge, 1948), 318–19.

A more recent study by Charles G. Sellers, Jr., while willing to treat the Whigs as a class party, contends that instead of being planter dominated, "the Whig party in the South was controlled by urban commercial and banking interests, supported by a majority of planters, who were economically dependent on banking and commercial facilities." "Who Were the Southern Whigs?" in *American Historical Review* (New York, 1895–), LIX (January 1954), 341–46.

[6] Jack, *Sectionalism and Party Politics in Alabama*, 31.

[7] Thomas P. Abernethy, *The Formative Period in Alabama, 1815–1828* (Montgomery, 1922), 146; Albert B. Moore, *History of Alabama* (Tuscaloosa, 1951), 160–61. According to Moore, "The two parties . . . rested upon social and economic foundations . . . The Whig party was the 'broadcloth' party; it drew its strength from the men of slaves and means who lived in the Black Belt and in the western counties of the Tennessee Valley and the business interests affiliated with them. The Democratic party," on the other hand, "was supported principally by farmers and the small business classes of the other parts of the State. Generally speaking, the Whig party was a south Alabama party and the Democratic party dominated north Alabama."

[8] Abernethy, *Formative Period*, 146.

also admits that "from the outset there was a considerable planter contingent in the Democratic party." [9]

How nearly correct, then, are the generalizations? Were the Alabama Whigs almost exclusively large planters and slave-holders; the Democrats small farmers and nonslaveholders? Do the county returns for the six presidential elections (1836 through 1856) in which there was a Whig nominee show that the Whigs were a class party? Do the background, education, occupations, and religious affiliations of the men elected to Congress and to the Alabama legislature suggest that the Whigs were "the party of the wealthier and more cultivated people"?

It cannot be denied that many Whig voters lived in the Alabama Black Belt; nor is it denied that the Democrats received more votes than the Whigs in most of the counties where there were few slaves. What has not been sufficiently emphasized, however, is that the Whigs did not receive votes just in the Black Belt or that areas of small farms were not the only Democratic strongholds. For twenty years the Whig party was a major political organization in Alabama with supporters in every county. Although never able to carry the state, Whig presidential nominees received 42 per cent of the votes cast in the six presidential elections between 1836 and 1856.[10] Some of the largest majorities given Whigs were polled in counties where there were few slaves, and some of the

Table 1. Whig Vote by Counties

Whig vote	0–45%			45–50%			50–55%			55–65%			65–100%		
Slave population of counties	over 50 %	30–50 %	0–30 %	over 30–50 %	0–50 %	0–30 %	over 30–50 %	0–50 %	0–30 %	over 30–50 %	0–50 %	0–30 %	over 30–50 %	0–50 %	0–30 %
1836	3	6	12	0	5	1	1	3	2	4	2	2	6	0	2
1840	2	5	13	1	4	1	2	0	1	8	6	2	1	1	2
1844	3	7	15	2	3	0	7	2	3	2	4	0	0	0	0
1848	1	2	12	1	1	0	2	3	2	5	3	3	2	1	1
1852	8	9	20	4	3	1	3	2	1	0	0	0	0	0	0
1856	8	8	17	1	4	2	5	0	0	1	1	1	0	0	1
Total	25	37	89	9	20	5	20	10	9	20	16	8	9	2	6

[9] Moore, *History of Alabama*, 161.

[10] Clanton W. Williams (ed.), "Presidential Election Returns and Related Data for Ante-Bellum Alabama," in *Alabama Review* (Tuscaloosa, 1948–   ), I (October 1948), 279–93; II (January 1949), 64–71.

largest majorities given Democrats were polled in counties where there were many slaves.[11] Covington and Madison counties are conspicuous examples. Ranking very low in slaveholding, Covington returned Whig majorities in every presidential election except one. Madison, with over half its population slave, gave the Democratic candidates large majorities in every election.

Whig strength was not based solely upon planters. An analysis of the presidential elections from 1836 through 1856 shows only slight correlation between slaveholding and the Whig vote.[12] In only three of the sixteen counties where over half of the population was slave did Whig candidates receive a majority in every election. In three of these same sixteen counties Democratic candidates also received a majority in every election. The other ten leading slaveholding counties were inconsistent in their loyalties, and frequently the contests were close—a shift of 5 per cent in the vote would have brought defeat in nearly half of the Whig and in 36 per cent of the Democratic victories.

Table 2.   Correlation Between Whig Vote and Slaves

1836	.534
1840	.583
1844	.671
1848	.523
1852	.630
1856	.492

Between 1835 and 1856, thirty-eight different individuals represented Alabama in the United States Congress—twenty-six Democrats, eleven Whigs, and one Know Nothing.[13] During the same

---

[11] See Table 1, which is based upon data found in *ibid.*

[12] See Table 2, which is also based upon *ibid.* The returns also show only slight correlation between Whig vote and (1) per capita wealth; (2) percentage of families owning slaves; and (3) average acreage per family. The formula used in determining correlation was

$$\rho = 1 - \frac{6 \Sigma D^2}{N(N^2 - 1)} \text{ (Spearman's rank correlation coefficient).}$$

[13] Allen Johnson, Dumas Malone, and Harris E. Starr (eds.), *Dictionary of American Biography* (21 vols. and index, New York, 1928–1944); hereinafter cited as *DAB;* Thomas M. Owen, *History of Alabama and Dictionary of Alabama Biography* (4 vols., Chicago, 1921); William Garrett, *Reminiscences of Public Men in Alabama* (Atlanta, 1872); Willis Brewer, *Alabama: Her History, Resources, War Record, and Public Men* (Montgomery, 1872); and *Biographical Directory of the American Congress . . .* (Washington, 1950), were used in gathering biographical data on these men. William R. Smith was a Union Democrat, a Union Whig, and a Know Nothing during his tenure in Congress. *Ibid.,* 1837; *DAB,* XVII, 367.

years, 990 men from fifty-two counties were elected to the state legislature.[14] Party affiliations for 414 (41.7 per cent) could be determined—244 were Democrats, 167 were Whigs, two were both Democrats and Whigs during their tenure, and one was a Know Nothing.[15]

Persons of varied background and personality sat in both Congress and the state legislature: college professor and carpenter; preacher and drunkard;[16] Catholic and Jew; a member of the Sons of Temperance and a glutton;[17] men from very wealthy families and men whose fathers were poor. The congressmen included such well-known Democratic figures as Vice President William R. King, blimp-like Dixon H. Lewis, and fire-eating William L. Yancey; and such Whigs as the able speaker and writer John Gayle, prematurely gray-haired Francis S. Lyons, and the brilliant and erratic Jeremiah Clemens, who confessed that "he was obliged to drink to bring his genius down to a level with Mr. Y[ancey]'s." [18] Capable

---

[14] Twenty-five congressmen, either before or after their terms in Washington, sat in the state legislature but, in order to avoid duplication, they are not included in the 990 (neither are the men who were elected to the legislature first as Whigs or Democrats and later as Know Nothings). Party affiliations could be determined for 48.3 per cent (seventy-seven Democrats and eighty-four Whigs) of the men who represented the sixteen counties where over half the population was slave; for 46.9 per cent (ninety-five Democrats and sixty-three Whigs) of the men who represented the fifteen counties where slaves comprised from 30 to 50 per cent of the population; and for 28.8 per cent (seventy-two Democrats and twenty Whigs) of the men who represented the twenty-one counties where less than 30 per cent of the population was slave.

[15] The principal sources used in gathering material on these men were: *Journal of the House of Representatives of the State of Alabama, 1835–1856; Journal of the Senate . . . of Alabama, 1835–1856; Garrett, Reminiscences; Owen, History of Alabama;* and Brewer, *Alabama.* Some information was also obtained from various county histories.

[16] President Polk recorded that his friend Felix G. McConnell committed suicide because "of the effects of intemperance." Allan Nevins (ed.), *Polk: The Diary of a President, 1845–1849* (New York, 1952), 145–47. It was also suggested that Jeremiah Clemens "colored his water a little too deeply." Lewy Dorman, *Party Politics in Alabama from 1850 through 1860* (Wetumpka, Ala., 1935), 41–42, 132n.; Brewer, *Alabama,* 363. According to Garrett (*Reminiscences,* 162) Whig legislator Henry C. Lea became a drunkard. And not only was Democratic legislator Hugh M. Rodgers charged with being a drunkard but also with being a thief. *Ibid.,* 280–81.

[17] Franklin W. Bowdon's "only enemy was his own appetite, which impaired his usefulness, and cut him off in the zenith of life." Brewer, *Alabama,* 540.

[18] *Ibid.,* 363.

and principled men could be found in both parties as could dema-
gogues and political chameleons. Of the latter types no better
examples can be suggested than Democrat W. R. W. Cobb, "friend
of the poor against the rich," who "sang homely songs which he
had composed for his stump speeches" (one began: "Uncle Sam is
rich enough to give us all a farm") and resorted to such tricks as
"the rattling of tinware and crockery to keep the attention of his
audiences" while winking and "punctuating his phrases by chewing
with great gusto a piece of onion and the coarsest 'pone' bread";[19]
and the "master stump speaker" Henry W. Hilliard, successively a
Whig, a Know Nothing, a Democrat, a Bell man in 1860, a Radical
Republican, a Greeley man in 1872, and finally an unsuccessful
Republican candidate for Congress in 1876.[20] Two Whig legislators
were notorious jokers. Exceedingly fond of playing pranks on his
friends, Robert Dougherty of Macon County allegedly rode an
alligator over a mile in the Alabama River.[21] Richard H. Ricks
of Franklin was also "noted for his eccentricities and his waggery."
Wearing "his hair and beard long, and a blouse coat, which drew
much attention upon him," Ricks was "so addicted to sport that,
on joint ballot of the Two Houses, he was apt to vote for 'John
Smith,' his favorite candidate." [22]

If the representatives of the people of Alabama varied in personality, they were remarkably alike in place of birth. The overwhelming majority of both congressmen and legislators were born
in the South.[23] Over half of the Whigs as well as the Democrats
were born in either the Carolinas or Georgia: more Democrats
were born in South Carolina than in any other state; more Whigs
in Georgia.

Biographical data were not found on the social origins of all
the Democratic and Whig congressmen and legislators, but the
information that was obtained makes it clear that a number of
both Democrats and Whigs had the advantage of being born into

---

[19] Dorman, *Party Politics in Alabama*, 58–59.

[20] *DAB*, IX, 54–55.

[21] Garrett, *Reminiscences*, 354.

[22] *Ibid.*, 505.

[23] See Table 3. Place of birth was determined for all of the Whig and
Democratic congressmen and for 281 (28.3 per cent) legislators—153 Democrats, 104 Whigs, and 24 men whose party was not determined.

wealthy families. It is also clear that often Democrats as well as Whigs were of humble origins. If the Democrats sometimes lent "common men" to Congress and to the state legislature, so did the Whigs—"poor boy" candidates were not restricted to one party. For example, the Democrats could boast of such congressmen as Edmund S. Dargan, who was so poor that he had to walk from North Carolina to Autauga County, Alabama, and who, despite his limited education, taught school while studying law;[24] or of Benjamin Fitzpatrick, who "never attended school more than six months" but was offered the choice of running for vice president on the Douglas ticket.[25] The Whigs could claim congressmen like William R. Smith, who began life as an orphan, "without means and without influential friends," and rose from tailor's apprentice to college president;[26] or George W. Crabb, who migrated from Tennessee with little more apparent equipment for success than a common-school education but returned to Alabama from the "Indian war in Florida . . . the idol of his men" and assured of political "preferment." [27]

In the state legislature sat such simple Whigs as Luke R. Simmons, a "plain farmer," [28] and poorly educated James Cain, one of the "class of men," according to William Garrett, "who have been aptly styled 'the bone and sinew of the country.' " [29] There, too, sat Benjamin H. Baker, who "grew up with grave disadvantages";[30]

---

[24] *DAB*, V, 74.

[25] *Ibid.*, VI, 439.

[26] Brewer, *Alabama*, 561–62; *DAB*, XVII, 367.

[27] Although only a lieutenant colonel in one of the Alabama regiments in the Indian War, Crabb was after the peace "immediately elected a Major-General." *Biographical Directory of Congress*, 1027; Garrett, *Reminiscences*, 53. Democratic legislator John H. Garrett of Cherokee County, who "was fond of talking of duels and the code of honor which prevailed among the chivalry" in his native South Carolina, also owed much of his political success to his popularity with the militia. "He had quite a taste for military life, and was elected a Major General of Alabama Militia." *Ibid.*, 179–80.

[28] Garrett, *Reminiscences*, 196–97.

[29] *Ibid.*, 239. Cain's simplicity was reported to have been a factor in his victory over Democrat Eldridge Mallard. Mallard's "family were fond of stylish display, hardly in keeping with the times, and this fact was used by his political opponent, James Cain, in defeating him in 1841 and 1842." James M. Dombhart, *History of Walker County, Its Towns and Its People* (Thornton, Ark., 1937), 275–76.

[30] Brewer, *Alabama*, 514.

George N. Stewart, son of a common sailor in the United States Navy;[31] and Henry W. Cox, who, as his biographer described his quest for legal training, "succeeded over many difficulties in getting to the bar." [32] Of "humble parentage" also was William H. Fowler, who worked "at different times with a tailor, a printer, and a druggist." [33] Such men certainly do not confirm the theory that the Whig party was made up of "blue bloods." Probably most of the congressmen and legislators—Whig and Democratic—came about as close to being "aristocrats" as did legislator Thomas McCarroll Prince, a Whig merchant of Mobile. While visiting in Europe, one story goes, he registered at a hotel as "Thomas McCarroll Prince of Mobile." Large crowds gathered, and he was treated as visiting royalty until it was discovered "that the absence of a punctuation mark, and not 'blue blood' " had made him one of the nobility.[34]

A sizable number of both Democrats and Whigs were college graduates, but, surprisingly enough, the Democrats appear to have had more formal education than the Whigs. Over half (51.5 per cent) of the Democratic congressmen and legislators whose educational background could be determined were college graduates,

Table 3. *Place of Birth and Educational Backgrounds*

	Place of birth by percentage			Educational background by percentage		
	Born in the South	Born in the North	Born else-where	Limited or only common schooling	More than common schooling but not college graduates	College graduates
Congressmen						
Whigs	90.9	9.1	—	36.4	27.2	36.4
Democrats	100.0	—	—	38.5	23.0	38.5
Legislators						
Whigs	92.3	7.7	—	30.8	25.3	43.9
Democrats	96.1	3.3	.6	20.3	25.0	54.7
Party						
Unknown	100.0	—	—	32.0	40.0	28.0

[31] Owen, *History of Alabama*, IV, 1622.

[32] *Ibid.*, III, 407.

[33] Brewer, *Alabama*, 269.

[34] *Ibid.*, 172; Garrett, *Reminiscences*, 193.

while only 43.1 per cent of the Whigs could claim degrees. Moreover, a higher percentage of Democrats (10.4) than Whigs (5.9) received degrees from Northern colleges.[35] Indeed, the only congressmen who attended colleges outside the South were Democrats—Eli S. Shorter received both academic and law degrees from Yale, and William L. Yancey attended Williams College but left before graduating.[36] Democrat Robert B. Lindsay, a graduate of St. Andrew's University, Scotland,[37] was the only legislator to attend a foreign university.

As would be expected in a group of successful politicians, over half of the congressmen and legislators were lawyers.[38] All eleven Whig and twenty-four of the twenty-six Democratic congressmen were lawyers. (No evidence could be found that wealthy Demo-

---

[35] See Table 3. Educational background was determined for all of the Whig and Democratic congressmen and for 244 (24.6 per cent) legislators— 128 Democrats, 91 Whigs, and 25 men whose party was not determined.

Sixty-five Democrats and thirty-eight Whigs were graduated from Southern colleges: nineteen Democrats and seven Whigs from the University of Alabama (also, Democrat C. C. Clay, Jr. received a law degree from the University of Virginia; Democrat Joseph P. Safford received a law degree from Yale; and Democrat Lewis M. Stone received a law degree from Harvard); thirteen Democrats and three Whigs from the University of Georgia (Democrat J. L. M. Curry also received a law degree from Harvard); ten Democrats and eight Whigs from South Carolina College, or the University of South Carolina; five Democrats and three Whigs from the University of Virginia; five Democrats and six Whigs from the University of North Carolina; two Democrats and two Whigs from the University of Tennessee; four Democrats and one Whig from La Grange College; two Democrats and four Whigs from Cumberland; two Democrats from Transylvania; one Democrat from Randolph-Macon; one Democrat from Greenville College; one Whig from Emory; one Whig from Louisville Medical College; one Whig from Charleston Medical College; and one Whig from St. Joseph College, Kentucky.

Fourteen Democrats and six Whigs received degrees from Northern colleges: two Democrats and four Whigs from Princeton; four Democrats and one Whig from Yale; two Democrats from Harvard; two Democrats from the Philadelphia Medical College; one Democrat from the University of Pennsylvania; one Democrat from Amherst; one Democrat from the United States Military Academy; and one Democratic and one Whig from Middlebury College, Vermont.

[36] Owen, *History of Alabama*, IV, 1551; *DAB*, XX, 592.

[37] Brewer, *Alabama*, 190.

[38] See Table 4. Occupations were determined for all of the Whig and Democratic congressmen and for 346 (34.9 per cent) legislators—182 Democrats, 131 Whigs, and 33 men whose party was not ascertained. A considerable number of men, however, had more than one vocation—it was not unusual to find as many as three occupations listed for one man. Each occupation is noted in Table 4.

crat William M. Payne had any other occupation than that of a "large scale" planter;[39] or that Democrat W. R. W. Cobb was more than a former "peddler of clocks" who became a rich merchant.[40]) Nearly all of the congressmen, however, had concomitant occupations. Besides being lawyers, two Whigs and five Democrats were also planters. Democrat David Hubbard combined his legal practice with merchandising, planting, and manufacturing.[41] Democrat James F. Dowdell was also a Methodist preacher; and Whig Joab Lawler was "a receiver of public money" and a Baptist preacher.[42] Democrats William L. Yancey and James E. Belser and Whig William R. Smith were editors as well as lawyers;[43] Whig Henry W. Hilliard was a professor of English literature at the University of Alabama; and litterateur Jere Clemens, also a Whig, wrote four novels.[44]

Planting was listed as an occupation of ninety-nine (47.6 per cent) Democratic and forty-nine (34.5 per cent) Whig congressmen and legislators. Nineteen Whigs and thirty-eight Democrats were described by their biographers as "planter of large means," or "extensive planter," or "planter of considerable wealth." Whig legislator Robert M. Patton, for example, is said to have owned over three hundred slaves, while Democratic legislator John W. Portis is reported to have owned "not less than 100,000 acres." [45]

A slightly higher percentage of Whigs than Democrats were professional men, but about the same percentage of Whigs as Democrats were in business. Sixteen Democrats and thirteen Whigs were merchants; seven Democrats and four Whigs were bankers; three Democrats and four Whigs were connected with railroads; and two Democrats and two Whigs were manufacturers. Eleven Democrats and five Whigs were listed only as businessmen, or their business was described too vaguely for specific classification.

---

[39] Garrett, *Reminiscences*, 100; Owen, *History of Alabama*, IV, 1331.

[40] Brewer, *Alabama*, 286; Garrett, *Reminiscences*, 395; Owen, *History of Alabama*, III, 357–58.

[41] Hubbard was also "the leading promoter of Alabama's first railroad." *DAB*, IX, 322.

[42] Owen, *History of Alabama*, III, 502; IV, 1015–16.

[43] Brewer, *Alabama*, 450; *DAB*, XX, 592–93; XVII, 367.

[44] *DAB*, IX, 54; IV, 191.

[45] Owen, *History of Alabama*, IV, 1328; Garrett, *Reminiscences*, 366–67.

Such, for example, was Democrat Eldridge Mallard, who was said to be "the keeper of a very popular house of entertainment." [46] Ten Democrats and eight Whigs were listed merely as farmers.

Table 4.   Occupations

| | Congressmen | | Legislators | | Party |
	Whigs	Democrats	Whigs	Democrats	Unknown
	%	%	%	%	%
Planter	18.2	23.1	35.9	51.1	36.4
Large	18.2	15.4	13.0	18.7	12.1
Farmer	—	—	6.1	5.5	—
Lawyer	100.0	92.3	55.0	54.4	51.5
Professional	36.4	11.4	23.7	14.7	15.2
Physician	—	—	12.2	6.6	6.1
Minister	9.1	3.8	3.8	3.8	9.1
Teacher	9.1	—	—	.5	—
Author	9.1	—	.8	—	—
Editor	9.1	7.6	6.9	3.8	—
Business	—	11.5	22.9	22.0	18.3
Merchant	—	7.7	9.9	7.7	6.1
Banker	—	—	3.1	3.8	6.1
Railroad	—	—	3.1	1.6	—
Hotel	—	—	.8	1.2	—
Insurance	—	—	.8	—	—
Manufacturer	—	3.8	1.4	1.2	—
Real Estate	—	—	—	.5	—
Other	—	—	3.8	6.0	6.1
Total number of men	11	26	131	182	33

Earlier in life a number of congressmen and legislators had pursued occupations not listed in Table 4. Before obtaining more suitable positions, eleven Whigs and eleven Democrats had taught school—often while they were studying law. Six Whigs and five Democrats had been store clerks; two Whigs had been printing apprentices; one Whig and two Democrats had worked on farms; one Whig had been an apprentice to a tailor; two Democrats had been mail riders; one had been a plantation overseer; another an apprentice to a cotton gin maker; one a carpenter; and one a saddler.

Many congressmen and legislators were charged with being godless men, like Whig legislator Hardin Perkins, who "seemed to manifest no concern whatever for his spiritual condition, or for the responsibilities of a future life." "Most of our public men,"

---

[46] Dombhart, *History of Walker County*, 275.

lamented Garrett, "instead of being selected for high moral virtue, seem to repudiate all qualifications of this nature." [47] Whatever the reason, church membership could be ascertained for only 14 per cent of the congressmen and legislators.[48] Most of the Whigs as well as the Democrats were Methodists or Baptists; there were few Episcopalians in either party.

Table 5. Religious Affiliations

	Congressmen		Legislators		
	Whigs	Democrats	Whigs	Democrats	Unknown
Methodist	2	2	16	34	6
Baptist	1	4	10	21	2
Presbyterian	2	0	9	17	0
Episcopalian	1	1	3	7	0
Catholic	1	0	0	0	0
Jew	0	1	0	0	0
Congregationalist	0	0	1	0	0
Unitarian	0	0	0	1	0
Lutheran	0	0	0	1	0

Both the presidential election returns and the background, education, occupations, and religious affiliations of the Alabama congressmen and legislators suggest that some of the general statements about the Whig party need qualification. To say that the Whigs were the party of the large planter and slaveholder seems to be too much of an oversimplification. The correlation between the Whig vote and slaveholding in Alabama is slight. Some of the largest Whig majorities were received in counties where there were few slaves. Moreover, if the Whigs had relied exclusively upon planter support, it would have been impossible for them to have polled 42 per cent of the vote. Less than a third of the people of Alabama owned slaves.

Certainly it cannot be proved by the men who sat in Congress and in the Alabama legislature that great social differences existed between the two parties. On the contrary, the successful candidates for whom biographical information was found appear to have been more alike than different. Generally they were born in the same part of the South; their education was similar, as were their occupations and religious affiliations. Both parties elected large

---

[47] Garrett, *Reminiscences*, 192.

[48] See Table 5. Religious affiliations were determined for fifteen (40.5 per cent) congressmen and 128 (12.9 per cent) legislators.

planters as well as plain farmers—"self-made" men as well as men born into wealthy families.

In the state as a whole it may have indeed been true that more large planters were Whigs than Democrats. But if the men they sent to Congress and to the state legislature are any indication, the Whigs were no more exclusively the "silk stocking" party in Alabama than the Democracy was exclusively the party of the "common man."

GLYNDON G. VAN DEUSEN*†

Major Party Thought and Theory

Glyndon G. Van Deusen is the leading student of the Whig Party and its leaders. In this essay he notes that Whig leaders had a number of convictions which clearly distinguished them from the Jacksonians. Stated principles were—as Marvin Meyers had suggested—an important clue to the real beliefs of political men. But the burden of Van Deusen's argument is the essential similarity of Whigs and Democrats, both in the composition of their constituencies and in their fundamental beliefs. "The divergencies that existed . . . were more over means than over ultimate ends."

DURING THE LAST one hundred years, a considerable number of historians and biographers have attempted to assay the character

---

* From Glyndon G. Van Deusen, "Some Aspects of Whig Thought and Theory in the Jacksonian Period," *American Historical Review*, LXIII (January, 1958), pp. 305–322.

† Joseph Dorfman and Bray Hammond have been kind enough to read this article, and I have profited by their critical suggestions. I am also indebted to J. Cutler Andrews for his critical comments. No one but myself, however, bears responsibility whatsoever for the views herein expressed.

of Jacksonian democracy. The results have been a series of conflicting interpretations. Some have seen the movement simply as the rising of the masses against aristocratic rule.[1] Others have depicted it as a glowing tribute to Jackson himself.[2] To Frederick Jackson Turner, Jacksonian democracy represented the essence of the frontier spirit.[3] Arthur M. Schlesinger, Jr., while regarding Western debtor elements as important in the formation of Jacksonian democracy, puts his chief emphasis on the working class elements congregated in the Eastern cities and portrays the Democratic party as a political organization imbued with the belief that there was "a deep-rooted conflict in society between the 'producing' and 'non-producing' classes—the farmers and laborers on the one hand, and the business community on the other."[4] Joseph Dorfman, on the other hand, regards Jacksonian democracy as a movement devoted to preserving a laissez faire society and, therefore, opposing high tariffs, corporations, and monopolies. It was, says Dorfman, essentially a middle class, free trade, reform movement.[5] Bray Hammond and Richard Hofstadter maintain that the most dynamic element in Jacksonian democracy was its rising business element, avid for state bank credit and resentful of the dominance of the conservative Whig capitalists.[6]

There is, in all of these interpretations of Jacksonian democracy,

---

[1] James Parton, *Life of Andrew Jackson* (Boston, 1866); Moiseĭ Ostrogorski, *Democracy and the Organisation of Political Parties* (New York, 1902); Hermann Von Holst, *The Constitutional and Political History of the United States* (8 vols., Chicago, 1876–92); William G. Sumner, *Andrew Jackson as a Public Man* (Boston, 1882); John B. McMaster, *History of the People of the United States* (8 vols., New York, 1883–1914); Cyrus Brady, *The True Andrew Jackson* (Philadelphia, 1906).

[2] William G. Brown, *Andrew Jackson* (Boston, 1900); Arthur Colyar, *Life and Times of Andrew Jackson* (Nashville, 1904); Augustus Buell, *History of Andrew Jackson* (New York, 1904).

[3] *The Frontier in American History* (New York, 1920). This was early Turner. The concept was later modified. See his *The United States 1830–1850* (New York, 1935).

[4] *The Age of Jackson* (Boston, 1945), pp. 306–307.

[5] *The Economic Mind in American Civilization* (2 vols., New York, 1946), II, 601–36 and "The Jackson Wage-Earner Thesis," *American Historical Review*, LIV (Jan., 1949), 296–306.

[6] Hammond, *Banks and Politics in America* (Princeton, N. J., 1957), *passim* and "Public Policy and National Banks," *Journal of Economic History*, VI (May, 1946), 79–84; Hofstadter, *The American Political Tradition and the Men Who Made It* (New York, 1948), pp. 55–58.

some measure of validity. The movement was a rising of the masses in support of one who symbolized for them the virtue, the essential "rightness," of the common man. It was the hope of many a stout mechanic—and of many even stouter bankers, businessmen, and middle-class-minded farmers and planters. It rallied thousands of voters on the frontier. It contained many idealists, and not a few hard-boiled realists whose main objective was getting into office and staying there. It was also, in the opinion of this writer, a movement so heavily imbued with archaic notions about corporations, currency, banking, and do-nothing national government, that it would sooner or later have gone down to political defeat, even without the aid of the great depression which it helped to bring on.

The pity is that, in the midst of all this furious contention over Jacksonian democracy, the ideology of the rival Whig camp has suffered from neglect. Although Dixon Ryan Fox and Louis Hartz have made real contributions to the subject, and E. Malcolm Carroll, A. C. Cole, Joseph Dorfman, Arthur Schlesinger, Jr., and Richard N. Current have touched on the Whig point of view at various angles,[7] so far as I am aware there has been no systematic attempt to analyze Whig thought and theory as represented by the writings and speeches of the Whig leaders of the period. This essay, an approach to such an analysis, deals with aspects of the thought and theory of prominent Whigs of the New England, Middle Atlantic, and Western states.

One outstanding characteristic of Whig thought was its optimism regarding the future of the country. From Thomas Corwin in the West to John Quincy Adams in the East, the prevailing note was one of confidence as the Whig leaders contemplated America's great natural resources, the energy and ingenuity of the American people, and the rapid progress of invention. Corwin saw limitless possibilities for development in the West and in the nation. Samuel Ruggles, in the midst of the depression of 1837, declared that New York State could safely incur a debt of $40,000,000 for internal improvements, an assertion which was characterized by John A. Dix as fit only to be classed with the Arabian Nights entertainment. Abbott Lawrence, on the slightest temptation, would launch into

---

[7] Fox, *The Decline of Aristocracy in the Politics of New York* (New York, 1919); Hartz, *The Liberal Tradition in America* (New York, 1955); Carroll, *Origins of the Whig Party* (Durham, N. C., 1925); Cole, *The Whig Party in the South* (Washington, D. C., 1913); Dorfman, *op. cit.*; Schlesinger, *op. cit.*; Current, *Daniel Webster and the Rise of National Conservatism* (Boston, 1955).

glowing predictions regarding the industrial future of the country and earnestly bid the South and the West to share in this industrial development.

To be sure, pessimism about the existing order sometimes reared its head amid the Whig ranks. More than one Whig succumbed to dark forebodings when there was a prospect of a reduction of the tariff; by the latter 1830's John Quincy Adams was full of gloom occasioned by the rise of controversy over slavery; Greeley was so startled by the panic of 1837, and so alarmed by its accompanying mob violence, that he turned from contemplation of the nation's economic potential to the search for an equation between progress and utopian socialism.

The dominant note, however, was one of stubborn and sometimes ecstatic cheer. Senator Asher Robbins of Rhode Island prophesied in 1830 that in the blaze of America's glory "the master states of the world will be lost, as stars are lost in the blaze of the noon tide sun." [8] Hezekiah Niles saw the free, democratic, enterprising American people making use of the tariff and internal improvements to become the greatest industrial nation in the world. [9] William Seward told the New York State solons in 1839 that "our race is ordained to reach, on this continent, a higher standard of social perfection than it has ever yet attained; and that hence will proceed a spirit which shall renovate the world." [10] And Webster, as usual, expressed the general conviction in magniloquent prose. "Our course, gentlemen," he said at a New York dinner in February, 1831, "is onward, straight onward, and forward ... Our path is marked out for us, clear, plain, bright, distinctly defined, like the milky way across the heavens. If we are true to our country, in our day and generation, and those who come after us shall be true to it also, assuredly, assuredly, we shall elevate her to a pitch of prosperity and happiness, of honor and power, never yet reached by any nation beneath the sun." [11]

It is not without significance that this Whig optimism was

---

[8] *Register of Debates,* 21st Cong., 1st Sess., VI, pt. 1, 438.

[9] *Niles' Register,* XXXV (Dec. 20, 1828), 259; XXXVII (Dec. 5, 1829), 237, (Feb. 2, 1830), 426.

[10] *State of New York Assembly Doc. No. 1* (62nd Sess.), Seward to the Legislature, Jan. 1, 1839.

[11] *The Writings and Speeches of Daniel Webster* (18 vols., Boston, 1903), II, 64. See Philip Hone, *Diary,* Tuckerman ed. (2 vols., New York, 1889), I, 14, 45; II, 127, for optimism of a Whig businessman.

closely linked to material development. The Jacksonian optimists were prone to dwell upon the glorious promise of American social and political democracy. Not so the Whigs. Occasionally a Seward or a Webster would emphasize the importance of self-government or of social improvement by cultural means as bases for confidence in a happy future, but the Whig slogan might well have been: "America is headed for a glorious destiny. It is bound to become the richest and most powerful nation in the world." At the rainbow's end there was definitely a pot of gold.

The happy future of the Whigs was not to be reached by radical or revolutionary steps. It was, rather, to be the result of orderly developments that would be respectful of what the Whigs chose to regard as fundamental rights. When Webster declared in 1834 that "The laws should favor the distribution of property to the end that the number of the very rich and the number of the poor should both be diminished," he was quick to add the proviso, "as far as practicable with the rights of industry and property." [12] This statement may be taken as a very fair representation of Whig dynamic in the direction of "leveling" legislation.

The Whigs were aware, sometimes uncomfortably aware, of the existence of the masses, but they refused to recognize society as divided into distinctly separated groups, and they waxed wroth over what they called Democratic efforts to kindle class hatred. The Whigs recognized the existence of something which they called "the masses," or "the lower classes," but when Webster, or Lawrence, or Nathan Appleton, or Hezekiah Niles spoke of the "laboring classes" they were wont (like our own Arthur Larson[13]) to lump together all who worked—mechanics, farmers, businessmen, and bankers. For there was, according to the Whig philosophy, a natural harmony of interest between all the groups that made up the American social order. Labor and capital were but complements of one another. "If there be any aristocrats in Massachusetts," said Webster, "the people are all aristocrats."

These premises led, naturally enough, to the conclusion that unions were unnecessary and that strikes could be harmful. The Whigs could see the importance of cheap labor, especially where

---

[12] *Writings and Speeches,* XVI, 241–42. Webster was reported as saying during the Bank controversy that if Congress takes care of the rich, "the rich will take care of the poor." This he denied.

[13] *A Republican Looks at His Party* (New York, 1956), p. 110.

competition in foreign markets was concerned, although they also recognized the social value of good wages and wanted the workers to become the owners of property. They saw the best guarantee of obtaining these desirable goals, however, not in social disturbance but in hard work, sober living, and consistent support of the Whig party and its policies.[14] They held that the opportunities in which America abounded made this course an entirely practicable one.

The Whig attitude toward labor synchronized nicely with their attitude toward suffrage. Generally speaking, they accepted universal manhood suffrage as a "going concern." Occasionally, as in the case of Niles, Seward, or Greeley, a Whig would speak with approval of general male possession of the right to vote. In New York State the Whigs championed the extension of suffrage to Negroes, a proposal that was fought bitterly and successfully by the Democrats. Tocqueville, nevertheless, found the wealthy (the majority of whom were undoubtedly Whigs) secretly opposed to democracy.[15] Some Whig thinkers were openly loath to accept suffrage as a natural right. Even Greeley declared, in 1842, that suffrage was not a right to be acknowledged but a duty to be imposed by those who already possessed it.[16] The Whig editors of the *American Review* repeatedly declared that self-government and popular suffrage were not natural rights. They were privileges and, ideally speaking, should be exercised only by those possessed of property and intelligence. The ignorant and the vicious, said the *Review*, should not feel that they had a *right* to vote; they had the vote simply because there was no remedy that was not worse than the disease.[17] Whig leadership in the Jacksonian period was too realistic to oppose universal manhood suffrage, but its acceptance

---

[14] Lawrence, *Letter to a Committee* (Boston, 1837), pp. 6–12; *Niles' Register*, XXXVI (Apr. 11, 1829), 101; XLVIII (Apr. 24, 1830), 155, (May 22, 1830), 231–32; Webster, *Writings and Speeches*, II, 149–50; III, 175–76, 535; IV, 6, 429, 437; V, 227; XV, 107; Robert L. Carey, *Daniel Webster as an Economist* (New York, 1929), p. 70; *Register of Debates*, 22nd Cong., 1st Sess., VIII, pt. 1, 493, speech of Senator Asher Robbins; Appleton, *Labor, Its Relations in Europe and the United States Compared* (Boston, 1844), pp. 3, 4, 10, 16; Springfield, Mass., *Republican*, Aug. 18, Oct. 6, 13, 1838; Dorfman, *Economic Mind*, II, 635.

[15] Tocqueville, *Democracy in America* (2 vols., New York, 1945), I, 179–80.

[16] Glyndon G. Van Deusen, *Horace Greeley* (Philadelphia, 1953), p. 75.

[17] *American Review*, II (Nov., 1845), 446–48; IV (July, 1846), 29; (Nov. 1846), 442; V (June, 1847), 625.

could scarcely be termed enthusiastic. *Vox Populi Vox Dei* was not a Whig slogan.[18]

If the Whigs had reservations about political democracy, they were more than dubious about the health and well-being of the nation's financial system. This attitude derived in part from their natural conservatism, in part from the decidedly fragile nature of Jacksonian economics, and in part from the general economic conditions of the period from 1820 to 1850.

The Jacksonian era was fertile with opportunities for industrial development; it was the heyday of Veblen's Captain of Industry. It was also an era when business was beset by hosts of dangers and difficulties. The early businessman was generally a pioneer. He had to contend with bad communications, uncertainty in the supply of raw materials, currency confusion, and stiff foreign competition. One may gather from Democratic as well as Whig sources the most dismal pictures of a business class afflicted from 1815 on by an almost constant succession of crises and depressions, with the mad inflation of the middle 1830's thrown in to add chaos to confusion.[19]

Added to these business vicissitudes were those imposed by the Jacksonians—the veto of the recharter of the Second Bank of the United States with the destructive impact of that move upon the currency system, the lamentable "pet bank" system, the shock administered by the Specie Circular, the advocacy of the Independent Treasury (a move by which the federal government largely threw overboard its responsibility for regulating the national currency), and the constant onslaughts by large portions of the Democratic press and by Democratic politicians upon paper currency, banks, and the corporate form of business structure.

---

[18] Typical of this Whig attitude toward the common man was Philip Hone's dislike of unions and of the great unwashed masses (*Diary*, I, 64, 200, 210; II, 69–70). Cf. also Everett's attitude, in 1825 and then in 1850, on the subject of *Vox Populi Vox Dei* (Everett, *Orations and Speeches*, [Boston], 1836 ed., pp. 88–89 and 1850 ed., I, 97, 118–19).

[19] *The United States Magazine and Democratic Review*, V (Feb., 1939), 153 (hereafter cited as *Democratic Review*); Robert Rantoul, *Memoirs, Speeches and Writings* (Boston, 1854), 535–36; Allan Nevins, *Abram S. Hewitt* (New York, 1935), pp. 11–14; *House Doc. No. 38*, 22nd Cong., 1st Sess., 1831–32, II, 6; Clive Day, "The Early Development of American Cotton Manufactures," *Quarterly Journal of Economics*, XXXIX (May, 1925), 457–58, and *The Rise of Manufacturing in Connecticut, 1820–1850* (New Haven, Conn., n.d.), pp. 20–28; Isaac Lippincott, *A History of Manufactures in the Ohio Valley* (New York, 1914), p. 70; George P. Fuller, "An Introduction to the History of Connecticut as a Manufacturing State," *Smith College Studies in History* (Northampton, Mass., 1916), I, 66.

The Whig leaders, as befitted the representatives of a respectable portion of the business class, had a very lively sense of the importance of a sound financial structure. They could see that there was simply not enough specie in the country to permit its widespread use as a circulating medium. They could see that to force such a currency to any significant extent would not only be extremely inconvenient (as the New York and Connecticut experiments proved) but would also be a most serious handicap to the expansion of business and to the settlement of the West.[20] They also saw clearly the value of the Second Bank of the United States as a means of currency regulation, as an aid through its exchange operations to the development of the nation's commerce, and as a means for injecting at least a measure of honesty into the operations of the state banks. This theme runs through the speeches, messages, letters, and editorials of Webster, of Clay and Seward, of Richard Henry Bayard and Nathan Appleton, of Hezekiah Niles, John P. Kennedy, and Horace Greeley. Again and again one finds this Whig refrain—the country's need of a sound, substantial, government-regulated circulating medium, a judicious mixture of specie and specie-backed paper.[21]

Whig devotion to the principle of a sound currency was paralleled by their interest in credit as a means of fostering the nation's economic life. Credit was necessary to provide for the industrial expansion of the East, to give the Southern planter an opportunity for expanding into the cotton lands of the Southwest,

---

[20] Flagg Papers, New York City Public Library, S. Allen to Flagg, May 5, 1837, Jesse Hoyt to Flagg, May 10, 1837 (Azariah C. Flagg was long a power in the Albany Regency and comptroller of New York State, 1834–39 and 1842–46); J. M. Morse, *A Neglected Period of Connecticut History* (New Haven, Conn., 1933), p. 302; H. R. Smith, *Economic History of the United States* (New York, 1955), pp. 139, 199, 201. Paul W. Gates, "Land Policy and Tenancy in the Prairie States," *Journal of Economic History*, I (May, 1942), 62–72, illustrates the West's need of capital.

[21] The regulation favored by the Whigs was sometimes by national, sometimes by state, action. Nationally, it would be through the charter provisions for a national bank; in the states, by legislative regulation of state banks. It is not without interest that, at one time or another, both Webster and John Quincy Adams favored eliminating small bills from circulation (Webster, *Writings and Speeches*, VI, 133; Adams, *Memoirs* [12 vols., Philadelphia, 1874–77], IX, 135, 237; see also *Niles' Register*, XLVI [Mar. 8, 1834], 20). It was certainly ironical, as John J. Crittenden pointed out, that Benton should accuse the Whigs of loving paper money while at the same time the Democratic destruction of the Bank of the United States was multiplying the issues of doubtful bank paper throughout the country (*Register of Debates*, 24th Cong., 2d Sess., XIII, pt. 1, 76–77).

and to develop, agriculturally and industrially, the whole vast Western region. It was important that this credit be ample; it was equally important that it be sound. The best way to provide credit was through the bank credits available in a well-managed banking system.[22]

The Whig leaders were aware of these fundamental principles. Nathan Appleton subscribed to them when he helped found the Suffolk bank system, which furnished a firm credit basis for New England's industrial expansion. Seward in New York and young Abraham Lincoln in Illinois alike based their support of the principle of a national bank, modified and safeguarded to protect the public interest, squarely upon the country's need for credit. Thomas Corwin saw good credit facilities as essential to the development of the West. "We owe more to credit and to commercial confidence," said Webster in 1838, "than any nation that ever existed; and ten times more than any nation, except England." Whig statesmen generally had a very clear conception of the part which sound credit plays in a nation's development.[23]

Zeal for a stable currency and ample credit facilities demonstrated Whig concern for the prosperity of the economy in general and of the business class in particular. In line with this attitude was the Whig position in regard to corporations, those "monopolistic" structures which were beginning to appear with increasing frequency in American society during the Jacksonian period.

It is perhaps significant that the evidence regarding the Whigs and corporations is not abundant. The party leaders were never vociferous about the Democratic hue and cry over these combinations of capital. Occasionally a prominent Whig like Hezekiah Niles or William Henry Seward would even sound a note of caution regarding them,[24] but when the Whigs did express themselves, it was usually in favor of the corporate form.

---

[22] *McLane Report,* 22nd Con., 1st Sess., 1831–32, *House Doc. No.* 308, II, 861; Guy S. Callender, "Early Transportation and Banking," *Quarterly Journal of Economics,* XVII (Nov., 1902), 114–31; Lippincott, *History of Manufactures,* p. 149.

[23] Arthur B. Darling, *Political Changes in Massachusetts, 1824–28* (New Haven, Conn., 1925), pp. 14–15; Nathan Appleton, *Remarks on Currency and Banking* (Boston, 1841), p. 13; William H. Seward, *Works* (5 vols., New York, 1853–84), I, 31–33; II, 198–99; Roy Basler, ed., *The Collected Works of Abraham Lincoln* (New Brunswick, N. J., 1953), I, 160–62; Josiah Morrow, ed., *Life and Speeches of Thomas Corwin* (Cincinnati, 1896), pp. 105–82; *Cong. Globe,* 25th Cong., 2d Sess., Appendix, 603, col. 3, Webster on the Sub-Treasury, Jan. 31, 1838.

[24] *Niles' Register,* XXXV (Dec. 21, 1828), 262; Seward, *Autobiography* (New York, 1891), p. 94; *Works,* II, 318.

The great Whig orator, Edward Everett, linked the accumulation of capital by corporations with the development of the nation's wealth and welfare.[25] John Quincy Adams evidently saw no harm in corporations. He regarded the Bank of the United States as a corporation entitled to all the rights before the law that a person would have, and he clearly implied that it should be regarded as under the protection of the fifth amendment.[26] Webster was quick to see the usefulness of the corporation in a country where capital was scarce and where economy in production was a much to be desired goal. The corporation, Webster held, not only increased property but also tended to "equalize it, to diffuse it, to scatter its advantages among the many, and to give content, cheerfulness, and animation to all classes of the social system." It was of special use to the laborer because it increased his earnings and thereby put him in the way of himself becoming a capitalist.[27] The *American Review*, in 1846, declared itself opposed to monopoly, of which it could detect some traces among the banks, but took the position that corporations in general were far from monopolistic. Everyone had the right to join them by purchasing their stock, and the *Review* implied that they were necessary to the development of the American economy.[28]

Viewed in historical perspective, the development of the corporation *was* essential if the country was to take that course of development which has made its economy one of the wonders of the modern world. The great permanent investments required to establish industrial concerns and banks and to build railroads and canals could scarcely have been acquired in any other way than by corporate accumulation, especially in view of the already well-developed American devotion to private enterprise and the lessons in foolhardy state expenditure that were brought home by the panic of 1837.[29]

---

[25] Everett, *Orations and Speeches* (Boston, 1870), pp. 294–95, 297 (a speech in Boston, Sept. 13, 1838).

[26] *Register of Debates*, 23rd Cong., 1st Sess., X, pt. 3, 3494–95, Apr. 4, 1834.

[27] *Writings and Speeches*, XIII, 72–76 (Nov. 11, 1836).

[28] IV (Dec., 1846), 639–40.

[29] Adolf Berle and Gardiner C. Means, *The Modern Corporation and Private Property* (New York, 1932), p. 4; Lewis H. Haney, *Business Organization and Combination* (New York, 1934), p. 115; Louis C. Hunter, "Financial Problems of the Early Pittsburgh Iron Manufacturers," *Journal of Economic and*

It is true that corporation charters, which were first granted largely by special acts of the state legislatures, often involved legislative corruption and sometimes guaranteed monopolistic or quasi-monopolistic privileges to the corporation involved. It is also true that the notes of banking corporations were not infrequently circulated at considerably less than their face value. Wage payments in such bank notes bred a hearty dislike of banks in general, and to many wage earners, as to Jackson himself, such terms as "corporation," "bank," and "monopoly" came close to being synonymous as well as opprobrious epithets, especially since the Dartmouth College case decision (1819) protected corporation charters from assaults by state legislatures.

But there was another side to the story of corporation charters. The amount of private capital was so small, and the need for economic development so great, that Democrats as well as Whigs encouraged corporations to develop. In Pennsylvania, even as the Democrats pointed the finger of scorn at "monopolies," they voted "yea" on scores of corporation charters. In New York during the 1830's Democratic legislators were conspicuous in their support of railroad corporation charters, and, in the words of Azariah Flagg, these same Democrats chartered banking monopolies "as if propelled by steam power." [30] The weight of the evidence indicates that the Democratic outcry against "monopoly" magnified its evils for the sake of political capital.[31]

Another reason for questioning the validity of the outcry against monopolies is the fact that the incorporated organizations (chiefly banks and internal improvement and manufacturing companies)

Business History, II (May, 1930), 520–44. Seventy-five years later Samuel Gompers (*Labor and the Common Welfare* [New York, 1919], pp. 90–91) recognized that the development of the corporate form was essential to the building of the modern American industrial structure.

[30] Flagg Papers, [A. Flagg] to "My Dear Sir," Dec. 20, 1838; Hartz, *Economic Policy and Democratic Thought, Pennsylvania, 1800–1860* (Cambridge, Mass., 1948), pp. 62–79; William Miller, "A Note on the History of Business Corporations in Pennsylvania, 1800–1860," *Quarterly Journal of Economics,* LV (Nov., 1940), 150–60.

[31] One of the aims of Democratic politicians in this period was to make it appear that there was a clear-cut distinction between the parties, that all aristocrats and Old Federalists were Whigs and all the genuine democrats Jacksonians. Michael Hoffman wrote to Azariah Flagg, Nov. 3, 1828 (Flagg Papers), bemoaning the tendency of the "Morgan affair" to blur this desirable distinction between the parties. It was, therefore, often much to the advantage of the Jacksonians to pose as the defenders of the people against these horrid contrivances of wealthy business interests.

were generally of modest size and, by their very nature, could scarcely be monopolistic. The banks bore the brunt of the monopoly charge, but the great majority of banking and insurance companies "were small concerns with less than $100,000 capital," and most of the manufacturing companies were still smaller. As the state banks multiplied, they tended to lose such monopolistic privileges as they possessed and even the Second Bank of the United States, as Walter B. Smith clearly demonstrates, was not monopolistic.[32]

The devitalization of "monopoly" occasioned by the increasing competition among banks was furthered by the appearance of means for controlling the privileges granted in charters. In one state after another, New York and Delaware for example, constitutional revisions provided for changing or repealing corporation charters,[33] and the Supreme Court decision in *Ogden* v. *Saunders* (1827), as Marshall's dissent clearly recognized, vitiated the obligation of contract clause in the Constitution, the clause upon which the Dartmouth College decision had rested.[34]

Still another means of handling the problem of individual charters has begun to develop, even before the 1830's. Acts of free incorporation for bank and other business concerns, acts generally welcomed by the business class, began to appear. New York State

---

[32] Callender, "Early Transportation and Banking," pp. 148–49, 154–56; William C. Kessler, "A Statistical Study of the New York General Incorporation Act of 1811," *Journal of Political Economy*, XLVIII (Dec., 1940), 877–80; Smith, *Economic Aspects of the Second Bank of the United States* (Cambridge, Mass., 1953), p. 251. Smith points out that in 1830, when the Bank of the United States was very prosperous, it made only 20 per cent of the total bank loans, its note circulation was only about one fifth of the total, it had only one third of the total bank deposits, and it held only about one third of the specie held by American banks.

[33] Carl R. Fish, *The Rise of the Common Man* (New York, 1927), pp. 50–61; Alfred Russell, *The Police Power of the State* (Chicago, 1900), p. 119.

[34] *Ogden* v. *Saunders* upheld the validity of state insolvent laws enacted after the date of contracts. Marshall contended that the decision established the principle that a law could enter into a contract so completely as to become a part of it. "If," said Marshall, "one law enters into all subsequent contracts, so does every other law which relates to the subject. A legislative act, then, declaring that all contracts should be subject to legislative control and should be discharged as the legislature might prescribe, would become a component part of every contract, and be one of its conditions." This, Marshall argued, would "prostrate" the obligation of contract clause in the Constitution. *Ogden* v. *Saunders*, Wheaton 12:332–58, especially 338–40 and 355–58; Charles A. Beard, *Contemporary American History, 1877–1913* (New York, 1914), pp. 55–56; Charles Warren, *The Supreme Court in United States History* (2 vols., Boston, 1928), I, 686–93; Carl B. Swisher, *Roger B. Taney* (New York, 1935), p. 349.

had such a law as early as 1811 for certain types of manufacturing companies. Webster, in 1836, supported the general incorporation act for manufacturers in Massachusetts. In 1837 the Hinsdale Act of General Incorporation for business was passed by the Connecticut legislature. It was a bipartisan act. In 1838 the New York State legislature passed a free banking act which destroyed whatever there was of monopoly in banking in the state. Governor Marcy, a Democrat, was for free banking, and Democrat Churchill C. Cambreleng applauded the measure in Congress, but the law was, nevertheless, a Whig law. The great majority of the Democrats in the New York State legislature voted against it, and the *Democratic Review* denounced it as a Whig trick.[35]

Free incorporation was no more a Democratic monopoly than was the corporation a Whig monopoly. Both were born out of the exigencies of the times. The chief difference between the Democrats and the Whigs on corporations was that the latter were more forthright than the former in their attitude toward this social instrument.

The Whig concept of government embraced other uses than those involved in establishing a sound currency, ample credit, and the corporate form of business activity. Government, the Whigs held, should always be regarded as an instrument for the promotion of the general welfare and was, therefore, susceptible to a great variety of uses. Webster professed himself aghast when, in September, 1837, President Van Buren warned that "all communities are apt to look to government too much," declared that relieving mercantile embarrassments or interfering with ordinary commercial operations would be unconstitutional, and proposed, by means of the Independent Treasury, to divorce the government from all relationship to banking. "I feel," said Webster, "as if I were on some other sphere, as if I were not at home, as if this could not be America when I see schemes of public policy proposed, having for their object the convenience of Government only, and leaving the people to shift for themselves . . ."[36] It is a not unwarrantable con-

---

[35] Webster, *Writings and Speeches*, XIII, 72–74; Hammond, "Free Banks and Corporations, The New York Free Banking Act of 1838," *Journal of Political Economy*, XLIV (Apr., 1936), 184–96; Morse, *Connecticut History*, pp. 297–302; *Cong. Globe*, 25th Cong., 2d Sess., Appendix, 598, col. 2, Biddle on the Sub-Treasury, May 15, 1838; *Democratic Review*, V (May, 1839), 427–46. The New York banking act required conformity to certain specified banking standards.

[36] James D. Richardson, *Messages and Papers of the Presidents* (Washington, D. C., 1899), III, 324–46; *Cong. Globe*, 25th Cong., 2d Sess., Appendix, 606, col. 3, Webster on the Sub-Treasury, Jan. 31, 1838.

jecture that Franklin D. Roosevelt, had he been miraculously trans-
ported back into the 1830's, would have shared Webster's dismay.
For the Whig attitude toward the function of government, at least
on the national level, bears a closer resemblance to that of the
New Deal than did the attitude toward government of Jackson and
Van Buren.

Government, said Webster and the other Whig leaders of the
North and West, was there to be used. Adams, Clay, Seward, Corwin, Niles, and the young Lincoln deemed it the duty of government to nurture the well-being of all classes of the people.

The Whigs looked upon the state governments as proper
agencies for promoting the welfare of society. State governments
controlled by Whigs were generous in making grants for roads and
canals. The records of leading Whigs, from Webster's speeches to
Hezekiah Niles' *Register,* show a general disposition to favor state
grants—and state ownership as well. Samuel Ruggles was scornful
of the idea that government should restrict itself to protecting
life, liberty, and property. Seward was enthusiastic over state
development of free education, prison reform, care of the insane,
provision for the blind, the deaf, and the dumb; he became almost
lyrical when contemplating the social results of internal improvements constructed by the state of New York. He even argued, in
1840, that expenditures for internal improvements should be continued because they were important means of sustaining the purchasing power of the masses and therefore were a benefit to the
population of the state as a whole.[37]

One of the most important spheres of state action, according to
the Whigs, was education, for the social value of schooling was a
cardinal point in Whig philosophy. Education, the Whigs held, was
essential if a democratic government was to function properly: it
went hand in hand with the building of moral character; by un-
leashing individual potential it would help to establish that equality
of condition so important in preserving a sound and vigorous democracy; it would foster intelligence and invention and thereby develop
the country's productive power.

There was, perhaps, an element of sophistry here—a belief on

---

[37] Rantoul, *Memoirs,* p. 150; Samuel B. Ruggles, *Report* (Boston, 1841),
p. 61; *New York State Assembly Doc. No. 1,* 62nd Sess., 18–23, Seward to the
Legislature, Jan. 1, 1839; Basler, *Works of Lincoln,* I, 40; Seward, *Works,* II,
212–25; *Niles' Register,* XXXVI (Aug. 22, 1829), 414; XXXVIII (Jan. 26 and
June 26, 1830), 317–19; XLIII (Nov. 10, 1832), 177; Dorfman, *Economic
Mind,* II, 624.

the part of some that education, properly handled, would serve as the opiate of the people—but, if so, it was not apparent in the writings or speeches of the Whig leaders. "I have no fear of the people learning and knowing too much," said Abbott Lawrence, who evidently pinned his faith on Christian morality as a counterbalance to any dangerous ideas that might develop in the schoolroom, and this appears to have been the prevailing attitude among the Whigs.[38]

If state governments were useful as social agencies, the national government was even more so to the Whigs, for it was only through the agency of the national government that Clay's American System could really come into being. With that system in operation, the tariff, by stimulating the manufacturing interest, would build up a market for agriculture and provide a great impetus to internal commerce. Distribution of the revenues from public land sales would hasten internal improvements and aid the states in making the contributions to the well-being of the people that lay within their province. Internal improvements would create a veritable commercial revolution (they did just that) by facilitating marketing of agricultural and industrial goods in all sections of the country. The chartering of a new national bank would provide the stabilization, at desirable levels, of currency and credit. Thus would be provided, through governmental activity, a harmonization of interests and a fructification of national wealth and power.

Nor was the American System the only means, in Whig eyes, by which the national government could exert a constructive influence upon society. Seward saw great benefit to be derived from commercial treaties that would foster international trade. He held it the duty of the national government, in times of stress and strain, to establish uniform bankruptcy laws and to give direct help to the states whose credit had been shattered by depression. Senator Richard Henry Bayard, speaking in 1838, demanded a construction of the welfare clause in the Constitution broad enough to enable

---

[38] Lawrence, *Letters from the Hon. Abbott Lawrence to the Hon. William C. Rives* (Boston, 1846), pp. 5–7; Springfield, Mass., *Republican*, Aug. 3, 1839; Arthur A. Ekirch, *The Idea of Progress in America, 1815–1860* (New York, 1951), pp. 187–88; Morse, *Connecticut History*, pp. 306–307; Webster, *Writings and Speeches*, II, 13, 253; *New York State Assembly Doc. No. 1*, 62nd Sess., 24–28, Seward to the Legislature, Jan. 1, 1839; Ruggles, *Report*, p. 7; Everett, *Orations and Speeches*, I, 307–28; II, 313–24, 335–62, 493–518; anon., *Importance of Practical Education and Useful Knowledge* (New York, 1847); Paul R. Frothingham, *Edward Everett* (Boston, 1925), pp. 136, 138–39; *Niles' Register*, XXXV (Nov. 22, 1828), 193, (Jan. 1, 1829), 361; XXXVII (Sept. 19, 1829), 49.

the national government to use its taxing power for the promotion of the general well-being. Webster believed that the government not only should act to stimulate private enterprise; it could and should, when occasion arose, place restrictions on private property "for the good of the whole community." It should take a comprehensive view of the needs of the country, he said in 1833, and then should proceed to do for the people and the states what they could not do for themselves.[39] Senator John P. Kennedy of Maryland, pleading for federal control of the banking system as both traditional and wise, declared that "without it, no system of banking could be devised that would be tolerated by the country." He lamented states' rights scruples about the employment of the federal government in the peoples' interest and urged Virginia to give up her dialectics and not, as Henry A. Wise put it, "die of an abstraction." [40] It is clear that belief in the federal government as an active agency in promoting the welfare of the nation was a cardinal principle of Whig thought.

It is, I think, significant that Whig thought in the Jacksonian period was so nationalistic in character. The advocates of protection were continually arguing that a high tariff was valuable because it benefited the country as a whole. John Quincy Adams' nationalist point of view has been conclusively demonstrated by Samuel F. Bemis.[41] It never appeared more clearly than in Adams' vision of the role of internal improvements as a means of binding the Union together.[42] Henry Clay believed with all the ardor of his impetuous nature that the American System was a national system, one that would bring a shower of blessings upon all parts of the Union. Webster spoke repeatedly of the existence within the nation of a harmony of interests, of the "stake in society" held by all citizens. His aim, and that of the Whigs, he constantly proclaimed, was to increase the stake of the ordinary citizen and so to promote the harmony and strength of the Union. Similar concepts are to be

---

[39] *Cong. Globe*, 25th Cong., 2d Sess., Appendix, 623–27, Mar. 9–10, 1838; Current, *Daniel Webster,* pp. 105–106; Webster, *Writings and Speeches,* II, 154 (Pittsburgh speech, July 8, 1833).

[40] *Cong. Globe*, 25th Cong., 2d Sess., Appendix, 594, col. 3, speech on the Sub-Treasury, June 22, 1838.

[41] *John Quincy Adams and the Union* (New York, 1956), *passim.*

[42] Adams, *Memoirs,* VIII, 316, 229, 536; Adrienne Koch and William Peden, eds., *The Selected Writings of John Quincy Adams* (New York, 1946), p. 389. Even Jackson's famous toast to the Union failed to allay Adams' fears that Old Hickory would somehow, some way, destroy the strength of the central government.

found in the Samuel B. Ruggles *Report* of 1838 to the New York legislature, in the writings and speeches of Edward Everett, Abbott Lawrence, Thomas Corwin, Hezekiah Niles, and Abraham Lincoln, and in the often fusty pages of the *American Review*. The thought of both William Henry Seward and Horace Greeley was essentially nationalistic in character.[43]

Whig nationalism was predominantly economic in form. It showed little trace of any constructive international outlook. It was as broad as the nation—no broader. But, within its limits, the Whig nationalists were dynamic and forward-looking, envisioning progress for all classes of society, and their ideas on banking, currency, internal improvements, and government spending were considerably ahead of their time.

A myth that has gained currency in modern historical thought is that the Whigs and the Democrats stood diametrically opposed during the Jacksonian period—that the Whigs represented a grasping, narrow-minded, money-conscious business class, while the Democrats, ever mindful of the demands of social justice, fought for the rights of the common man. To a certain extent, this myth has a basis in reality. The Jacksonian Democrats professed to be, and many of them were, more interested in political democracy, in social justice, and in the maintenance of a general condition of liberty and equality than were the Whigs. Many of them accepted the Jeffersonian dictum that political democracy, if it were to flourish and endure, must be securely based upon economic democracy. They were more alive than were the Whigs to the potential menace of privilege that existed in specially chartered corporations and particularly in the Second Bank of the United States, and it is certainly possible to argue that the Democracy acted as a salutary restraint upon the "Captains of Industry" and the probusiness leaders of the Whigs.

But even their most ardent admirers must admit that, if the Jacksonians were the heirs of Jeffersonian idealism, they were also the heirs of Jeffersonian agrarianism, strict construction, and the neophysiocratic ideas of John Taylor of Carolina, concepts which lay like a heavy hand upon their shoulders. Yearning for the equality that can be found, alas, only in simple societies, the Jacksonians sought it by attempting to destroy all privilege, real or fancied.

---

[43] See particularly Everett, *Orations and Speeches*, I, 196; II, 144–45; Frothingham, *Edward Everett*, p. 119; Van Deusen, "The Nationalism of Horace Greeley," in *Nationalism and Internationalism*, ed. Edward M. Earle (New York, 1950), pp. 431–54.

At the same time, their narrow view of the function of the national government repeatedly kept them from using the government for constructive ends.[44] They turned a suspicious eye, and sometimes a warring hand, upon the new economic order that was shaping around them. In the name of liberty and equal rights, they destroyed the Second Bank of the United States, and thus did much to turn a nation that had been in the van of progressive banking development into a nation whose banking practices lagged well behind those of western Europe.[45] Their hard money ideas were negative and inadequate for dealing with the problem at hand—how to establish a currency and credit that would be both sound and ample. The Independent Treasury was also negative in character, a semi-retreat from the national government's constitutional duty of currency regulation.

The Whigs, on the other hand, were less interested than were the Democrats in the constant maintenance of equality and less alive to the potential threat to equality of opportunity that lay in the great bank and in the corporate form. Anxious to leave the road open to those with vision and merit, they were too prone to stress the "stake in society" concept, too prone to visualize social harmony and justice as goals that would be almost automatically attained if the economic order developed to their liking. But they did grasp more clearly than did the Democratic leadership the value of sound economic practice, whether in basic aspects of finance or in the development of the corporate form of business organization.

It would be a mistake, however, to conclude that the Whig and Democratic parties of the Jacksonian period were at opposite poles of political or even economic thought. They were very evenly balanced in numerical strength, a fact that in itself indicated a lack of division along class lines. The *Democratic Review* declared in 1839 that it was on the rural elements "that the main reliance of our party has always rested"; that in the towns and cities not only the mercantile and professional classes, but "extensive" elements, a "large proportion," of the laboring class were Whig; and that this had been so from the time of Jackson's first election.[46] Modern re-

[44] A classic exposition of this general point of view is to be found in the *Democratic Review*, VI (Sept., 1839), 208–17.

[45] Smith, *Economic Aspects of the Second Bank of the United States*, p. 263; Oliver M. W. Sprague, "Branch Banking in the United States," *Quarterly Journal of Economics*, XVII (Nov., 1902), 242–45.

[46] *Democratic Review*, VI (Dec., 1839), 500–502.

search tells us how often businessmen and bankers voted Democratic and how frequently laborers and farmers ranged themselves under the Whig banner. We know how strong protectionist sentiment was among the Democrats of New England and Pennsylvania; we know that there were many Democrats in these same areas who supported the Second Bank of the United States; we know that many of the state banks supported the Democratic party and were in turn supported by it.[47]

The composition of the parties shows class lines definitely blurred—one may even say almost completely blurred. The stand of the parties on major issues shows some rather interesting similarities of aim. Both parties wanted a sound financial system. Both favored free banking and, generally, free incorporation for business firms.[48] Both accepted universal manhood suffrage and both be-

---

[47] W. Dean Burnham, *Presidential Ballots, 1836–1892* (Baltimore, 1955), pp. 1–10, 15–20, 163 ff.; see *Tribune Almanac*, I (New York, 1868), *passim*, for the large Whig vote rolled up in the agricultural areas and for scattered but significant voting statistics. As to the working class votes, see *Democratic Review*, VI (Dec., 1839), 500, 502; William A. Sullivan, *The Industrial Worker in Pennsylvania, 1800–1840* (Harrisburg, Pa., 1955), pp. 159–207, and "Did Labor Support Andrew Jackson?" *Political Science Quarterly*, LXII (Dec., 1947), 575–80; Edward Pessen, "Did Labor Support Jackson: The Boston Story," *Political Science Quarterly*, LXIV (June, 1949), 262–74; William Trimble, "Diverging Tendencies in New York Democracy in the Period of the Locofocos," *American Historical Review*, XXIV (April., 1919), 396–421; Darling, "The Workingmen's Party in Massachusetts," and "Jacksonian Democracy in Massachusetts," *American Historical Review*, XXIX (Oct., 1923), 81–86 and (Jan., 1924), 271–87; Andrew C. McLaughlin and Albert B. Hart, *Cyclopedia of American Government* (3 vols., New York, 1914), III, 23–26. Gubernatorial and congressional elections in the various states show the parties divided at the most by a few thousand votes. In the presidential election of 1836 the three Whig candidates received 49 per cent of the total vote while Van Buren mustered 50.8 per cent, scarcely a landslide victory. In 1840 Harrison had 52.8 per cent of the total, Van Buren 46.8 per cent, Birney .4 of 1 per cent. In 1844 Polk had 49.3 per cent of the total, Clay 48.1 per cent, and Birney 2.3 per cent. In 1848 Taylor had 47.3 per cent, Cass 42.5 per cent, Van Buren 10.01 per cent. An analysis of the vote on the recharter of the Second Bank of the United States shows 41 of the 141 Jacksonian Democrats in Congress voting for the Bank and shows the very considerable strength the Bank had among the Democrats of New England and the Middle Atlantic states. "Ike" Hill was out to get votes for Jackson in the campaign of 1828 and would have been as quick to plaster the opposition as the tool of vested interests as he was to plaster it with the epithet "Federalist." But if Hill really was convinced that the business class, as such, had interests opposed to those of the people, his *New Hampshire Patriot* did not disclose the fact.

[48] The Democrats argued that the Sub-Treasury, by collecting revenues only in specie, would effectively create a sound currency. See *Democratic Review*, III (Nov., 1838), 227. The *Democratic Review* declared repeatedly that the Democratic party was not opposed to corporations as such, but only to the monopolistic abuses that derived from special charters. See especially II (June, 1838), 212; V (Jan., 1839), 97–98, (Feb., 1839), 152; IX (Dec., 1841), 579.

lieved in education for the common man. Both used the spoils system, while decrying its use by the opposition. Neither, it may be added, did anything substantial to satisfy the crying need of the small farmer and the small businessman for long-term credits at moderate rates of interest. The divergencies that existed, and there were divergencies, were more over means than over ultimate ends. Thus the Democrats stressed the importance of safeguarding the liberty and the equality of opportunity of the common man; the Whigs saw as of paramount importance a national economic growth that would raise the general level of prosperity and thus develop the opportunities and promote the happiness of the individual members of society. Both sought the prosperity of the people as a whole, and both parties oriented, just as the two major parties do today, around a middle-class norm.

The view of the parties which I have just outlined was not unknown in the Jacksonian period. It is implicit in Tocqueville's description of the American political system,[49] and it was acknowledged as just by men of judgment within the Democratic party itself.

In the summer of 1832, that hectic presidential election year, Robert Rantoul, lawyer-reformer, Jackson supporter, antagonist of corporations, upholder of the Bank veto, had this to say of the parties:

> We cannot help admitting the obvious truths, that our party contests have not that intrinsic importance, with which the lively fancies of the heated partisans often invest them; that they are often in a great degree struggles for office, and that if the party out of power always strives to fight itself in, by the vindication on all occasions of certain leading popular principles, it is by no means certain how far those principles will be exemplified in its practice after it shall have prevailed by zealously professing them. That, however great may be the inconsistencies in the political conduct of individuals, even if beyond parallel in any other country, still the fluctuations of the government are temporary, and of lesser magnitude than they at first appear to be.[50]

Five years later, the *Democratic Review*, official organ of the Democratic party, stated in its first issue a similar point of view:

> There is a great deal of mutual understanding between our two parties; but in truth, there does not exist in the people, with reference to its great masses, that irreconcilable hostility of opinions

---

[49] *Democracy in America*, I, 177–78.

[50] Rantoul, *Memoirs*, p. 175.

and leading principles which would be the natural inference from the violence of the party warfare in which we are perpetually engaged.[51]

Again, in 1842, the *Democratic Review* acknowledged that among "vast numbers" of the Whigs, a "considerable portion" of that party, there was to be found "as much of the democratic sentiment and spirit as among any portion of our own [party]." [52]

The political conflicts of the Jacksonian period were fought more often with a view to gaining control of the government than out of devotion to diametrically opposed political and social ideals. "We are," wrote Levi Woodbury to Azariah Flagg in 1834, "but *one* people and . . . the success of a part is in some degree the success of the whole.[53] A realization of the fact that this was the case in Woodbury's day as well as in our own will help us to better understand both Whig and Democratic thought and theory in the Jacksonian period.

---

[51] I (Oct., 1837), 1.

[52] XI (July, 1842), 96.

[53] Flagg Papers, Woodbury to Flagg, Jan. 22, 1834.

MAJOR L. WILSON*

Dissimilarities in Major Party Thought

In this most stimulating essay Major L. Wilson holds that while the parties had unique outlooks, they both were liberal and devoted to freedom. But they differed in their appraisals of the extent of or quality of freedom in the United States. In Wilson's reading, Jacksonians were convinced that the essentials of freedom had been accomplished in their time and they therefore focused on expanding the "area of freedom" and on the present. "The Whigs confronted the Jacksonians with a far more positive appreciation of the quantitative dimensions of time." One Whig group—"the party of memory or order"—stressed the importance of traditions, while the Whig "party of hope" looked to a future in which the quality of the Republic would be enhanced.

𝕏𝕏

THAT A SUBSTANTIAL or rational dialogue obtained during the two decades after 1828 has been seriously questioned in many recent studies. In the name of a liberal consensus, Louis Hartz

* From Major L. Wilson, "The Concept of Time and the Political Dialogue in the United States, 1828–48," *American Quarterly*, XIX (Winter, 1967), pp. 619–644. Reprinted with the permission of the publisher, the University of Pennsylvania. Copyright © 1967, Trustees of the University of Pennsylvania.

dismisses the old "Progressive" frame of reference.[1] Conflict between the rich and the poor, the few and the many, property rights and human rights did occur, he admits, yet agreement on the fundamentals of a free society underlay the conflict and fixed its limits. Because John Locke came to the American wilderness without a dialectical foil, indeed, both democratic and capitalistic impulses were "bound to make themselves felt . . ." [2] The two elements worked against each other at first, it was true, because the Federalists and their immediate successors thought of the people as a "mob," while the people condemned their adversaries as scheming "aristocrats." But this manner of framing the issue of political conflict reflected less of eternal enmity, Hartz insists, than of the political confusion which came from importing European categories into a land lacking a feudal tradition. The irrationality of the process ended with the triumph of Whiggery in the "log cabin" campaign of 1840, in any case, and the resulting synthesis of democratic capitalism anticipated the full sway of Horatio Alger after the Civil War.

Essential agreement with this position has also come from other quarters. Russell Kirk, unlike Hartz, claims that some conservative Burkean elements also entered the American political tradition. But he concedes that with the demise of the Federalist party, effective debate was no longer possible. Things were rather "in the saddle" and the "unreasoning forces" of democracy, secularism and industrialism leveled all before them. Far from being "a high-principled party of the Right," Clinton Rossiter likewise argues, the Whig party made "a highly profitable peace" with the new order and vied with the Democracy in expressing the equalitarian passions and in feeding the materialistic lusts of the people.[3] Since the values of society were assumed to be "given," as Daniel Boorstin phrases the matter, conflict could take place only over the ways to realize

---

[1] For a concise statement of the Progressive position see Arthur M. Schlesinger, *Paths to the Present* (New York, 1949), p. 81.

[2] Louis Hartz, "The Whig Tradition in Europe and America," *American Political Science Review*, XLVI (Dec. 1952), 989. Hartz develops the consensus view most fully in *The Liberal Tradition in America: An Interpretation of American Political Thought since the Revolution* (New York, 1955).

[3] Russell Kirk, *The Conservative Mind from Burke to Santayana* (Chicago, 1953), p. 4; Clinton Rossiter, *Conservatism in America* (New York, 1955), p. 121. Daniel Aaron, in "Conservatism, Old and New," *American Quarterly*, VI (Summer 1954), 101, agrees with Kirk and Rossiter that by the 1840s "a political conservatism had degenerated into the negations of Whiggery that so disgusted Emerson."

commonly held goals. Glyndon G. Van Deusen thus concludes that the divergencies of the two parties, "and there were divergencies, were more over means than over ultimate ends." [4]

A great deal of light has been thrown on the period from 1828 to 1848 by this stress on the things which Americans held in common. It is surely inadequate, for example, to equate the "business community" with conservatism and "the other sections of society" with liberalism.[5] At the same time, little of conservatism in a Burkean sense can be found to challenge the prevailing liberalism. Whatever there was of debate, then, must have taken place within a common frame. But it is precisely at this point that the limitations of a consensus view become most apparent. Preoccupation with agreement obscures the real meaning of the differences separating Americans. To start with the assumption that profound debate among liberals was not even possible is to deny that men of the nineteenth century earnestly disagreed about the nature of their freedom. Triumphant democracy and capitalism, it would seem, made closed questions out of such matters as the nature of man, society and human destiny. Reality somehow got flattened out into two dimensions and the vision of man within a temporal process lost. The facile distinction between ends and means hence could be made, along with the judgment that efforts at intellectual clarification were essentially irrational.

One possible method, by contrast, for recovering the substance of the dialogue among liberals is to make fully explicit the concepts of time found in their pleadings. The way statesmen at any moment think about their relation to other men within a temporal process is surely of great significance. In a perceptive work on the fiction for the period, R. W. B. Lewis finds a meaningful debate about man in time and space.[6] A kindred study of the politics is here undertaken

[4] Daniel J. Boorstin, *The Genius of American Politics* (Chicago, 1953); Glyndon G. Van Deusen, "Some Aspects of Whig Thought and Theory in the Jacksonian Period," *American Historical Review*, LXIII (Jan. 1958), 321.

[5] Arthur M. Schlesinger Jr., *The Age of Jackson* (Boston, 1946), p. 505.

[6] R. W. B. Lewis, *The American Adam: Innocence, Tragedy and Tradition in the Nineteenth Century* (Chicago, 1955). "Every culture seems, as it advances toward maturity, to produce its own determining debate over the ideas that preoccupy it: salvation, the order of nature, money, power, sex, the machine and the like. The debate, indeed, may be said to *be* the culture, at least on its loftiest levels; for a culture achieves identity not so much through the ascendancy of one particular set of convictions as through the emergence of its peculiar and distinctive dialogue." (2). Lewis identifies the parties in the

with the belief that the past becomes fully meaningful only when the differences among people no less than their agreements are made clear.

Behind the conflict of interests, it is supposed, and vitally involved in the accompanying theories of man and society are fundamentally different concepts of time. How free is each individual or each generation to shape its own destiny? To what degree, on the other hand, is the pursuit of happiness collective and cumulative in nature and the state a corporate entity subsisting through time? How relevant are past institutional solutions, and to what extent should the solution of present problems be regarded as a prescription for posterity? Is man a political animal caught up in time, or can he claim immunity from time? Should the historical process be taken as a series of discrete points or as a continuum along which qualitative changes occur?

For two reasons these questions would seem to have peculiar relevance to the United States in the years from 1828 to 1848. Because most Americans were avowedly liberal, and hence disposed to claim great freedom from time, any differences of degree might be especially revealing. The differences would bulk larger, furthermore, because the society was still in the process of being built across unsettled space. Put another way, the debate was not alone over the ways to govern the existing society: it involved the far more seminal matter of ends, of the kind of liberal society to be built. When seen in this light, the consensus distinction between ends and means breaks down. Within the process of time, different means simply could not conduce to the same ends. It mattered greatly whether one brought to the task of building society a view of freedom as something complete at the beginning or at the end of the process—whether one started with pre-political atoms or with the view of man as a political animal. In the one case freedom might lead to unfreedom in the "thickening" of society and its involvement in time; in the other case a more perfect freedom would come as richer social conditions were created.[7] In pleading

---

dialogue as those of Hope, Memory and Irony—those who claimed freedom from the past and looked to the future only; those who looked to the past; and those, chastened by the prescriptive force of time, who yet harbored a sober and mature hope. For the purposes of the present study, however, these categories are not precise enough. In the political dialogue, the division into the past, the present and the future seems more valid.

[7] For a keen analysis of this point see Glenn Tinder, "Is Liberalism out of Date?" *Journal of Politics*, XXIV (May 1962), 258–76. The liberal urge for "protecting the person from the world," he well argues, often conflicts with

for a positive system of policies to develop the country, Representative Luther Severance of Maine defined the issue with great precision. "The question is not whether things shall be done or not," he noted in 1846, "but *how* they shall be done." [8] This issue was at the heart of the nullification controversy and of the extended debate in the following decade over internal improvements versus external expansion. The very nature of the Union and its destiny came in for profound consideration.

In larger perspective, to apply the analysis Guido de Ruggiero uses for Europe, the debate among Americans can best be understood as one between the different aspects or moments of the liberal mind.[9] Jacksonian democracy, attaining full self-consciousness during the nullification controversy and aggressive formulation in the decade of the 1840s, embodied liberalism's negative moment or phrase. The impulse to larger liberty, for freedom from essential control, disposed it to regard the task of building a liberal society as one of removing obstacles and repelling the enemies of freedom. An important qualification was made to the Jeffersonian dictum that each generation constituted a nation, it was true, for President Andrew Jackson confronted the Nullifiers with the view of the Union as an absolute. Within its spacious frame, however, he sought to gain for his age and to secure for later generations the freedom of an eternal present. Frequent use of the veto expressed an iconoclastic attitude toward efforts by the government to define or prescribe the life of the nation. The prospects for future control met his opposition no less than the policies of the American System inherited from the past. Freedom as a political good for the individual in the Union was the kind of thing to be possessed in its entirety at the time.

In like fashion the Union of freemen was to be considered an entity with its essential character already fully realized. Its future could only reproduce the present, in quantitative terms, become

---

the equally liberal imperative for "so shaping the world that the individual can be at home in it" (pp. 260, 261). Also relevant here is a perceptive article by Eric L. McKitrick, "Conservatism Today," *American Scholar,* XXVII (Winter 1957–58), 49–61. His defense of "otherdirectedness" at the present time involves the assumption that "a greatly heightened perception of the institutional side of American life" is a good thing. By implication, the "innocence" of the "free individual" in the nineteenth century represented a misuse of freedom (pp. 49, 53).

[8] *Congressional Globe,* 29 Cong., 1 Sess., App., 490 (Mar. 13, 1846).

[9] Guido de Ruggiero (trans. R. G. Collingwood), *The History of European Liberalism* (Boston, 1959), pp. 347–69, *passim.*

more of the same. By "extending the area of freedom" Jacksonians meant the development of the Union across space rather than through time.[10] In describing "the great nation of Futurity," to be sure, a contributor to the *Democratic Review* in 1839 hinted at qualitative change. But his very manner of speaking betrayed a predilection for freedom from time. "We are entering on its *untrodden space*," he said of the *"expansive"* future, "with the truths of God in our minds, beneficent objects in our hearts, and with a clear conscience unsullied by the past." [11] The idea of freedom as a function of space here clearly prescribed expansion as an alternative to putting the nation on a course of improvement through time. World without end, as Representative Alexander Duncan of Ohio stated the matter in 1845, the nation's destiny had "the love of liberty for its means, liberty itself for its own reward, and the spread of free principles and republican institutions for its end." [12]

The Whigs confronted the Jacksonians with a far more positive appreciation of the qualitative dimensions of time. Daniel Webster, standing "as in the full gaze of our ancestors and our posterity," called for his generation in 1838 to think of itself as but part of a larger corporate whole. A contributor to the June issue of the *Whig Review* in 1846 could thus deplore the mad hostility Jacksonians were showing toward everything established. "It is high time for us to have settled something," he insisted, "to be ready to take something for granted." In opposition to the urge for the freedom of the eternal present he protested that "this everlasting beginning will be the ruin of us." [13] Looking to the future, Senator Albert S. White of Indiana likewise condemned the Democrats for their reluctance to commit the nation to a positive course. "Is this confederated Government," he asked in 1841, "a mere machine to run in an endless cycle

---

[10] Jackson coined the phrase himself in a letter to Aaron V. Brown on Feb. 9, 1843. *Correspondence of Andrew Jackson,* ed. John Spencer Bassett (7 vols.; Washington, D. C., 1926–35), VI, 201.

[11] *United States Magazine and Democratic Review,* VI (Nov. 1839), 427. Henceforth cited as *Democratic Review.* Italics mine.

[12] *Congressional Globe,* 28 Cong., 2 Sess., App., 178 (Jan. 29, 1845).

[13] "Second Speech on the Sub-Treasury," Mar. 12, 1838, Daniel Webster, *The Writings and Speeches of Daniel Webster* (Nat. Ed.; 18 vols.; Boston, 1903), VIII, 237; *The American Review: A Whig Journal of Politics, Literature, Art, and Science,* IV (July 1846), 30. Henceforth cited as *Whig Review.* Charles Grier Sellers Jr. argues convincingly in opposition to many earlier studies that an underlying unity of outlook did obtain among the Whigs. "Who Were the Southern Whigs?" *American Historical Review, LIX* (Jan. 1954), 335–46.

of inanity?" Governor William H. Seward of New York explicitly dismissed the "specious theory" of Jefferson that each generation should have essential autonomy in the pursuit of happiness. The great resources of the country impressed him rather with the peculiarly collective and cumulative nature of the nation's destiny. While working within the context of "causes anterior to his own existence," Seward wanted his generation to place the nation on a course whose consequences would be as "distant as its dissolution." [14]

Here was to be found a much keener sense of man as a political animal. The distinction liberals usually made between government and society was now less sharp and clear. "It is a Republic that is necessary to virtue and not virtue to a Republic," a Whig partisan argued; "the State is for the aid of virtue, and not virtue for the State." [15] The political task of freemen was not alone to destroy: the job of preserving and of building remained. Having gained freedom from the bad authority of the past, the Whigs wanted to impose a new authority over themselves and thus create the social conditions for a better common life. The Union, in these terms, was less a political arrangement for pre-existing society than a richer society which by positive means could be called into existence. The federal government amounted to far more than a mechanism for preventing wrong; it was a corporate instrument for realizing a larger positive good. Qualitative change through time rather than quantitative growth across space marked the true destiny of such a nation of freemen. Far from being conservative in any traditional sense of clinging to an existing order, the Whigs sought to draw out a new order from the unsettled possibilities in America.[16]

In their attitudes about the thrust and direction of change within the corporate dimensions of time, however, the Whigs assumed a Janus-like pose.[17] While sharing a common belief that the govern-

---

[14] *Congressional Globe*, 26 Cong., 2 Sess., App., 78 (Jan. 19, 1841); William H. Seward, "Annual Message," Jan. 7, 1840; *The Works of William H. Seward*, ed. George E. Baker (3 vols.; New York, 1853), II, 240, 241.

[15] *Whig Review*, VI (Sept. 1847), 242.

[16] Kirk specifically denies that the goal of national consolidation was a conservative one. *The Conservative Mind*, p. 203. Marvin Meyers clearly underscores this nonconservative aspect of the Whigs in comparison with the Democrats: "the Whig party spoke to the explicit hopes of Americans as Jacksonians addressed their diffuse fears and resentments." *The Jacksonian Persuasion: Politics and Belief* (Stanford, Calif., 1957), p. 9.

[17] On this point, Lee Benson's fine work on the period is inadequate. He does find significant debate between Whigs and Democrats, between what he terms positive and negative liberalism. But he fails to appreciate the dual aspect of Whig thought as a whole, that is, its backward looking as well as its

ment should foster "all the virtues of men, active and passive," they differed among themselves about which of the two should be fostered the most. The group of Whigs who placed primary stress on promoting the passive virtues might best be called the party of memory or order. Their emphasis was ever on the importance of the judiciary, established constitutions and the educating effect of the law considered as "a Great Idea." By supporting the American System of policies, at the same time, they hoped to continue the process of consolidating the new society in America—to "knit together its various sections by the indissoluble bonds of a common interest and affection." A greater sense of nationality, "a fixed and decided national character," would then develop.[18] The Jacksonian prescription for new territorial acquisition, in these terms, posed no less a threat than the laissez-faire policies at home. "There must be some limit to the extent of our territory," Webster protested in the debate over annexing Texas, "if we would make our institutions permanent." [19]

A second group of Whigs comprised what Seward wanted to claim for all of them, namely, "the party of hope, of progress, and of civilization." Assuming the work of consolidating the Union essentially complete, they looked prospectively to the task of realizing the vast potential of freemen on the richly-endowed continent. The call for positive policies to develop and diversify the economy pointed to a teleological concept of civilization where, as John Quincy Adams put it, "all the powers of the body and all the faculties of the mind of every individual, from the cradle to the grave," might be exercised to the fullest extent. Nor did this goal necessarily rule out further territorial expansion, if new areas could be acquired by peaceful and honorable means. "The highest civilization," Henry C. Carey rather observed in 1848, "is marked by the most perfect individuality and the greatest tendency to union...." [20]

---

prospective temper. *The Concept of Jacksonian Democracy: New York as a Test Case* (Princeton, 1961), pp. 329–38, *passim*.

[18] *Whig Review,* VI (Sept. 1847), 242; I (Jan. 1845), 3, 2; II (Oct. 1845), 447.

[19] "The Admission of Texas," Dec. 22, 1845, Webster, *Writings and Speeches,* IX, 56.

[20] "Mass Meeting of Whigs," Auburn, N. Y., Feb. 22, 1844, *Works of Seward,* III, 245; John Quincy Adams, *Whig Review,* II (July 1845), 87; Henry C. Carey, *The Past, the Present, and the Future* (Philadelphia, 1848), p. 416.

Whig partisans of memory and hope thus complemented the Jacksonian predilection for freedom in the eternal present. The differing emphases on preservation, creation and destruction gave rounded form to the dialogue of liberals. By 1848, however, the issue of the expansion of slavery anticipated the final disruption of that debate. The corporate vision of the nation's destiny—and the Whig party holding it—would become, as a consequence, the chief victim.

This was necessarily the case because the slavery issue tended to polarize debate along the temporal spectrum no less than along sectional lines. The issue here joined between an illiberal feature of the past and the claims of freemen in the present would, as the debate grew more intense, serve to obscure a concern for the future in concrete and corporate terms. The call for free soil, on the one hand, made southern leaders see more clearly that in the peculiar institution they held hostages in time. Their aggressive determination to preserve slavery, on the other hand, made the temper of the free soilers more destructive. By securing freedom in the present for the territories, it was true, Jacksonians might look again to territorial expansion while Whig advocates of free soil sought to resume the task of internal improvement. Because political necessities compelled them to mute past differences, however, it became ever easier to suppose that the fulfillment of the nation's destiny required only the removal of the slave power obstacle. In the nature of things, the free soil movement became increasingly Jacksonian in tone.[21] The government, in the meantime, began to take on the character of a genial broker. Since most slaveholders had come to favor a rather inflexible policy of laissez faire, a positive role for the government could now appear as the true interest of freemen. But it was to act, not as a shaper of the future, but more as the giver of good things in the present.

While the issue of slavery threatened by 1848 to disrupt the earlier debate among liberals, it had been South Carolina spokesmen for slavery twenty years before who precipitated the profound dialogue over the nation's destiny. With the *Exposition and Protest* in 1828, John C. Calhoun provided a systematic challenge to the pro-

---

[21] Here, it would seem, Harry V. Jaffa misreads the nature of the free soil issue as it came into the 1850s. He contends, in *Crisis of the House Divided: An Interpretation of the Issues in the Lincoln-Douglas Debates* (Garden City, N. Y., 1959), pp. 344, *passim,* that the debate was essentially one between Whig and Democrat. In terms of the concepts of time, the debate can best be understood as one between two formulations of freedom in the eternal present.

tective tariff and its related policies.[22] Hailing the impending retirement of the national debt as a seminal moment for doing so, he
argued that a change in the fiscal system would represent a true
restoration of the Union. It was a Union, he insisted, which the
fathers had intended to be a partnership for pre-existing societies.
But a continuation of the consolidating tendencies of the American
System, he warned, threatened to create a new society in their
stead. He wanted to effect a moratorium on change in the Union,
for change menaced the peculiar institution which he took to be an
ultimate determinant in his society. In order to secure an eternal
present in the Union congenial to this absolute prescription of the
past, Calhoun favored a veto power for each member in the partnership firm. And beyond nullification he looked to secession. It was
this urgency to be free from future change which found lodging in
his formula that liberty was dearer than the Union.

An overwhelming chorus for the Union shouted down these
views. "Liberty *and* Union," as Webster formulated the matter in
1830, were "one and inseparable." [23] Agreement with his position
came from all parts of the country. The debate which followed thus
did not hinge at all on the issue of Union or no Union. It can best
be understood as a dialogue among freemen about the nature of
their Union and its destiny. In terms of the concept of time, it was a
debate among the parties of memory, hope and the eternal present.

Webster, for the party of memory, spoke first.[24] In answer to
the partnership concept, he adduced a corporate view of the Union.
It was a view which rejected the stark distinction Calhoun was
making between things social and things political. Webster thought
of the Union in a much more complex way. It was for him both a
new national society coming into existence and the efficient political
means for making the process an orderly one. Freemen at any moment comprised only a part of its reality, for as a corporate entity
embracing all of the generations the Union comprehended a wider

---

[22] "Exposition and Protest," Dec. 1828, *The Works of John C. Calhoun,* ed.
Richard K. Crallé (6 vols.; New York, 1883), VI, 1–59. In two other formal
statements Calhoun developed these ideas fully: Fort Hill Address, July 26,
1831, and Fort Hill Letter, Aug. 28, 1832, *ibid.,* pp. 59–94, 144–93.

[23] *Register of Debates in Congress,* 21 Cong., 1 Sess., 80 (Jan. 27, 1830).
For an extended analysis of the nullification debate in somewhat different
terms see an article by the present writer, " 'Liberty and Union': An Analysis
of Three Concepts Involved in the Nullification Controversy," scheduled to
appear in the Aug. 1967 issue of the *Journal of Southern History.*

[24] His dramatic replies to Senator Robert Y. Hayne on Jan. 20 and 27,
1830, were followed with many public addresses and the confrontation with
Calhoun in the Senate on Feb. 16, 1833.

span of time. During the debate with Calhoun over the Force Bill in 1833 Webster gave a clear and rounded definition of the Union:

> The Union is not a temporary partnership of States. It is the association of the people, under a constitution of Government, uniting their power, joining together their highest interests, cementing their present enjoyments, and blending, in one indivisible mass, all their hopes for the future. Whatsoever is steadfast in just political principles, whatsoever is permanent in the structure of human society, whatsoever there is which can derive an enduring character from being founded on deep laid principles of constitutional liberty, and on the broad foundations of the public will—all unite to entitle this instrument to be regarded as a permanent constitution of Government.[25]

While the grand corporation of the Union surely comprehended the future, Webster would direct much of its course by the guidelines of the past. The judiciary was indispensable to the perpetuation of the Union, in this view, because it interpreted truly the collected will of all generations. Freedom for each individual or generation was not the sort of thing abstracted from space and time, he protested, but a good within the temporal process with a history and a pedigree. It was, he noted, "our established, dear bought, peculiar American liberty." [26] Webster's view of the Constitution as an "executed contract" also embodied this spirit of prescription. He had argued earlier in the Dartmouth College case that the charter amounted to an irreversible grant which brought a private corporation into existence and stamped it with perpetuity. The Constitution, in like fashion, represented an irreversible grant from the people as a whole creating the perpetual corporation of the Union. In the same way that a law reflected the result of an agreement rather than the agreement itself, he thought of the Constitution as a supreme prescription, made at some point in time yet binding on all who followed.[27]

---

[25] *Register of Debates*, 22 Cong., 2 Sess., 571 (Feb. 16, 1833). Webster's language here does savor of Edmund Burke, whom both Hartz and Kirk consider the fountain of conservative thought. But concepts of man as a social animal and of the state as a corporate entity are not necessarily illiberal. With his "harmonic conception" of the state, for example, L. T. Hobhouse could easily accommodate Webster under the liberal banner. *Liberalism* (New York, 1911), pp. 130, *passim*.

[26] *Register of Debates*, 22 Cong., 2 Sess., 553 (Feb. 16, 1833).

[27] "The Dartmouth College Case," Mar. 10, 1818, Webster, *Writings and Speeches*, X, 195–233; *Register of Debates*, 22 Cong., 2 Sess., 564 (Feb. 16, 1833).

Webster's views on public policy betrayed as well this predilection for existing arrangements. While many were looking to the end of the public debt as an opportunity for placing the nation on a new course, he pleaded for the reigning policies of the American System. By its very nature, he strongly urged, a protective tariff involved a corporate concept of the pursuit of happiness. As a commitment by the nation at some point in the past—1816 or 1824—it redirected employments in some degree and induced organic changes in economic life which only time could fully mature. Webster looked upon it thus as the "settled course of public policy." He also invoked this same preservative principle in behalf of the Second Bank of the United States.[28] Over the new and emerging interests of the country, meanwhile, he stood ready to extend the protecting arm of government. By appropriations for internal improvements and by a more liberal land policy he hoped to "incorporate" the interests of the new states "closely in the family compact." And not the least advantage of a tariff, he ever observed, was the way the protection of laborers would help them acquire "a stake in the welfare of that community." Harmony in the present could be achieved by such positive measures, while they would serve over the long run to forge stronger bonds of Union and develop a "national character" more fully.[29] Because Webster looked to change, to a developing national community, he cannot be classified a conservative in many ways the term is used. Yet his kind of liberal outlook was one that embraced a tactic of change through essential preservation.

John Quincy Adams, by contrast, displayed during the nullification controversy the constructive moment or phrase of the liberal mind. While no less aware than Webster of the qualitative dimensions of time, Adams viewed the corporate destiny of freemen in far more prospective terms. He welcomed the end of the debt as a "day of jubilee" for it freed his generation for grand tasks. In another significant figure he thought of Americans, now disciplined and consolidated, as in a position "to survey from the top of Pisgah" the promised land to be enriched by their labors.[30] A concept of

---

[28] *Register of Debates*, 21 Cong., 1 Sess., 60 (Jan. 27, 1830); 22 Cong., 1 Sess., 1222 (July 11, 1832).

[29] "Reception at Buffalo," June 1833, Webster, *Writings and Speeches*, II, 134; "Public Dinner at New York," Mar. 10, 1831, *ibid.*, II, 57–58, 46.

[30] *Register of Debates*, 22 Cong., 1 Sess., App., 80 (May 23, 1832). For fuller perspective on Adams' views on progress see: Arthur Alphonse Ekirch Jr., *The Idea of Progress in America, 1815–1860* (New York, 1951), pp. 73–75;

progressive development toward a higher level of civilization here informed his thought about the nature of those labors. By a measure of control he would maintain a compact population, diversify economic pursuits and effect a balance of agriculture and industry. While retaining for these purposes the tariff and the Bank, he placed key emphasis on the policies relating to the public lands and internal improvements. Roads and canals, in this way of thinking, would provide some direction to the settlement of the country. By enhancing the value of the lands, at the same time, they would enrich the treasury for patronizing the arts and education. Thus by progressive stages through time a richer social milieu could be created by freemen, in turn conducing "to their own elevation in the scale of being." Because the pursuit of happiness was so collective and cumulative in nature, Adams conceived of the Union in corporate terms as "an union of all classes, conditions, and occupations; an union coextensive with our territorial dominions; an union for successive ages, without limitation of time." [31]

The destiny of the nation was hence a teleological one. Qualitative improvement would mark its progress through time. The nature of the two enemies saw to the Union help to explain his corporate vision more fully. One of them was the democratic spirit. It was a temper, he feared, which ill-prepared the people to see themselves within a temporal process or to assume the discipline which such a vision prescribed. "Democracy has no forefathers, it looks to no posterity," he complained. "It is swallowed up in the present and thinks of nothing but itself." [32] The slave power, as a second enemy, became a spoiler because it gazed too much upon the past.[33] The determination to preserve the peculiar institution which had come to them from the fathers made most slavery spokesmen implacable foes of all present efforts to shape the course of the people. As the presumed bases of support for the triumphant

---

Charles A. and Mary R. Beard, *The American Spirit: A Study of the Idea of Civilization in the United States* (New York, 1942), pp. 152–62; Samuel Flagg Bemis, *John Quincy Adams and the Union* (New York, 1956), pp. 55–70; Wendell Glick, "The Best Possible World of John Quincy Adams," *New England Quarterly*, XXXVII (Mar. 1964), 3–17.

[31] *Register of Debates,* 22 Cong., 2 Sess., App., 46, 59 (Feb. 28, 1833).

[32] *Memoirs of John Quincy Adams: Comprising Portions of His Diary from 1795 to 1848,* ed. Charles Francis Adams (12 vols.; Philadelphia, 1876), VIII, 433 (Dec. 11, 1831).

[33] *Register of Debates,* 22 Cong., 2 Sess., App., 53 (Feb. 28, 1833).

Jackson, the two enemies of Adams threatened to throw away the great opportunities freemen enjoyed on the unsettled continent. By seeking to dismantle the American System, Adams bitterly charged, the President was embracing "a complete system of future Government for this Union directly tending to its dissolution." [34]

The political prescription for dividing and conquering his enemies would threaten, however, to involve Adams in a profound dilemma. By allying with the democratically-minded people, success would surely come in removing the slave power as an obstacle to the fuller realization of the Union. Yet in their very present-mindedness, the new allies might also remain after the victory as an obstacle. The tactic for creating the alliance would, indeed, lend great likelihood to that result. In 1833, for example, Adams sought to show how the slave power, as a foe of positive government, constituted an enemy to the true and present interests of the people. By opposing the tariff, he warned, the slave power sought "to rob the free workingman of the North of the wages of his labor, to take money from his pocket and put it into that of the southern owner of machinery." [35] But once befriended to the idea of positive government, the people would not necessarily conceive of it as a shaper and a planner of the future. It might rather appear to them as the giver of good things, as a genial broker in the present for whatever the people wanted. A preoccupation with the task of removing the slave power obstacle in order to gain freedom of action in the present thus worked against the corporate vision of the future.

President Andrew Jackson, no less than Webster and Adams, stood ready to save the Union at all hazards. In the proclamation to the people of South Carolina on December 10, 1832, he rejected the partnership concept that the freedom of an eternal present involved the ultimate freedom to dissolve the Union itself. Yet in resisting Calhoun's theory, Jackson adduced an idea of the Union far different, indeed, far more absolute than the corporate view. His was a Union in many ways above space and time, a transcendental entity, in itself a kind of eternally present being. [36] The proof

---

[34] *Memoirs of John Quincy Adams*, VIII, 503 (Dec. 4, 1832).

[35] *Register of Debates*, 22 Cong., 2 Sess., App., 59 (Feb. 28, 1833).

[36] For a very suggestive discussion of Jackson's thought that is relevant here see John William Ward, *Andrew Jackson: Symbol for an Age* (New York, 1955), pp. 101–32, *passim*. Extremely significant in this same connection is the fact that President Abraham Lincoln's concept of the Union was far more transcendental and Jacksonian than corporate and Whiggish. Edmund Wilson, *Patriotic Gore* (New York, 1966), pp. 99–130.

of its absolute value was hence to be found less in subtle legal reasoning or in the glories of a planned future than in the hearts of its present members. The "united voice of the yeomanry of the country" in response to his proclamation gave great assurance. Representative Churchill C. Cambreleng of New York, alarmed at many "federalist" heresies in the proclamation, yet clearly perceived that the people liked it because its sentiments "make them think and feel like men." [37] The Union was not deemed so valuable because of anything which it did; to the contrary, Jackson wanted to free the people from past policies and future controls. It was an absolute rather because it gave meaning and identity to a growing number of Americans like Jackson who were becoming orphaned in time. In the order of Providence, Jackson thus affirmed, the Union constituted "the only means of attaining the high destinies to which we may reasonably aspire." [38]

Within the spacious frame of the Union, however, Jackson sought to realize the Jeffersonian goal of freedom for each individual and generation in the pursuit of happiness. In the fourth annual message to Congress on December 4, 1832, Jackson provided a systematic statement of policies. Delivered only six days before the proclamation that would save the Union, this message called for the government of the Union to devolve much of its power on the states and the people and thus relinquish efforts at controlling the nation's course. Jackson defended anew in the message his earlier vetoes of internal improvement bills and of the measure to recharter the Bank. To this list of discredited legislation for the privileged few he now added the protective tariff. The most crucial of his proposals—the one which embodied most fully his concept of freedom—was the one recommending the reduction in the price of the public lands to a level barely sufficient to cover the costs of administration. With it he clearly challenged the plan of Adams for using land revenues and internal improvements to direct in some degree the development of the country. The "speedy settlement of these lands," Jackson rather affirmed, "constitutes the true interest of the Republic." [39] It served, by multiplying freemen across

---

[37] Jackson to Joel R. Poinsett, Jan. 24, 1833; Cambreleng to Martin Van Buren, Dec. 18, 1832, *Correspondence of Jackson,* V, 11; IV, 505 note.

[38] "Proclamation," Dec. 10, 1832, *A Compilation of the Messages and Papers of the Presidents,* comp. James D. Richardson (18 vols.; New York, 1913), III, 1219.

[39] "Fourth Annual Message," Dec. 4, 1832, *ibid.,* p. 1164.

space, to turn back the threat to freedom contained in the Whiggish policy of consolidation.

It was here as well that Jackson differed most from Calhoun. By nullification and secession the South Carolinian stood ready to destroy the Union in order to secure freedom. President Jackson, by contrast, sought to secure the freedom of an eternal present within the Union through a process of growth. By continued expansion the Union would be able to reproduce its existing character across space rather than to undergo qualitative changes through time.[40] It was very revealing, in this light, that the "one absurdity out of thousands" which Jackson found in Calhoun's theory was one pertaining to a new part of the Union and not to the old thirteen. The fathers had not purchased Louisiana, Jackson insisted, in order that territorial peoples might at statehood secede and assume a separate destiny. As people moved across the great valley and recreated the miracle of freedom, he supposed, the Union would grow ever stronger. Jackson's efforts at the time to acquire Texas also savored of this outlook, for, as he put it, "the god of the universe had intended this great valley to belong to one nation." [41]

With his views Jackson actually served as the great compromiser in the nullification controversy. While no less prepared than Webster and Adams to save the Union, he also shared Calhoun's opposition to a corporate definition of policies. But Jackson's policies represented far more than the mere response of a "compromiser" to conflicting pressures. They comprised instead a positive affirmation made possible by the end of the debt. By devolving power and control, Jackson sought to secure the freedom of an eternal present for his age and for posterity. "In regard to most of our great interests," he thus noted, "we may consider ourselves as just starting in our career, and after a salutary experience about to fix upon a permanent basis the policy best calculated to promote the happiness of the people and facilitate their progress toward the most complete enjoyment of civil liberty." [42]

---

[40] For a perceptive analysis on the point See William T. Hutchinson, "Unite to Divide, Divide to Unite: The Shaping of American Federalism," *Mississippi Valley Historical Review*, XLVI (June 1959), 3–18.

[41] Jackson to Van Buren, Dec. 23, 1832, *Correspondence of Jackson*, IV, 505; Jackson to Van Buren, Aug. 12, 1829, *ibid.*, p. 57.

[42] "Fourth Annual Message," Dec. 4, 1832, *Messages and Papers*, III, 1168–69. That Jackson rather than Henry Clay was the great compromiser is argued fully in an article by the present writer, "Andrew Jackson: The Great Compromiser," *Tennessee Historical Quarterly*, XXVI (Spring 1967), 64–78. Clay's views of the Union had much of Jackson's western flavor, while on matters of public policy he stood somewhere between Webster and Adams.

These triumphant Jacksonian views also pointed to the more aggressive formulation of the nation's manifest destiny in the following decade.[43] By removing the Indians and by dismantling the American System, Jackson hoped to do away with the internal obstacles to true freedom. But any outside obstacle to the further territorial expansion of a growing nation would also create a crisis of freedom. If "personal liberty is incompatible with a crowded population," as Alexander Duncan of Ohio told the House in 1845, then to be "circumnavigated by British power" in Texas, Oregon and California meant density and unfreedom just as surely as the consolidating policies of the Whig party. Another representative from Ohio, Joseph J. McDowell, thus declared that growth was "the normal state" of the Union. More than that, Representative John A. McClernand of Illinois added, extension constituted "the condition of our political existence." [44]

By 1848, a triumph over both the internal and the external foes of freedom seemed assured. The renewed effort by the Whigs in 1842 to establish the American System was undone four years later by the Walker Tariff, the Independent Treasury and presidential vetoes of measures for internal improvements. The flag of the nation was, in the meantime, advancing to the Pacific with the annexation of Texas, undisputed control of Oregon south of the 49th parallel and the likely acquisition of New Mexico and California. In good earnest, Americans would then be able to answer the call made earlier by Representative Chesselden Ellis of New York for "filling up the grand outlines of a territory intended for the possession and destiny of the American race—an outline drawn by the hand of the Creator himself." [45]

Involved in all such arguments was the urge to gain immunity from time. This came out very clearly, first of all, in the unusual

---

[43] Albert K. Weinberg overstates the case when he argues that the ideals of democracy and expansionism did not become linked together until the 1840s and only then "as a defensive effort to forestall the encroachment of Europe in North America." *Manifest Destiny: A Study of Nationalist Expansionism in American History* (Baltimore, 1935), pp. 109, *passim.* The spatial, atemporal concept of freedom lodged in Jacksonian thought, it would rather appear, made expansionism one of its essential attributes. Frederick Merk, by his analysis of the inherently expansive nature of federalism, likewise takes issue with Weinberg. *Manifest Destiny and Mission in American History: A Reinterpretation* (New York, 1963), pp. 24–60.

[44] *Congressional Globe,* 28 Cong., 2 Sess., App., 178 (Jan. 29, 1845); 29 Cong., 1 Sess., App., 76 (Jan. 5, 1846); 29 Cong., 2 Sess., App. 104 (Jan. 15, 1849).

[45] *Congressional Globe,* 28 Cong., 2 Sess., App., 138 (Jan. 28, 1845).

anxiety many advocates of manifest destiny professed for the well-being of posterity. Their seminal sense of responsibility did not indicate, of course, any plan for defining or prescribing the future. They wanted instead to secure the freedom of each succeeding generation to make a fresh start in the pursuit of happiness. Every new acre of territory, Representative Duncan thus observed, comprised "an additional guaranty" for freedom. John L. O'Sullivan likewise pointed to the needs of "our yearly multiplying millions," while a representative from Illinois stated the matter with fullest force. "This great Republic was not created for the few people who were in it at the Revolution," John Reynolds declared in 1843, "nor for the few who are *now* in it, in comparison to the hundreds of millions of souls who will hereafter exist in it." [46]

The praises which President James K. Polk sang to the federative nature of the Union also reflected this predilection for freedom in an eternal present. The federal Union was suited to indefinite expansion across space, he exulted, because the decentralization of power enabled it to comprehend that which it did not control. Freemen, going north to settle new areas without direction from the center, could yet be integrated into the Union at the time of statehood. The very nature of the Union made expansion possible, and expansion in turn strengthened the Union for extending the area of freedom still farther, world without end. A policy of consolidation, by contrast, would presumably commit the nation in time and wreck the Union. "It may well be doubted," Polk argued in the inaugural address, "whether it would not be in greater danger of overthrow if our present population were confined to the comparatively narrow limits of the original thirteen states." [47] Many studies, to be sure, have discounted the reality of open space as a safety valve. But the idea itself surely exercised compelling influence, for it provided a basis for relinquishing efforts at directing the nation through time. It postponed the encounter of the American Adam with time.[48]

----

[46] *Congressional Globe*, 174 (Jan. 29, 1845); *Democratic Review*, XVII (July 1845), 5; *Congressional Globe*, 27 Cong., 3 Sess., App., 111 (Jan. 30, 1843).

[47] "Inaugural Address," Mar. 4, 1845, *Messages and Papers*, V, 2230.

[48] Henry Nash Smith, *Virgin Land: The American West as Symbol and Myth* (Cambridge, 1950), pp. 205–6; Carter Goodrich and Sol Davison, "The Wage Earner in the Westward Movement," *Political Science Quarterly*, L (June 1935), 161–85. Joseph Shafer, in "Was the West a Safety Valve for Labor?" *Mississippi Valley Historical Review*, XXIV (Dec. 1937), 299–314, takes issue here, but only in a limited way.

This spatial concept of freedom also prescribed a politics of conflict. As Marvin Meyers well puts it, Jackson himself supposed the people he represented to be "the great social residuum after alien elements have been removed." The chief domestic concern of the statesman, in this view, was to isolate the aristocratic foes of freedom who would, by the use of the government, establish interests and commit the nation in time. "Legislation has been the fruitful parent of nine-tenths of all the evil, moral and physical, by which mankind has been afflicted," one Democratic partisan declared. By the operation of a protective tariff, Representative David Wilmot more fully explained, "the lords of the spindle" sought to enslave the operatives. "True independence consists in freedom from restraints," he affirmed, "untrammeled to all things not morally wrong." [49] Another saw in internal improvements a threat to freedom, for one generation could so easily run up the debt and become the "mortgagers of posterity." Having triumphed over the consolidating policies of the Whig party, President Polk yet warned that new efforts would be made to revive the whole system of special legislation. [50] Horace Greeley among others resisted this view of politics as a "Social War" and bitterly disclaimed the label of "aristocrat" for those favoring positive legislation. That the Whigs were aristocratic in a European sense few would maintain. But the effort to prescribe the course of the nation did have a savor of establishment uncongenial to the Jacksonian concept of freedom. [51]

A belligerent attitude toward outside foes of expansion matched this politics of conflict at home. In geopolitical terms, Great Britain was here reckoned to be the ultimate threat to freedom, for she opposed the further growth of the United States on the continent. "We cannot bear that Great Britain should have a Canedy on our west as she has on the north," Jackson thus argued in behalf of annexing Texas. In like spirit, John A. McClernand of Illinois displayed "several beautifully colored maps" in the House to show how a cordon of British power stretching from Canada through Oregon and California to Mexico and the Caribbean posed a deadly peril. Senator Lewis

---

[49] Meyers, *The Jacksonian Persuasion,* p. 15; *Democratic Review,* I (Oct. 1837), 6; *Congressional Globe,* 29 Cong., 1 Sess., App., 769 (July 1, 1846).

[50] *Democratic Review,* XXI (Oct. 1847), 332; "Fourth Annual Message," Dec. 5, 1848, *Messages and Papers,* VI, 2503–13.

[51] *Whig Review,* II (Aug. 1845), 115. With his consensus view, of course, Hartz can only regard as irrational this Democratic cry of aristocracy. *Liberal Tradition in America,* pp. 89–113. It does make sense, however, when seen in the context of an earnest dialogue about time.

Cass invoked the law of growth. The nation's course must be onward across the continent, he warned, else "we shall find ourselves in the decrepitude of age, before we have passed the period of manhood." [52] But far more than the natural effect of the law of growth threatened the country, Sam Houston advised the Senate in a speech opposing compromise over Oregon. Because of her hatred for free institutions, Great Britain was determined to drive the nation back "within the limits of the good old thirteen States." One concession would lead to another, Houston predicted, until freemen were ousted "from every outpost of the Republic." It would be much better, Cass agreed, to fight for the first rather than the last inch of territory.[53] More aggressively Stephen A. Douglas vowed "to drive Great Britain and the last vestiges of royal authority from the continent of North America, and extend the limits of the republic from ocean to ocean." [54] A full decade before Lincoln formulated the idea of a house divided between slavery and freedom advocates of a manifest destiny here found a similar conflict between "monarchy and freedom." [55]

War to remove an obstacle to national growth would help to secure freedom for the future. To freemen of the present, at the same time, war might prove very attractive as a moral equivalent, if not a moral superior, to peace. Because "personal enfranchisement" was the essence of nationality in the Jacksonian view, little in the way of common purposes and common discipline remained to foster and sustain that sense of community.[56] "It was a maxim of the venerable Macon," Houston perceptively remarked, "that war was

---

[52] Jackson to Francis P. Blair, May 11, 1844, *Correspondence of Jackson*, VI, 286; *Congressional Globe*, 29 Cong., 1 Sess., App., 278 (Jan. 8, 1846); 427 (Mar. 30, 1846).

[53] *Congressional Globe*, 639 (Apr. 15, 1846); 29 Cong., 1 Sess., 45 (Dec. 15, 1845).

[54] *Congressional Globe*, 28 Cong., 2 Sess., App., 68 (Jan. 6, 1845).

[55] Senator Daniel Dickinson of New York in a speech on the Oregon question, *Congressional Globe*, 29 Cong., 1 Sess., App., 327 (Feb. 24, 1846). This very close kinship of manifest destiny and free soil again passes over Jaffa, because he persists in the view that the debate between Lincoln and Douglas was essentially one between Whig and Democrat. *Crisis of the House Divided*, p. 88.

[56] *Democratic Review*, VI (Nov. 1839), 427. In *American Nationalism: An Interpretative Essay* (New York, 1957), Hans Kohn well notes that the essence of American nationalism has been the idea of freedom. But he fails to distinguish clearly enough among the different concepts of freedom.

necessary to such a government as ours at least once in every thirty years." By calling on the people to "pay a price for their freedom," it provided a means for recreating and regenerating the first principles of the nation.[57] In a negative way, war would discipline turbulent spirits and enable other individuals to transcend the "selfishness and mediocrity" which ever threatened to overtake a country of free individuals. "It would only be in such a conflict that the sinews and strength of freemen could be fully displayed," McClernand of Illinois stated more positively, "that the moral sublimity of republicanism would loom forth as a phoenix from the smoke and thunders of war." The two wars with Britain, Cass agreed, had pushed the country forward "in character and position" in the world.[58] President Polk made the same claim for the Mexican War. A fuller sense of national identity would also come from the knowledge that, as Representative McDowell put it, a victory by republican arms might spark "a great moral explosion" for liberating Europe from the thralldom of monarchy. "Young America" was here beginning to contemplate more aggressive means for fulfilling the mission of freedom.[59]

Whigs confronted the affirmations of a manifest destiny for the nation in ways which reflected the differences in their own ranks. A decidedly defensive posture was taken by those who stressed order in the process of emerging national community. Rapid settlement of the western lands already placed enough strain upon the corporate Union, Representative Joseph R. Ingersoll of Pennsylvania protested, because "a want of nationality" generally characterized the people from new areas. To acquire even more territory and strange peoples would surely wreck the delicate task of building a homogeneous nation, complained another partisan, and "we shall not know ourselves or know our country." [60] In explaining his opposition to further acquisitions, Webster confessed that the theme of his entire career had been to make Americans *"one people,* one

---

[57] *Congressional Globe,* 29 Cong., 1 Sess., App., 640 (Apr. 15, 1846).

[58] *Democratic Review,* XVI (June 1845), 532; *Congressional Globe,* 29 Cong., 1 Sess., App., 276 (Jan. 8, 1846); 430 (Mar. 30, 1846).

[59] "Fourth Annual Message," Dec. 5, 1848, *Messages and Papers,* VI, 2481–82; *Congressional Globe,* 29 Cong., 1 Sess., App., 76 (Jan. 5, 1846). On the aggressive sense of mission, see Merle Curti, "Young America," *American Historical Review,* XXXII (Oct. 1926), 34–55.

[60] *Congressional Globe,* 28 Cong., 2 Sess., App., 56 (Jan. 4, 1845); *Whig Review,* VII (May 1848), 440.

in interest, one in character, and one in political feeling." Departure from this goal would "break it all up," he lamented, and transform the Union into "a deformed monster." The true destiny of the country, Robert C. Winthrop agreed, was one to be fulfilled within "the old and ample homestead which our fathers bequeathed us." To lay down permanent boundaries, he elsewhere argued, would be to take "a bond of fate for the perpetuation of our Union." [61]

A resumption of domestic policies for building a "more substantial Union," Winthrop further noted, comprised the true alternative to indefinite expansion. Henry Clay agreed that the American System alone could bring to the people "additional security to their liberties and to their Union." [62] By its "constant endeavor to identify the interests of the people with those of the government," another Whig affirmed, his party sought to create through time a more homogeneous nation. The appearance in the files of the *Whig Review* of an organic theory of Union to challenge the "fiction of a social compact" also underlined this urgency to order.[63] Society was based on a contract, to be sure, but it was a contract of nature reflecting the absolute moral and physical needs of man as a social being. "The aim of this contract, nay, its very essence is nationality," so went the argument, "the union of as many as can be bound by the ties of kindred, country, language, and a common destiny." [64] This concept of nationality stood in sharpest contrast to that of the Jacksonians. Whereas the latter would free the individual in time and develop the Union across space, the party of memory wanted to fix bounds to the Union and to realize more fully its elements of solidarity.[65]

---

[61] "Objects of the Mexican War," Mar. 23, 1848, Webster, *Writings and Speeches*, X, 32; "River and Harbor Improvements," Mar. 12, 1846, Robert C. Winthrop, *Addresses and Speeches on Various Occasions* (4 vols.; Boston, 1852–86), I, 500; "The Conquest of Mexican Territory," Feb. 22, 1847, *ibid.*, p. 599.

[62] "River and Harbor Improvements," Mar. 12, 1846, *ibid.*, p. 500; Henry Clay to James F. Babcock and others, Dec. 17, 1844, Calvin Colton, *The Life, Correspondence, and Speeches of Henry Clay* (6 vols.; New York, 1864), IV, 514–15.

[63] *Whig Review*, VII (Apr. 1848), 330; *Whig Review*, II (Nov. 1845), 440.

[64] *Whig Review*, IX (Mar. 1849), 225. Clay, like many other Whigs of the time, privately found much to commend in Native Americanism. Clay to John S. Littell, Nov. 17, 1846, Colton, *Life of Clay*, IV, 536.

[65] Merk clearly perceives the nature of Whig nationalism here, yet he tends strongly to deny that the Jacksonian position was nationalistic at all. *Manifest Destiny and Mission*, p. 57.

Other Whigs defined the alternative to manifest destiny in more hopeful and prospective terms. This came out clearly in the way Seward used organic theory. While admitting that the Union was "secured at first by compact alone," he now took it to be an effectively organized national community answering to the needs of Americans as social beings. The statesman, in this view, was thus free to look beyond the task of consolidation to ways for enriching the common life. Economic policies for that purpose should enable the nation to produce "within its own limits all articles requisite to its own sustenance and comfort, *so far as nature has interposed no obstacle.*"[66] Economic self-sufficiency would obviously bring greater security from outside powers. The realization of the goal through time would also create, as Senator Rufus Choate noted, "fountains of national wealth and civilization" within the country. Because the pursuit of happiness was corporate in nature, he argued that progressive social mastery over nature would enrich the lives of all freemen. An iconoclastic laissez-faire policy, by contrast, threatened to discard the accumulating skills of society like an old bow "which none of this generation knows how to bend . . ."[67]

Spokesmen for the party of hope insisted, however, that the collective mastery over nature "must be the supremacy of man over nature as *man* . . . " They regarded the policy of economic nationalism as a necessary means for creating a higher level of civilization—for "expanding and cultivating of all the powers and capacities of man considered as a social being . . . "[68] Only a richly diversified society could detect "the slightest shade of individuality," Choate explained, or develop the widest possible variety of "national mind." In awakening the "dormant power" of the human mind, Representative George P. Marsh of Vermont agreed, society best exemplified the law of progress. Seward warned, in the same vein, that "our righteous national prejudice" against elites of any kind must not be a stumbling block to the elevation of standards in higher education.[69] In the name of "a complete man," one spokesman for the Democracy railed against the specialization of life which threatened to reduce

---

[66] "Speech at a Whig Mass Meeting," Yates County, N. Y., Oct. 29, 1844, *Works of Seward*, III, 266; *Whig Review*, IV (Sept. 1846), 218.

[67] *Congressional Globe*, 28 Cong., 1 Sess., App., 642 (Apr. 12, 1844).

[68] *Whig Review*, VII (Feb. 1848), 149; *Whig Review*, III (June 1846), 616.

[69] *Congressional Globe*, 28 Cong., 1 Sess., App., 646 (Apr. 12, 1844); 29 Cong., 1 Sess., App., 1012 (June 30, 1846); "Education," Westfield, N. Y., July 26, 1837, *Works of Seward*, III, 147.

the individual to "a supplementary being" of society. But Whigs answered that only from "a fixed center of thought" could the individual realize his full potential. In this view, the good society was one which realized most fully its elements of diversity.[70]

A profoundly revealing difference here obtained between the hopeful Whigs and their adversaries. It has been noted that the Whigs, while entertaining a more cosmopolitan concept of civilization, sought to fulfill it by avowedly nationalistic policies. Civilization was something which took time, Choate observed, and much conscious effort. The Democrats, by contrast, tended to take opposite grounds. They pursued a more cosmopolitan economic policy of laissez faire, yet they displayed a stronger inclination to cultural nationalism. While disclaiming essential responsibility for shaping national life by positive policies, they were disposed to defend the cultural result as uniquely American and therefore uniquely good. In negative moments, to use the terms of Henry Nash Smith, many Democratic spokesmen chose American "primitivism" over European "civilization." [71] Senator Lewis Linn of Missouri, for example, rejected that "high state of civilization" which involved compacted population, elegance and refinement for the few, or "great corporations . . . for enabling one set of men to lord it over another." The "rigorous morals and stern virtue of a republic," argued another partisan, comprised a true alternative to civilization. The "rough carol" of a Mississippi boatman or the sound of an axe, he explained, were "better guaranties for the stability and perpetuity of our republican institutions" than the trill of a cavalier or the songs of the gondoliers.[72] The non-civilization in America, it would appear, assured the continued existence of the Union for more non-civilization. When Democratic spokesmen did accept the idea of civilization as

[70] Democratic Review, XVIII (Jan. 1846), 13; Whig Review, I (Apr. 1845), 423. For the fullest and most systematic statement by a hopeful Whig of the social conditions necessary for the highest pursuit of happiness, see John Quincy Adams, Whig Review, II (July 1845), 80–89.

[71] Smith, Virgin Land, pp. 250–60, passim. Two recent studies have amended Smith's view by showing that the American ideal lay on the spectrum between "primitivism" and "civilization." In The Machine in the Garden: Technology and the Pastoral Ideal in America (New York, 1964), Leo Marx develops the concept of "pastoralism." John William Ward develops the idea of "cultivated nature." Andrew Jackson: Symbol for an Age.

[72] Congressional Globe, 27 Cong., 3 Sess., App., 154 (Jan. 26, 1843); Democratic Review, XXI (Nov. 1847), 425.

something which evolved progressively through time, they most often supposed that its conditions would somehow automatically arise. The satisfaction of physical wants engendered a demand for higher things and evoked the supply to fulfill it. "The demand for artists, poets, and philosophers expands," the argument thus ran, "science becomes a distinct pursuit, literature is made profitable, and all the more delicate and ennobling modes of exerting human faculties receive invigorating rewards." [73]

With their temporal concept of freedom, finally, many Whigs saw in positive efforts to shape national life a moral equivalent to war. The spirit of restlessness pervading the land, Horace Mann supposed, truly reflected the "unexampled energies" released by republican institutions. But with the force of "traditional feelings of respect for established authority" spent, he argued that his generation must impose a new authority over itself. Abraham Lincoln expressed the fear, however, that constructive policies of government could not provide the needed discipline. The ambitious spirit of the age sought to express freedom not in building on the work of the fathers but in tearing down. "It sees *no distinction*," he noted, "in adding story to story, upon the monuments of fame, erected to the memory of others." Another observer who shared the same insight damned the Jacksonians for abetting no less than reflecting this urge to destruction.[74] William Seward was far more hopeful. He believed that freemen could, by positive means, "constantly renovate and regenerate society." He clearly perceived that "action is the condition of our existence" and that action could be directed by the government "to pursuits consistent with public order and conducive to the general welfare." He revered the fathers in the first instance not as heroes who destroyed enemies of freedom but as freemen of one generation who made great sacrifices to enrich the life of the larger corporate whole. "The principle of internal improvement derives its existence," Seward observed, "from the generous impulses of the Revolutionary age." With the "arts of peace" Representative Marsh of Vermont likewise wanted to con-

---

[73] *Democratic Review*, VI (Sept. 1839), 215.

[74] "The Necessity of Education in a Republic," 1838, *Life and Works of Horace Mann*, ed. Mrs. Mary Mann (5 vols.; Boston, 1865–68), II, 150, 168; "Address before the Young Men's Lyceum of Springfield, Illinois," Jan. 27, 1838, *The Collected Works of Abraham Lincoln*, ed. Roy P. Basler (9 vols.; New Brunswick, N. J., 1953), I, 114; *Whig Review*, VII (Feb. 1848), 207–9.

tinue "the conquest of nature" rather than make war on trumped-up enemies of freedom.[75]

The Whigs were unable to prevent a war in the 1840s, but they did persist in opposing to the concept of manifest destiny a vision of freemen within a process of time. By 1848, however, the issue of slavery expansion was threatening to disrupt the dialogue about the destiny of the nation in time and space. The southern urge to preserve one peculiarly crucial aspect from the past served in a dialectical fashion to engender stronger claims for freedom in the present. Intense focus on the conflict between freedom and slavery—on the issue of the present versus the past—thus tended to remove from consideration the corporate outlook of the Whigs.

The initial response of most northern Whigs, to be sure, was one which resisted this tendency. While overwhelmingly in favor of freedom for the territories, they opposed, as one put it, "the one-idea school" which would make the issue an end in itself. They wanted rather to make free soil but a part of the "great system of the Union" for shaping its future.[76] Representative Winthrop affirmed in 1847 that the Wilmot Proviso was "the great conservative principle of the day" because it divided northern from southern expansionists and thus enabled the nation to fix its needed permanent boundaries. But if there was to be more expansion, Webster argued for free soil on the further ground that it would at least call a halt to the growth of unequal political power provided by the three-fifths representation of the slaves. Such added power in the councils of the Union would surely doom all hopes for directing the future course of the country.[77] Seward, among a smaller number of Whigs, defended a policy of freedom in the territories on yet another ground. He embraced in a positive way "the popular passion for territorial aggrandizement," but he wanted to inform it with more conscious purpose. With the energizing principle of freedom in new areas and the continued direction of the government from the center, he hoped to build a great empire for perfecting freedom in

---

[75] "To the Whigs of Orleans," Auburn, N. Y., May 13, 1844, *Works of Seward,* III, 395; "Annual Message," Jan. 1, 1839, p. 205; "Annual Message," Jan. 7, 1840, p. 242; *Congressional Globe,* 29 Cong., 1 Sess., App., 1012, 1013 (June 30, 1846).

[76] *Whig Review,* VIII (Aug. 1848), 193; VIII (Oct. 1848), 340.

[77] "The Conquest of Mexico," Feb. 22, 1847, Winthrop, *Addresses and Speeches,* I, 599; "Objects of the Mexican War," Mar. 23, 1848, Webster, *Writings and Speeches,* X, 20–21.

America and for carrying forward the republican mission to the rest of the world.[78] Because free soil was a means to this larger end, Seward resisted the efforts of the radical third party in 1848 to make it an end in itself. Only under the banner of the Whig party, he protested, could the highest destiny of the Union be achieved.[79]

From the outset, by contrast, Jacksonian advocates imparted to the issue of free soil much of the flavor which came to predominate in the 1850s. They made the slave power to appear the chief enemy of freedom and the removal of that obstacle the remaining task for the nation. David Wilmot argued, in the first place, that white laboring men seeking open space and freedom could not live with dignity among masters and slaves. A ban on slavery in the territory, furthermore, provided a real choice for freemen at the time of statehood. The probable rejection of slavery, in turn, assured the increase of free states and paved the way for further acquisitions. A cordon of slave states to the Pacific would otherwise block the southward spread of freedom and abort the manifest destiny of the country. A free soil policy thus assured freedom from "the lords of the lash" in the territory, while the expansion which it made possible also assured freedom from "the lords of the loom" back in the settled areas. In geopolitical terms, the domestic slave power here began to replace monarchial Britain as the chief enemy of freedom.[80] Senator Hannibal Hamlin added a final twist to this line of argument which clearly anticipated Lincoln's concept of the house divided. By going to the territory, Hamlin reasoned, the slave power hemmed in freemen. But worse than that, a malignant slave power posed the danger of doubling back to overspread the existing areas of freedom in the states. "After you have overrun your territories," he asked ominously in 1848, "what power can prevent the slaveholders from coming into the free States with his slaves?" [81]

Finally, a radical third party in 1848 gave form to the free soil

---

[78] "To the Chautauqua Convention," Auburn, N. Y., Mar. 31, 1846, *Works of Seward,* III, 409; "The True Greatness of Our Country," Baltimore, Dec. 22, 1848, pp. 11–24.

[79] This came out with great clarity in Seward's speech in the Western Reserve of Ohio during the presidential campaign of 1848. He pleaded with Whigs to leave the Free Soil party and return to their old loyalty. "The Election of 1848," Cleveland, Oct., 1848, *ibid.,* pp. 293–302.

[80] Wilmot outlined these ideas in two speeches given in the House. *Congressional Globe,* 29 Cong., 2 Sess., App., 315–17 (Feb. 8, 1847); 30 Cong., 1 Sess., App., 1076–79 (Aug. 3, 1848).

[81] *Congressional Globe,* 1146 (July 2, 1848).

position which would virtually obscure the corporate concept in the following decade. While it did in some degree effect a synthesis of Whig and Democratic elements, the Free Soil party embodied more nearly the Jacksonian urge to freedom in the eternal present. On its Democratic side, the platform defined a politics of conflict between "free labor" and "the aggressions of the slave power." The call to rescue the federal government from this enemy of freedom represented, as Salmon P. Chase ever argued, the "paramount" issue.[82] "Freedom is the only question before the American people," Charles Sumner agreed, "the question of questions." On the Whig side, to be sure, the Free Soil platform called for more positive action by the government. But underlying this demand was the assumption that in "forgetting all past political differences" the former Democrats and Whigs ceased to regard the specific measures once separating them as of seminal importance.[83] "If we are wrong on the Tariff, it can be righted in twelve hours," one delegate explained the order of priorities. "But if we are wrong on the subject of slavery, it never can be righted." [84] Along with a tariff of protection which involved, as the Whigs once supposed, a temporal concept of freedom, the Free Soilers could thus adopt a homestead provision which obviously expressed a spatial concept of freedom. Here was to be found, however, less of Babel among conflicting ideas than a new view of the government as a genial broker. Whereas Jacksonians once wanted the government to leave the people alone and the Whigs wanted it to help shape the future, Free Soilers now would make the power of the government available in the present for whatever the people might desire.

---

[82] Edward Stanwood, *A History of the Presidency from 1788 to 1897* (Boston, 1928), p. 239; Salmon P. Chase to Charles Sumner, Nov. 26, 1846, S. H. Dodson, comp., *Diary and Correspondence of Salmon P. Chase, Annual Report* of the American Historical Association, 1902 (2 vols.; Washington, D. C., 1903), II, 113.

[83] "Massachusetts Convention of Worchester," June 28, 1848, Charles Sumner, *The Works of Charles Sumner* (15 vols.; Boston, 1875), II, 83; Stanwood, *History of the Presidency*, p. 239.

[84] The delegate to the Free Soil convention was Judge Nye. Quoted in Julian P. Bretz, "The Economic Background of the Liberty Party," *American Historical Review*, XXXIV (Jan. 1929), 258–59. For further background on the Free Soil party in 1848 see Theodore Clarke Smith, *The Liberty and the Free Soil Parties in the Northwest* (New York, 1897), pp. 121–38, *passim*. Paul C. Nagel, in *One Nation Indivisible: The Union in American Thought, 1776–1861* (New York, 1964), pp. 104–44, provides useful analysis of the absolute and majoritarian concept of the Union at which many Free Soilers had arrived by the end of the 1840s.

If the foregoing analysis is valid, it was this "free soil synthesis" which disrupted the earlier dialogue of American liberals about space and time. The debate of the 1850s between Lincoln and Douglas was to be between two forms of negative liberalism, for little of the corporate sense of freemen within a temporal process remained.[85] By 1858, Lincoln could define the chief task of the nation as that of removing an obstacle to freedom, while the platform of the Republican party in 1860 constituted a classic example of the new broker state politics. By his support of the principle of popular sovereignty, at the same time, Douglas supposed that freedom in the present already obtained. Free soil constituted an enemy to freedom, in this view, because it would prove to be a stumbling block to further expansion. Horatio Alger—the symbol Hartz uses for the synthesis of democratic capitalism—went chiefly with the free soil cause. His triumph came, not in the log cabin in 1840 as Hartz supposes, but in the great conflict over slavery. Consensus among liberals followed and did not precede the demise of the Whig party.[86] Not the least price paid by the nation in coming to grips with the issue of slavery was the loss for a generation at least of an effective corporate vision of its destiny.

---

[85] For an extended argument that the debate still reflected Whig versus Democrat see Jaffa, *Crisis of the House Divided*. But Jaffa's analysis lacks any fundamental sense of the different concepts of time.

[86] Hartz makes the very damaging admission that his "liberal society analysis" cannot account for the great conflict over slavery. By that measure his consensus view of the liberal tradition in America breaks down, since it is not able to explain the most "liberal" event in the nation's history. *Liberal Tradition in America,* p. 19.

PART   III

...AND THE MINOR

EDWARD PESSEN*

The Working Men's Party Revisited

*The closest thing to ideological parties in the Jacksonian era were such
"third parties" as the Working Men. The following article argues that for
all the questions that have been raised concerning their authenticity, the
Working Men's parties were for the most part bona fide organizations led
by uncommonly radical men. While occasionally supporting Jacksonian
policy, the Working Men not only remained aloof from the Democratic
organization but typically attacked it as vigorously as they did its major
party opponents. "Humbugs, both," charged the Working Men's leaders,
in referring to the major parties.*

xxxxxxxxxxxxxxxxxxxxxxxxxxxxxxxxxxxxxxxxxxxxxxxxxxxxxxxxxxxxxxxxx

THE UNIQUE FEATURE of the American labor movement
during the Jacksonian era was the establishment of Working Men's
parties. Beginning in Philadelphia in 1828, a Working Men's movement spread throughout the country, reaching its climax in the
1830s. For the only time in American history, workers formed
separate political organizations, largely independent of the major
parties. Since one of the classic features of the modern American

* From Edward Pessen, "The Working Men's Party Revisited," *Labor
History*, IV (Fall, 1963), pp. 203–226.

labor movement is precisely the extent to which it has eschewed independent politics, the appearance of this movement is obviously a matter of much significance. This essay will examine some of the important aspects of the Working Men's parties, as well as some of the issues still in controversy concerning them.

If no attempt will be made here to give a blow-by-blow account of the rise and fall of the Working Men's parties, it is because it is by now a much-told tale. A fairly substantial literature has appeared since George Henry Evans and his contemporaries first chronicled the activities of the New York Working Men.[1] To this date the most comprehensive, and probably still the most valuable, study remains

[1] George Henry Evans, "History of the Origin and Progress of the Working Men's Party in New York," in the *Radical*, 1842–1843; Hobart Berrien, *A Brief Sketch of the Origin and Rise of the Working Men's Party in the City of New York* (Washington, n.d.); Amos Gilbert, "A Sketch of the Life of Thomas Skidmore," *Free Enquirer* (New York), Mar. 30, and April 6, 13, 1834; Jabez D. Hammond, *History of Political Parties in the State of New York*, 2 vols. (rev. ed.; New York, 1850), vol. II, 330–331.

For the New York area, the most recent study—and in my opinion, a most valuable and judicious volume, despite my questions about some of its interpretations—is Walter Hugins' *Jacksonian Democracy and the Working Class* (Stanford, 1960). Also invaluable is Seymour Savetsky's "The New York Working Men's Party," unpubl. Master's essay (Columbia University, 1948). Also see Edward Pessen, "Thomas Skidmore, Agrarian Reformer in the Early American Labor Movement," *New York History*, vol. XXV (July, 1954); Frank T. Carlton, "The Working Men's Party of New York City, 1829–1831," *Political Science Quarterly*, XXII (Sept., 1907), 401–415. For Philadelphia, see William A. Sullivan, "Did Labor Support Andrew Jackson?" *Political Science Quarterly*, LXII (Dec., 1947), 569–580; and, by the same author, "Philadelphia Labor During the Jackson Era," *Pennsylvania History*, vol. XV (Oct., 1948), No. 4, 1–16; Louis Arky, "The Mechanics' Union of Trade Associations and the Formation of the Philadelphia Working Men's Movement," *Pennsylvania Magazine of History and Biography*, LXXVI (April, 1952), 142–176; and Edward Pessen, "The Ideology of Stephen Simpson, Upperclass Champion of the Early Philadelphia Workingmen's Movement," *Pennsylvania History*, XXII (October, 1955), 328–340. For New Jersey, see Milton J. Nadworny, "New Jersey Workingmen and the Jacksonians," *Proceedings of the New Jersey Historical Society*, LXVII (July, 1949), 185–198; and, by the same author, "Jersey Labor and Jackson," unpubl. Master's essay (Columbia University, 1948). For Boston and New England, see Edward Pessen, "Did Labor Support Jackson? The Boston Story," *Political Science Quarterly*, LXIV (June, 1949), 262–274; and Arthur B. Darling, "The Workingmen's Party in Massachusetts, 1833–1834," *American Historical Review*, XXIX (October, 1923), 85–86. On the Working Men's parties in general, see Joseph Dorfman, *The Economic Mind in American Civilization* (New York, 1946), vol. II, chap. xxiv; and, by the same author, "The Jackson Wage-Earner Thesis," *American Historical Review*, LIV (Jan., 1949), 296–306; Arthur M. Schlesinger, Jr., *The Age of Jackson*, (Boston, 1945), chap. xi; Nathan Fine, *Labor and Farmer Parties in the United States, 1828–1928* (New York, 1928); Alden Whitman, *Labor Parties, 1827–1834* (New York, 1943); and Edward Pessen, "The Working Men's Movement of the Jacksonian Era," *Mississippi Valley Historical Review*, XLIII (Dec., 1956), 428–443.

the pioneering effort of Helen Sumner, written for Commons' *History* in 1918. In many respects it remains the basic structure on which all later works have built.[2]

The modern discussion, focusing as it has on a few major cities, has perhaps obscured what Miss Sumner's researches long ago uncovered: the ubiquitousness of the Working Men's parties. Operating under a variety of names—"Working Men's Party," "Working Men's Republican Association," "People's Party," "Working Men's Society," "Farmer's and Mechanic's Society," "Mechanics and Other Working Men," and just plain "Working Men"—they appeared in most of the states of the Union. Pennsylvania was the home of the first known group, of course, the Philadelphia party of 1828, which developed out of the Mechanics' Union of Trade Associations. Other groups in that state, some of them unknown to Miss Sumner, were organized in Phillipsburg, Lancaster, Carlisle, Pike Township in Clearfield County, Pottsville, Harrisburg, Erie, and in Allegheny and Mifflin Counties.

In New York State the leading and certainly the most interesting group was organized by Thomas Skidmore and others in New York City. Brooklyn had its own organization, in which the later trade unionist John Commerford played a leading role. Parties also appeared in Troy, Albany, Rochester, Buffalo, Genesee, Utica, Salina (Syracuse), Schenectady, Geneva, Ithaca, Auburn, Batavia, Brockport, Hartford in Washington County, Canandaigua, Kingsbury, Lansingburgh, Glens Falls, Palmyra, and Saratoga. A Working Men's party convention in 1830 was attended by delegates from the counties of New York, Albany, Rensselaer, Cayuga, Oneida, Washington, Onondaga, Tioga, Tompkins, Montgomery, Kings, Cortland, and Ontario. It was reported that a number of other counties also had chosen delegates, who for some unknown reason did not attend.[3]

In New Jersey, groups formed not only in Newark and Trenton, as Miss Sumner noted, but in Hanover (Morris County), Centerville, Caldwell, Peterson, and in Orange and Essex Counties, as well.[4] Organizations, albeit questionable ones which may have been "Working

---

[2] Miss Sumner wrote Part Two, "Citizenship (1827–1833)," in John R. Commons and Associates, *History of Labour in the United States* (2 vols., New York, 1918), I, 169–332.

[3] *Ibid.*, p. 265. Based on a report in the *Farmers', Mechanics' and Workingmen's Advocate*, Sept. 1, 1830.

[4] Nadworny (*op. cit.*, f.n. 1, above) corrects Miss Sumner with regard to the New Jersey movement, for she believed that it was confined to Newark and Trenton (see *ibid.*, p. 287).

Men" in name only, were started in Washington, D. C., and in Canton, Ohio. Working Men also formed in Zanesville and in Columbiana County, Ohio. In Delaware, there were branches in Wilmington, Brandywine, and Red Clay Creek, and in New Castle County.

New England had a lively movement featured by the Association of Farmers, Mechanics and Other Working Men. In addition to this group, whose members came from a number of states, Working Men were organized in Boston, Dedham, Northampton, Dorchester, and in Hampshire and Franklin Counties in Massachusetts; in New London and Lyme in Connecticut; Dover, New Hampshire; Portland and Brunswick in Maine; and in Woodstock, Burlington, Middlebury, and Calais in Vermont.

Most of our information concerning these parties comes from the pages of the dozens of journals which sprang up in this period in support of Working Men. According to the *Delaware Free Press,* one of these journals, by August, 1830, there were at least twenty newspapers in a number of states that might be classified as pro-labor.[5] Miss Sumner found that "some 50 different newspapers in at least 15 States" had expressed approval of the movement at one time or another between 1829 and 1832. These papers varied, naturally, in the degree of support or attention they gave to the workingmen's cause, but a substantial number of them that I have examined can properly be described as organs of the political movement, so completely were they dedicated to the Working Men's issues both in their coverage and in their slant of the news.

In the case of several of the leaders of this movement, their identification with labor consisted precisely in the fact that they edited such journals. George Henry Evans was such a figure. Another was William Heighton, an Englishman who came to this country as a youth, became a cordwainer, the founder of the Philadelphia Mechanics' Union of Trade Associations, and early in 1828, the chief editor of the *Mechanic's Free Press,* the official journal of the Philadelphia movement. This weekly has been described as the "first of the mechanics' newspaper in this country edited by journeymen and directed to them." [6] In Philadelphia, Heighton's journal prodded workers "along the path of reform and into politics," thus helping

---

[5] Commons, *History of Labour,* I, p. 286. Also see Edward Pessen, *"La Première Presse du Travail: Origine, Role, Idéologie," La Presse Ouvrière, 1819–1850,* ed. by Jacques Godechot (Paris, 1966), pp. 43–67.

[6] Louis Arky, "The Mechanics' Union of Trade Associations and the Formation of the Philadelphia Working Men's Movement," p. 163.

to initiate the political movement. More typical was Evans' *Working Man's Advocate* in New York City, which appeared shortly *after* the Working Men organized there. In many cases the journal followed so soon after the party that the two were practically simultaneous, as in Newark, where a Newark *Village Chronicle and Farmers, Mechanics and Working Men's Advocate* came out immediately after the political movement started.

Louis Arky's description of the *Mechanic's Free Press* could apply to numerous other papers as well: "Its pages presented a spectrum of reform, from Pestalozzian educational ideas and co-operative store suggestions to the views of free thinkers and reprints from works like [John] Gray's Lecture [*Lecture on Human Happiness*, London, 1825, a socialistic tract]." [7] In addition, the journals would carry accounts of workingmen's activities in other cities as well as their own, announcements of future activities, romances, advertisements, literary excerpts, and a potpourri of other material. From the point of view of the student of American labor, however, most rewarding were their editorials, the letters of contributors—so often polemical and therefore piquant as well as informative—and their listings of the demands and the programs of the Working Men's parties. Students of the history of American journalism and those who are interested in our social history also will find a treasure-trove in the *New England Artisan and Farmer's, Mechanic's and Laboring Man's Repository*, the New York *Daily Sentinel*, the Indianapolis *Union and Mechanics' and Working Men's Advocate*, and the other labor journals of the period.

If the worth of Miss Sumner's contribution endures, it is also true that the recent discussion, certainly that of the past two decades —based as it is on new evidence and reflecting new scholarly interests and frames of reference—has not only added to our knowledge but in many cases severely modified and brought into serious question her conclusions concerning important matters. In this respect perhaps the trend is similar to that in American historical writing in general: an iconoclastic revisionism which accepts no previous interpretations as sacred, inspired as it is by a relativism to which all old judgments are merely the ephemeral reflections of a forever bygone time.

It would be understatement to describe the main questions raised by the recent literature as a challenge to the traditional thesis. For these questions concern nothing less than the fundamental

---

[7] *Ibid.*

nature of the Working Men's movement. They ask simply: Was the movement authentic? Was it composed of bona fide wage earners battling in the interests of wage earners? Or was it spurious, consisting instead of wily politicians who wrapped themselves in the Working Men's mantle only to hide their real identity?

According to Miss Sumner the issue that divided the true Working Men's parties from the fraudulent was the tariff. For although her study expressed few doubts about the authenticity of most of the organizations which carried the title, she did believe that in some cases "advocates of a protective tariff assumed without warrant the popular name—'mechanics and workingmen.'" Adding to her suspicions was the fact that these "associations of so-called workingmen which favored protection generally avoided committing themselves to the usual demands of the Working Men's party." [8] But if the organization were for free trade and in addition raised the "usual demands," her study accepts it at face value.

In challenging the authenticity of these parties, critics have focused on a number of issues. One bone of contention has been the party's origins, since the way in which the organization was started, the nature of the men involved, and the issues propelling them into action obviously tell us whether the organization was of and for workingmen or whether it was something else again—at least in its infancy.

The political movement in Philadelphia grew out of a decision by the city's Mechanics' Union of Trade Associations to enter into politics in order to promote "the interests and enlightenment of the working classes." The latter organization, the "first union of all the organized workmen of any city," had been organized largely through the energetic activity of the cordwainer William Heighton. It included the individual unions—or societies as they were then called—of journeymen bricklayers, painters, glaziers, typographers and other trades, as well as the journeymen house carpenters whose strike for the ten hour day in the summer of 1827 spurred the formation of the broader union. There can be little doubt as to the authenticity of the Mechanics' Union, whose appeal to its constituent societies rested primarily on its down-to-earth promise of financial support to journeymen on strike against their masters.[9] A few months after it was organized, the bylaws of the Union were

---

[8] *Op. cit.*, pp. 294–295.

[9] Arky, *loc. cit.*, pp. 155–158.

amended to provide that three months prior to general elections the membership should "nominate as candidates for public office such individuals as shall pledge themselves . . . to support and advance . . . the interests and enlightenment of the working classes." [10] The new bylaws took immediate effect. Several months later the *Mechanic's Free Press* reported that "at a very large and respectable meeting of Journeymen House Carpenters held on Tuesday evening, July 1st [1828], . . . the Mechanics' Union of Trade Associations is entering into measures for procuring a nomination of candidates for legislative and other public offices, who will support the interest of the working classes." Thus was born the Working Men's party of Philadelphia, in the promise by some journeymen workers to support at the polls individuals sympathetic to the working class. The most skeptical observer can hardly deny the true workingmen's character of the party, at least at the time of its birth. [11]

In New York City a Working Men's party appeared for the first time in 1829 when in the elections for the State Assembly held early in November, eleven candidates nominated by the new party made a remarkable showing. The decision to run Working Men's candidates on a separate ticket was made at a general meeting of mechanics on October 19, 1829. In addition to approving a number of other resolutions presented by the executive body, known as the Committee of Fifty, the meeting resolved "that past experience teaches that we have nothing to hope from the aristocratic orders of society; and that our only course to pursue is, to send men of our own description, if we can, to the Legislature at Albany; . . . [that] we will make the attempt at the ensuing election; and that as a proper step thereto we invite all those of our fellow citizens who live on their own labor and none other, to meet us . . ." [12]

This Committee of Fifty had been elected at the second of two meetings of journeymen mechanics held earlier that year in the last

---

[10] *Mechanics' Gazette,* Jan. 19, 1828, cited in *ibid.,* p. 162.

[11] William A. Sullivan, who raises a number of questions about the validity of the Philadelphia political movement on the basis largely of the candidates it was to nominate, nonetheless concedes that a long list of "economic, political and social ills" precipitated this bona fide movement of "the Philadelphia workingmen into politics"; "Philadelphia Labor During the Jackson Era," *Pennsylvania History,* XV (October, 1948), 4. For Sullivan's suspicions regarding the "Working Men" of western Pennsylvania, see his *The Industrial Worker in Pennsylvania 1800–1840* (Harrisburg, 1955), pp. 181–193.

[12] *Working Man's Advocate,* Oct. 31, 1829; New York *Evening Journal,* Oct. 30, 1829.

week of April, to give leadership in the struggle to protect the ten hour day against an alleged employers' plot to lengthen it.[13] The first meeting of the mechanics, which was in fact to lead directly to the nomination of candidates—and which can therefore properly be described as constituting the first meeting of the New York Working Men's party—had been called in order to combat "all attempts to compel them to work more than ten hours a day." [14] It would appear then that in its origins the political movement of the New York Working Men was clearly a response of bona fide workers to an attack on their working conditions.

Seymour Savetsky, however, after a close study of this movement, which appeared to establish the intimate relationship between both the leaders and the supporters of the new movement with the Republican [or Jackson] party, concluded that "the explanation for the origin of the . . . party is to be found in the bitter internal dissensions and schisms that were wrecking the Republican Party of New York. In the fractionalization of the Republican party . . . resides the explanation for the appearance of the New York Working Men's Party." [15] While there is evidence that the emergence of the New York movement owed something to the disenchantment of some Republican (or Democratic) voters with the Tammany machine, it seems to me that it is impossible to disagree with Walter Hugins that the party's "initial impetus was economic, a protest against unemployment and a defense of the ten-hour day." [16] Even Jabez Hammond's contemporary account, while stressing the complexity and heterogeneity of the State movement, saw the beginnings of the New York City party as essentially due to the concern of mechanics in the building trade with onerous economic conditions.[17] My own research into the New York Working Men has centered on the roles of Robert Dale Owen, George Henry Evans, and Thomas Skidmore, only the latter of whom might be classified as a worker. Although

---

[13] On the origins of the party, see the New York *Morning Courier*, the New York *Commercial Advertiser*, and the New York *Free Enquirer*, all for April 25, 1829; and the *Radical*, Jan., 1842.

[14] New York *Morning Courier*, April 23, 1829.

[15] Seymour Savetsky, "The New York Working Men's Party," pp. 109–110. Lee Benson's *The Concept of Jacksonian Democracy: New York as a Test Case* (Princeton, 1961), accepts Savetsky's view.

[16] Walter Hugins, *Jacksonian Democracy and the Working Class*, p. 11.

[17] Jabez Hammond, *History of Political Parties in the State of New York*, vol. II, 330.

these men were to steer this movement in directions determined largely by doctrinaire philosophies, this fact in no way contradicts another: the New York Working Men's party originated in a movement of journeymen mechanics to defend their position against an anticipated attack by masters and employers.

For Boston, as for Newark and other towns in New Jersey, the evidence is not clear. The program adopted by the Boston Working Men's party, the methods advocated to attain it, and the candidates nominated to represent the organization politically all raise doubts as to the nature of the movement. But according to the correspondents who reported on its first meetings in the summer of 1830, these were attended by large numbers of "men, who from appearances, were warm from their workshops and from other places of daily toil, but who bore on their countenances conviction of their wrongs, and a determination to use every proper means to have them redressed." [18]

There is much fuller information on the origins of the much more significant New England Association of Farmers, Mechanics and Other Working Men. Described by Miss Sumner as a "new type of labour organization, in part economic and in part political," this association was formed when delegates from the New England states, convening in Providence in December, 1831, agreed to hold the first convention the following spring in Boston. The advertisement for the first convention emphasized that "the object of that convention is to mature measures to concentrate the efforts of the laboring classes, to regulate the hours of labor by one uniform standard." [19] This was in fact a call for the ten hour day. It is no coincidence that the date set by the first convention for the establishment of the ten hour system—March 20, 1832—happened to be precisely the date on which the Boston shipyard workers began their strike for the ten hour day. Certainly the workers went on strike not because the Association's constitution so directed them. Rather, the Association incorporated the idea of a ten hour system, a strike to achieve it, a war chest to finance it, and expulsion of all those who would work more than ten hours per day after March 20, because of the great influence that Boston's shipyard workers and their allies had in its councils. [20] It was the defeat of the ten hour strike that led

---

[18] Boston *Advocate,* Sept., 1830, cited in Commons, *op. cit.,* p. 291; Boston *Courier,* Aug. 11, 28, 1830.

[19] *Columbian Centinel,* Feb. 15, 16, 1832.

[20] See articles 3, 4, 5, and 9 of the Association's constitution; *Working Man's Advocate,* March 3, 1832. Also see *Boston Traveller,* March, 1832.

the delegates to the second convention held at Boston in September to modify the clause calling for the expulsion from the Association of those who worked more than the ten hour day.[21] It appears incontestable that New England's most important Working Men's party was organized by workingmen to achieve—in contrast to its New York City counterpart, which sought to maintain—the ten hour day.

The sharpest questions as to the authenticity of the Working Men's parties have been provoked by the accumulating evidence on the social and economic backgrounds of their members and leaders. The organ of the Philadelphia Working Men liked to think that in contrast to the two major parties—the Federalists, made up of law-yers and aristocrats, and the Jackson party, composed of bank specu-lators and office hunters—"on the Working Men's ticket . . . the candidates from first to last have been taken from the ranks of the people." But William Sullivan has shown that during its four years of existence the Philadelphia party nominated and supported very few workers as candidates for office. According to his tabulation of the party's one hundred candidates, only ten were workingmen. Twenty-three were professional men, fifty-three were merchants and manufacturers, eleven were "gentlemen," and three had no occu-pation recorded. Among these were some of the wealthiest men in the city, including Charles Alexander, publisher of the conservative *Daily Chronicle*. These facts lead Sullivan to doubt that the Phila-delphia organization was a true workingmen's party.[22] Louis Arky, on the other hand, found a high percentage of its early leaders, better than 75 per cent, workers or artisans.[23] The contradiction may be more apparent than real. The men who actually ran the party were themselves workers. If the candidates were wealthy that fact was not disconcerting to a party whose interest was confined to the views— not the bank accounts—of its nominees.

Milton Nadworny, the leading student of the New Jersey move-ment, found little solid information as to the occupations or incomes of the leaders and candidates there, although for Newark he ventures the understatement that "undoubtedly, not all of the men in the group were pure, unadulterated workingmen." Despite his findings

---

[21] See the letter from a Boston delegate in the *Working Man's Advocate*, Sept. 15, 1832.

[22] William A. Sullivan, "Did Labor Support Andrew Jackson?" p. 375; and Sullivan, *The Industrial Worker* . . . , pp. 178–179.

[23] Louis Arky, *loc. cit.*, p. 173.

that small businessmen and merchants often played leading parts in the movement, he nonetheless accepts it as essentially authentic.[24]

The New York City Working Men split into at least three factions shortly after their remarkable political success in the fall of 1829. There can be little doubt that the most numerous of these had little in common with true workmen. But prior to the infiltration of the party by opportunistic elements, culminating in their ascendancy over it by the time of the 1830 elections, the evidence indicates that bona fide workers were active in its ranks. Of the eleven candidates put up for the State Assembly in 1829, ten were workers. The other, a physician, got significantly fewer votes than all the rest of his colleagues in the election.[25] In its early stages, according to George Henry Evans, the party sought not only to confine leadership to workingmen but to see that these were journeymen rather than masters. That it was not successful, however, is shown by the fact that by 1830 even Evans' faction was supporting manufacturers as candidates for political office.

For that matter, Evans' definition of a workingman was rather broad. According to him, only one member of the seventy-man General Executive Committee of the New York party of 1830— a broker—was not a workingman. Evidently, to Evans, the five grocers, the two merchant-tailors, the oil merchant, the teacher, and the farmer were workers. The complete occupational breakdown for this committee unfortunately does not distinguish between masters and journeymen, but it does range over a broad category of occupations, including carpenters, smiths, masons, painters, pianoforte makers, sash makers, and porter housekeepers. Savetsky, who is not inclined to take this Party's claims at face value, nonetheless concedes that on this committee "a majority ... belong to the laboring element in the community." His close study of the property owned by this group established that just under 50 per cent were propertyless, another 10 per cent had only personal property, while only three individuals owned property assessed at more than $10,000.[26] For the years after 1831 it has been rather conclusively shown, both by Jabez

---

[24] Milton Nadworny, "Jersey Labor in the Age of Jackson," pp. 58, 59–60, 75–76.

[25] *Working Man's Advocate*, Nov. 7, Dec. 25, 1829.

[26] According to Savetsky, the findings on the property holdings of the General Executive Committee members were based on a careful reading of fourteen volumes of tax rolls for the year 1830 (*loc. cit.*).

Hammond in 1846, and Walter Hugins, in 1960, that the New York Working Men included a wide variety of social and economic types.

The Boston Working Men's party did not last long, but while it lasted it showed no animus toward men of wealth. Years ago I did a study of the social position of the candidates it supported in the municipal election of 1830 and in the state congressional contest of 1831. Their mayoralty candidate, Theodore Lyman, Jr., was a wealthy shipowner, while four of their seven aldermanic candidates were among the wealthiest men in Boston. Thirty-five of their sixty choices for the State Assembly belonged to that elite group whose property was valued in excess of $2,600.[27] Since fewer than two thousand persons in a population of seventy-eight thousand had this amount of property, it would appear that forty of the party's sixty-eight nominees belonged to the wealthiest segment of the community. I must admit, however, that I am now not so sure of what I wrote then, that these figures "do not imply anything fraudulent," and that they reflect "middle class aspirations and a certain naïveté" more than they raise doubts "as to the true workingmen's character" of the Boston Working Men's party.[28] Doubts as to the actual nature of the party are indeed raised by such figures.

Doubts have also been raised by the programs of the Working Men's parties. Joseph Dorfman has not been alone in noting that some of the measures they advocated bore no relation to the economic needs of workingmen. But it is true of course that working-men had needs that ranged beyond the economic. That Working Men's parties raised aloft a standard which included a wide variety of political, social, intellectual, occasionally even religious, as well as economic issues, does not testify necessarily to anything but their breadth of interests and hopes.

The programs of the parties were amazingly similar. For as Miss Sumner observed, "substantially the same measures were advocated by the workingmen in most of the western and southern cities, as well as in New Jersey, Delaware and New England, as were advocated by their comrades in Philadelphia and New York." [29] The program of the Philadelphia Working Men was to become the nucleus of the program everywhere. It included above all a call for a free,

---

[27] These figures are based on the study *List of Persons, Copartnerships and Corporations who were taxed twenty-five dollars and upwards in the City of Boston for the year 1834* (Boston, 1835).

[28] Edward Pessen, "Did Labor Support Jackson? The Boston Story," p. 267.

[29] *Op. cit.,* p. 296.

tax-supported school system to replace the stigmatized "pauper schools," which according to Sullivan provided a "highly partial and totally inadequate system of education for their children." The final copies of the *Mechanic's Free Press* contained on the masthead these additional reforms: abolition of imprisonment for debt; abolition of all licensed monopolies; an entire revision or abolition of the prevailing militia system (the burden of which fell most heavily on workers); a less expensive law system; equal taxation on property; no legislation on religion; a district system of election.[30] In addition, the Philadelphians intermittently protested against the unsanitary and overcrowded housing conditions of workingmen; the high cost of living; the long hours, low wages, and poor conditions of labor, as well as the low esteem in which manual work was held; the hostility of the major parties toward labor; the mistreatment of labor unions; the lottery system—"the fruitful parent of misery and want to numberless heart-broken wives and helpless children, who have beheld the means of their subsistence lavished in the purchase of lottery tickets"; the "pernicious operating of paper money"; and such down-to-earth grievances as insufficient "hydrant water for the accommodation of the poor," and "the failure of the city to clean the streets in the remote sections of the city where the workingmen reside." And earlier they had pressed successfully for the passage of a mechanics' lien law to assure workingmen first claim on their employers' payrolls. Nor does this exhaust the list; from time to time there were criticisms of the sale of liquor, of banks and banking, of charitable institutions, of conspiracy laws as used against unions, the use of prison labor, and the general complexity of the laws and of the legal system.

The Working Men of New York and of other cities did not of course slavishly follow the Philadelphia program, even though they put forward grievances and demands which concentrated on the same essentials.[31] In New York City, for example, Thomas Skidmore early won the Working Men over to support of an "agrarian" program calling for "equal property to all adults," a plank which was supported until the expulsion of Skidmore from the party at the end of 1829. Later, Robert Dale Owen, George Henry Evans, and their supporters championed a unique educational system known as "State

---

[30] Cited in Sullivan, "Philadelphia Labor During the Jackson Era," pp. 9–10.

[31] For a useful and comprehensive modern discussion of the New York program, see Hugins, *op. cit.*

Guardianship," under which working class children not only were to receive an improved education under a tax-supported program but were to board out in the new public schools as well. At one time or another, the party also stressed anticlericalism, compensation for jurors and witnesses, direct election of the mayor, smaller electoral districts, the payment of certain political officials (for the classic reason later emphasized by the English Chartists, that otherwise only wealthy property owners could afford to hold office), reduction of salaries in some cases, civil service reform, abolition of capital punishment, pensions for Revolutionary War veterans, a single municipal legislative chamber, and free trade. With regard to the half dozen or so issues which were more emphasized, the mastheads of the labor journals which proclaimed them could have been interchanged without notable difference. On many occasions the New York *Working Man's Advocate* and the Philadelphia *Mechanic's Free Press* carried precisely the same slogans.

Some programs, as has been indicated, were related to local problems and issues. The New England Association reflected its rural composition by calling for a reform in land tenure laws, and its sympathy with factory operatives by insistence on factory legislation. The Working Men of Boston advocated a reduction of the fees charged by professionals, while calling also for decreases in what were considered exorbitant expenditures of the state government. And in Cincinnati the Working Men added "improvements in the arts and sciences" to the classic appeal for equal universal education and the abolition of licensed monopolies, capital punishment, unequal taxation on property, the prevalent militia system, and imprisonment for debt.

There is no question but that this was a broad program, substantial portions of which were supported by men and groups having nothing to do with labor. Imprisonment for debt, for example, was opposed by many people outside of the Working Men's movement, on broad humanitarian grounds, in some cases, and on grounds of economic inefficiency, in others. Its victims were not always the "laboring poor." Yet it would be an economic determinism of a very rigid sort, indeed, to insist that authentic labor organizations confine their programs to economic issues advantageous only to workers.

Much of the Working Men's program was in fact concerned with the economic interests of labor. Workers did of course seek a larger slice of the pie. But they also sought improved status in society, and some of them organized in order to support the perfectionist demands put forward by their idealistic leaders as the means of achieving this status. The programs of the Working Men's parties reveal them to have been champions of social justice and a truer democracy, as well as critics of every kind of social abuse.

Still other questions as to the authenticity of the Working Men have been raised over the alleged closeness of their relationship with the Jacksonian party. Where Arthur M. Schlesinger, Jr., sees a coalition between the two movements, some critics of his thesis have interpreted the same evidence as indicating the essential fraudulence of the Working Men's parties, which were thus only front organizations for the Democrats. It is perhaps a source of comfort to these critics that their charges are similar to those made one hundred and thirty years ago by some National Republican leaders and publishers.

With regard to this issue, as with others, the evidence is either inconclusive or too complex to permit of black and white generalizations. Assuredly, from time to time and with regard to certain issues, the two movements behaved as one. The organ of the Newark Working Men, the Newark *Village Chronicle and Farmers, Mechanics, and Workingmen's Advocate,* admitted in April of 1830 to its sympathy with the Jacksonians. And there seemed to be more than coincidence in the decision by the two parties in New Jersey that year to hold their nominating conventions for the state legislature in the same small town on the same date. It is not surprising that after the fall elections critics denounced the collusion between the two parties. Five years later the Newark Democrats still evidently depended to a large extent on the political support of the Working Men, while in 1836 the two groups jointly supported a number of legislative candidates. The leading student of the New Jersey Working Men concludes that they consistently supported the Democrats and their candidates.[32]

In New York City the striking political success achieved by the Working Men in 1829 seems to have been the result largely of a shift in the voting habits of people who ordinarily voted for the "Republican" or Jackson party.[33] The New York party broke into several splinter groups shortly after the 1829 election. The so-called *Sentinel* or *Advocate* wing, named after the journals published by Robert Dale Owen and George Henry Evans, supported much of the Democratic program, especially its antimonopoly features. In fact,

---

[32] Nadworny, *loc. cit.,* pp. 55, 68–69, 75.

[33] This is the conclusion of Savetsky, according to whom the Working Men were essentially Democrats grown disenchanted with Tammany (*loc. cit.,* pp. 110, 115).

according to Savetsky, this faction was simply absorbed or assimilated into the New York Jacksonian organization after its defeat in the elections of 1830.[34]

In New England the decision in 1833 of the New England Association to support as their gubernatorial candidate, Samuel Clesson Allen, erstwhile supporter of Andrew Jackson and opponent of the Bank of the United States, led more than one Whig journal to denounce the unholy alliance of Working Men and Jackson men. The same fact is the basis for Schlesinger's conclusion that at this time the Massachusetts Working Men increasingly threw themselves behind Jackson's monetary program.[35] Yet this same New England Association convention urged the formation of a pro labor national political organization. When the Association again nominated Allen for Governor at its last convention in September, 1834, at Northampton, it simultaneously urged rejection of the candidates of the major parties for state office. A close study of its programs, conventions, resolutions, and actions indicates that from its birth in Providence in December, 1831, until its demise not three years later, this organization was little concerned with, let alone sympathetic to, the Democratic party. As for the Boston Working Men's party, it showed no support whatever for the Jacksonian party. Its slate of candidates for the Board of Aldermen and the State House of Representatives included a goodly number of National Republicans.[36] Although its mayoralty candidate, Theodore Lyman, Jr., had worked for Jackson's victory in 1828, he had broken with Old Hickory's party well before the 1830 municipal elections. The nonsupport of the Democrats by the poorer wards in the 1831 elections provoked David Henshaw, Jackson's appointee to the strategic collectorship of the port of Boston, to charge that Boston workingmen were the enemies of the Democratic party. (The evidence indicates that workmen were no great friends to the Working Men's party either.)

In New York City not only Skidmore but Evans, Owen, and

---

[34] *Ibid.*, p. 60.

[35] *The Age of Jackson,* p. 158.

[36] Two of its seven candidates for alderman were National Republicans, according to the Boston *Courier,* Dec. 9, 1830, and the Boston *Daily Advertiser and Patriot,* Dec. 11, 1830. Fifteen of the sixty state candidates were also nominated by the National Republicans, while a number of the remainder were prominent members of the party, according to the *Columbian Centinel,* May 7, 1831.

their supporters as well, regularly voiced their opposition to both major parties. Despite their occasional agreement with the Democrats on a particular issue, their press warned that Jackson had no interest in important reform. If old Hammond can be believed, the men who "flocked to the standard of the Workingmen" in New York were "opposed to the Albany Regency and the Jackson party." [37]

The Philadelphia Working Men had no objections to supporting candidates of whatever social background or political persuasion. Yet their journal saw no contradiction in denying any connection with either of the major parties. In fact, it stressed the danger represented by the Democrats, "for as most of us are deserters from their ranks they view us with the same sensation as the mighty lord would the revolt of his vassals: there cannot be so much danger from the Federalists as, generally speaking, we were never inclined to trust them." [38] In the elections of 1829, the one year in which the Philadelphia Working Men achieved an outstanding success, they combined with the anti-Jacksonians in support of eight local candidates, while endorsing only one Jackson supporter. Sullivan has concluded that "an analysis of the [Philadelphia] Working Men's Party reveals that both in its composition and its predilections, it was amazingly regular in its support of the anti-Jackson forces." [39]

Even for New Jersey the situation was more complex than the allegations of some National Republicans would make it appear. The original platform of the New Jersey Working Men refused to align the group in support of Jackson. As the Working Men of Morris showed in 1834, they had no compunctions about nominating a Whig to office. His success goaded the Democrats into charging that the Whigs used the Working Men as tools! The following year an election rally of Newark's Working Men's party expressly stated that it preferred neither of the major parties. And although in 1836 there was a degree of cooperation between the two groups, before the year was out there was evidently a falling out that may have been due to the Working Men's resentment at being used by the Jackson party.[40]

Two points need to be stressed. The programs of the Working

---

[37] Jabez Hammond, *op. cit.*, p. 331.

[38] *Mechanic's Free Press*, April 12, 1828, cited in Sullivan, "Did Labor Support Andrew Jackson?" p. 571.

[39] Sullivan, "Philadelphia Labor During the Jackson Era," p. 13.

[40] Nadworny, *loc. cit.*, pp. 67, 69–73.

Men's parties called for reforms that in most cases went unmentioned by the Democrats, whether on local, state, or national level. This would indicate that the organizers of the new movement were motivated precisely by the failure of the Democrats—not to mention the National Republicans—to work toward goals that were regarded as of the highest importance. Something new in the form of a Working Men's party was added because it was believed it was needed. In addition, despite the attempt by some historians to treat the political issues and the major parties of the era in striking ideological terms, as though they represented diametrically opposed social and class viewpoints, the facts are otherwise. As Charles Sellers, Glyndon Van Deusen, Bray Hammond, Richard Hofstadter, and others have shown, the major parties had similar views on many important issues, differing more in tactical approaches than in fundamental objectives, with neither party dedicated to a drastic alteration in the fabric of society. Of course there were Democrats and Democrats. But Jackson himself and the leaders of the Democratic party in most of the states, were practical men of pragmatic temper. All of which is to say that it is to misinterpret the nature of the Democratic state machines or the national Democratic party of Andrew Jackson's day, to believe that so loose, opportunistic, all-inclusive, and eclectic a coalition would devote itself to the kinds of reform urged by the Working Men.

What is to be concluded concerning the relationship between the Working Men—led by radicals who often sharply criticized the Democratic party—and Jacksonian Democracy? To the extent that it, too, opposed aristocratic privilege and monopoly, the Working Men's movement may perhaps be interpreted as part of a broadly defined "Jacksonian Revolution." But neither organized nor unorganized workingmen became a fixed part of a Democratic political coalition. And if the Jacksonian movement was in fact a movement primarily devoted to achieving a freer competitive capitalism, the Working Men clearly had demands which went far beyond that objective.[41] Yet, according to the large view which seeks to impose a pattern on an era, reforms of varied character, championed by diverse groups, each seeking the achievement of its own objectives, somehow merge in a broad, all-embracing reform movement. It is

---

[41] See Richard Hofstadter, *The American Political Tradition* (New York, 1948), p. 56; Bray Hammond, *Banks and Politics in America from the Revolution to the Civil War* (Princeton, 1957), *passim;* Joseph Dorfman, *The Economic Mind in American Civilization,* II, chap. xxiii; Richard B. Morris, "Andrew Jackson, Strikebreaker," *Amer. Hist. Rev.,* LV (Oct., 1949), p. 68.

only in this general sense that the Working Men of the Jacksonian era can be said to have been a part of a large, sweeping movement, toward whose political expression—the Democratic party—they often displayed indifference, if not actual hostility.

Examination of the various controversies concerning the authenticity of the Working Men's parties establishes one thing clearly: it is impossible to generalize about the movement, as though its constituent parts were alike in all particulars. The origin of some Working Men's parties was obscure; of others, dubious. Some arose out of economic struggles; others, out of concern for status. Some came to be dominated by opportunists, others by zealots. The only safe generalization perhaps would be that no two parties experienced precisely similar careers.

Yet it is also clear that despite inevitable differences in their circumstances and behavior, these organizations, arising more or less simultaneously and calling for like reforms, had much in common. Common to the Working Men's parties in the major cities was their authenticity—at least for part of their history. By authenticity is meant that they were formed by workers or men devoted to the interests of workers, explicitly sought workers as members or at least supporters, devised programs promoting the causes and welfare of workers, and entered politics in the hope of goading the major parties to concern themselves with important reforms heretofore ignored. The authenticity of the party was not compromised when, evincing no interest in their social status or the size of their bankrolls, it backed candidates who promised support of the Working Men's program or important elements of it. Nor was there anything suspect on those occasions when nonworkers gave their support to portions of the party program.

The origins of the Working Men in Philadelphia, New York City, Newark, and the cities of New England, revealing as they do either the working class backgrounds or aims of the founders, strengthen the belief that the parties were not misnamed. It is true that these parties contained many men who by present definitions would not qualify as workers. But the definition of that earlier day was much more flexible. The prevailing concept was that all who performed "honest toil" were workingmen. Even to such a radical as George Henry Evans, only lawyers, bankers, and brokers could be designated as persons not engaged in the kind of useful occupation qualifying them for membership either in the Working Men's party or the working class. (It is interesting testimony to the growing conservatism of the New York City Working Men that a

NEW PERSPECTIVES ON JACKSONIAN PARTIES AND POLITICS

resolution incorporating Evans' sentiments was defeated as too restrictive. In the fall of 1829, on the other hand, there was strong support for the principle of confining leadership in the party to journeymen and, in Evans' words, denying a vote to any "boss who employed a large number of hands.") Additional light on this issue is thrown by the similar discussion that arose among the Philadelphia Working Men. According to the *Mechanic's Free Press*, early in the party's history, in the summer of 1828, it was decided that while employers might be present at meetings, they could not hold office. Yet one year later its Ricardian Socialist editor, William Heighton, could write: "If an employer superintends his own business (still more if he works with his own hands) he is a working man. . . . If this view of things be correct, shall we look with a jealous eye on those employers who prefer being considered working men? Who are willing to join us in obtaining our objects?" Not only for political candidates but for mere membership in the party, as well, the important issue evidently had become simply whether the man would join in "obtaining our objects."

It is also true that at a certain point in its career the New York party seemed to be in the hands of men who had little sympathy with its expressed program. But these elements infiltrated the party only after its dramatic success in the 1829 elections; and they suc- ceeded in taking it over only by the use of money, intra party in- trigue, extra legal tactics, and newspaper excoriation, accompanied by continuous lip service to reform. The New York Working Men underwent a *transition* that shows that in its heyday it was not only an authentic but also an impressive organization, even frightening to some politicians. Perhaps nothing more dramatically suggests that this and other Working Men's parties were bona fide than the oppo- sition, to put it mildly, they inspired in Democratic and National Re- publican politicians alike, and above all in most of the press. The Boston *Courier* was not alone in arguing that "the very pretension to the necessity of such a party is a libel on the community." The un- derlying thought of the editors, the Buckinghams, was that rich and poor, publishers and lowly typesetters alike, we are all workingmen: therefore, what need was there for a separate Working Men's party?

In the nation's cities a Working Men's party did appear. It burst forth on the political community like a meteor, either electing its candidates or achieving a balance of power on its second try, as in the City of Brotherly Love, or immediately after putting forward its original slate, in other cities. In New York City, for example, a ticket nominated for the State Assembly less than two weeks before the election, elected one and came near to electing several other candidates, amassing better than 6000 out of 21,000 votes cast. And yet in this, as in other cases, the political success was decidedly ephemeral. Decline set in almost immediately, culminating in a few brief years in the party's demise and disappearance.

What accounted for the almost immediate downfall of the Working Men's party? From that day to this, attempts at explanation have not been lacking. Some Philadelphia leaders bitterly blamed workers themselves both for their blindness to their own true interests and for their lack of courage. Other sympathizers attributed party failure to the mistaken policy of supporting wealthy candidates personally sympathetic to monopolies.[42] Thomas Skidmore, himself cashiered out of the New York party for his radical views and his uncompromising way of fighting for them, charged that the party's doom was sealed by its permitting rich men to take over, men who had no business in the party. His onetime opponent Evans later came to agree with him.[43] Hammond also noted that the New York State party contained within its ranks men who made their living doing what they professed to criticize, not excluding banking. By his view, "this party, if it deserves the name of a political party, was too disjointed and composed of materials too heterogeneous to continue long in existence." [44] New York friends of the Boston Working Men's party, on the other hand, attributed its pathetic political showing to preoccupation with issues, such as religious infidelity, that were not properly the concern of a workingmen's political organization.[45]

In her summary of causes for the failure of labor parties, Miss Sumner listed "changes from industrial depression to prosperity which turned the workers' attention from politics to trade unionism"; dissension—"legitimate" when resulting from heterogeneity, "illegitimate" when started and nurtured by "professional politicians of the old parties, who worm themselves into the new party"; the inexperience of the leaders in regard to the practical problems in

---

[42] The columns of the *Mechanic's Free Press* for 1830 and 1831 carry many of these post mortems.

[43] The *Working Man's Advocate*, March 6, and April 17, 1830; *Free Enquirer*, March 20, 1830; the *Radical*, Jan., 1842; the *Friend of Equal Rights*, April 14, 1830, cited in the *Working Man's Advocate*, April 17, 1830.

[44] Jabez Hammond, *op. cit.*

[45] See *Working Man's Advocate* for May, 1831, especially the issue of May 11.

managing a political party; the hostile activities of open enemies of the party; and "the taking up of some of its most popular demands by one of the old parties." [46] The authors of the most recent literature tend to confirm many of her judgments. For New York, both Hugins and Savetsky before him stress the way in which Tammany and the Democrats absorbed the program, especially its antimonopoly features. Savetsky also calls attention to the lack of dynamic and energetic leadership such as might have been provided by a person like Frances Wright—erroneously designated by contemporary opponents of the party as its high priestess, with an eye toward tarring it with the same infidelity brush that was applied to her. Arky emphasizes the Philadelphia party's inept machinery: "For political purposes the movement was clumsily organized." Sullivan stresses the lack of class consciousness of its members, threats made by employers against those who supported it, and above all, the very nature of the party and its candidates. It is the provocative conclusion of Arthur Schlesinger, Jr., that the Working Men disappeared because "their own parties were engaged in kindhearted activity on the periphery of the problem," on such issues as education, imprisonment for debt, and clericalism; whereas the Democrats stressed the core issues that really counted. Thus, "during the Bank War, laboring men began slowly to turn to Jackson as their leader, and his party as their party." [47] Not the least questionable feature of this interpretation is its assumption that the Working Men's parties and "laboring men" were one and the same thing. If most laboring men did not vote for Jackson, it is also sadly true that, apart from a few exceptional cases, at no time did they vote even as a significant minority for the parties organized in their behalf.

It is hard to disagree that their own political ineptness and inexperience, internal bickering, heterogeneous membership, and lack of funds, together with infiltration of their ranks by men interested only in using them, the opposition of the press, and the shrewdness and adaptability of the Democrats, all played an important part in bringing about the downfall of the Working Men. Several related points might also be mentioned. Better than the major parties then or now, the Working Men's party represented the Burkean definition of a political party as a group of men united in behalf of certain

---

[46] *History of Labour*, I, 326.

[47] Schlesinger, Jr., *The Age of Jackson*, p. 143.

political, social, and economic principles. Its membership may have been broad, but the party's program was not all things to all men, a grab bag designed primarily to win office for those who professed to support it. In the American Society of the Tocqueville era such clarity of program worked against the chances of success at the polls.

When the Working Men's party did open its lists to individuals of opposing viewpoints, it failed to shake the following of the traditional parties, which were much more adept at practical politics. Perhaps by this stratagem the party that presumed to speak out for labor fatally blurred its image—at least in the eyes of workingmen.

Speak out the Working Men did, in a message that was idealistic and radical. As the message became clearer, an American public seeking the main chance and increasingly optimistic about its possibilities lost interest in the nay-saying of the radical dissenters who formulated the Working Men's program. It may well be, then, that a reform party was doomed to failure in an American society bemoaned by James Fenimore Cooper—a society in flux, whose characteristic members quivered in anticipation of material fortunes to be made. Such optimism when shared by workers is the stuff that kills off ideological politics.

A final assessment of the Working Men's parties cannot fail to note their significance, notwithstanding their failings and their ephemeral vogue. Immediately after the remarkable showing of the New York Working Men became known, the Democrats promised to pass the lien law that the new party was agitating for. Nor was it a matter of a lien law alone. Even in the short run, the Democrats, in New York and elsewhere, hastily showed greater concern than ever before for the various reform provisions of the Working Men's program.[48] Thus, one of the factors that helped accomplish their disappearance as a separate political entity also was an indication of their strength. If it is the function of radical parties in America to act as gadflies, to goad and influence, rather than win elections, then the Working Men succeeded admirably.

Of course the degree of success they enjoyed is hard to measure.

---

[48] Walter Hugins sees a smashing victory accomplished by the New York State Working Men in 1834, several years after they had formally disbanded as a separate party. In his words, "though forced by circumstances to disband as a political party, the Workingmen had reached the climax of their power and prestige. The party of Jefferson and Jackson had seemingly embraced the principles (antimonopoly) of the party of 'Mechanics and Working Men'"; (*op. cit.*, p. 35).

The Working Men were not alone in championing public education, abolition of imprisonment for debt, banking reform, reform of the militia system, factory laws, general incorporation laws, recognition of labor's right to organize unions, shorter hours of work for labor— to name some of the leading issues. It is impossible to fix with precision their contribution in comparison with that of other individuals and groups who supported one or another of these measures. But there would seem to be no question that the role of the Working Men's parties was an important one, in some cases even greater than is usually believed. In the struggle for the creation of a public school system free from the stigma of charity or pauperism, for example, it has long been the fashion, certainly since Frank Carlton pointed it out, to accord much credit to the Working Men. Yet, as Sidney Jackson has shown, not only did the Working Men agitate for the establishment of such a system but they also advocated sophisticated qualitative measures that seem remarkable for their prescience. Among the changes they sought were an improved curriculum, less concerned with pure memory and "superannuated histories," less emphasis on strict discipline, better physical conditions for children, better trained and better paid teachers, and better equipped schools, free of clerical influences.[49] In sum, Helen Sumner's generous estimate does not seem overdrawn: "The Working Men's party, in short, was a distinct factor in pushing forward measures which even conservative people now recognize to have been in the line of progress toward real democracy." [50]

It has been suggested that one of the factors working against the long-run popularity of the Working Men's party was a radicalism not congenial to opportunistic Americans. But on the other hand, the party's relative popularity, brief though it was, suggests that some of their contemporaries were receptive to the voice of protest. That a Thomas Skidmore, who favored a redistribution of property, could win acceptance as a leader of the New York party, or that the program of the "conservative" Cook-Guyon faction, which came to dominate this party, continued to pay lip service to radical reform, indicate not only that an important minority in the Jacksonian era were disenchanted with their society and its institutions, but that it

---

[49] Sidney Jackson, "Labor, Education and Politics in the 1830's," *Pennsylvania Magazine of History and Biography*, LXVI (July, 1942), 282–284.

[50] *History of Labour*, I, 332.

was considered politic by some astute men to cater or defer to this mood. A final significance then of the Working Men's party lay in the testimony its career afforded that the United States of the Jackson era was not altogether devoid of the sense of alienation that in England and on the continent provided fertile ground for the spread of Owenite, Chartist, Fourierist, and other socialist doctrines.

CARL N. DEGLER*

The Less than Radical Locofocos

Conservative opponents of the Jacksonians had a field day in the mid-1830s, labelling them the "Locofoco" party. For the Locofocos, who were the anti-Tammany wing of the New York City Democracy, had a reputation for extreme radicalism. In actuality this short-lived party had a most stormy relationship with the dominant wing of the Democracy. In this essay Carl N. Degler examines the complex economic beliefs of the notorious faction. He shows that "wedded to private property and profits as they were, the Locofocos were no socialistic opponents of capitalism like the Owenites or Brook Farmers."

𝕩𝕩

I

MOST STUDENTS OF Jacksonian America are familiar with the Locofocos of New York through the interesting and informative history of the party which its secretary, Fitzwilliam Byrdsall, pub-

* From Carl N. Degler, "The Locofocos: Urban 'Agrarians,'" *Journal of Economic History*, XVI (September, 1956), pp. 322–333.

lished in 1842.[1] But Byrdsall himself was primarily interested in the anti-monopoly features of his party's program, and therefore his history all but ignores the even more significant monetary policy of the Locofocos. At the present time in historical writing, it is fashionable to emphasize the role played by the Jacksonian movement as a whole in liberating the expanding American economy from the fetters of a dying mercantilistic approach to business enterprise.[2] There is much to be said for such an interpretation. But the Jacksonians faced toward many meccas, and one of the most articulate and widely known groups which rallied around the Jackson standard —the Locofocos—cannot be trimmed to this pattern.

While the antimonopoly planks of the Locofocos are quite in keeping with the antimercantilistic or "liberating" interpretations often applied to the Jacksonians, the party's monetary principles point in precisely the opposite direction. It is the Locofocos' monetary views which most clearly reveal that the group was not a part of the expansionist pattern currently alleged to be characteristic of the Jacksonian movement. The activities of two Locofoco Assemblymen in the New York legislature of 1837 spell out in unmistakable terms the lack of concern the Locofocos and other hard-money Jacksonians felt for the needs of an expanding economy.

Robert Townsend, Jr., and Clinton Roosevelt were well-known leaders of their party when, with the aid of the Whigs, they were elected to the Assembly in 1836. Townsend, a carpenter by trade, had been active in the General Trade Union Convention of 1834.[3] He became associated with the Locofocos in June 1836, after a protest meeting by the party in support of several workers who had been convicted for striking. Roosevelt was a lawyer by profession and an economist and newspaper editor by avocation. In 1833 he published a pamphlet urging the elimination of the Banking System, as he called it, because it raised prices and thereby permitted foreign

---

[1] F. Byrdsall, *History of the Loco-Foco, or Equal Rights Party* (New York: Clement and Packard, 1842).

[2] See, for example, Fritz Redlich, *Molding of American Banking* (New York: Hafner Publishing Company, 1951), Part I, Chaps. vi and vii; Richard Hofstadter, *American Political Tradition* (New York: Alfred A. Knopf, 1948), Chap. iii.

[3] John R. Commons *et al.*, *History of Labour in the United States* (New York: Macmillan Company, 1926), I, 427–29.

goods to evade the protective tariff.[4] He was also the editor of the Locofoco paper, *Democrat,* which began to appear in 1836.

Though this was the first term which either man served in the legislature, both were active in behalf of their Locofoco principles.[5] Two days after the session opened Roosevelt offered a resolution demanding the formation of a select committee to investigate the banking situation in New York, a move in which he was supported by a petition from his Locofoco constituents.[6] This first effort to inject Locofoco monetary doctrine into the Assembly, however, garnered no results.

Prevented from airing their views on monetary matters, the two Locofoco Assemblymen consistently registered their opposition, in true Locofoco fashion, to the granting of special privileges through acts of incorporation. Again and again they were lone dissenters in votes to incorporate railroad, bridge, or turnpike companies.[7] Insurance companies did not carry the same opprobrium, it would seem, for both voted for them. They also supported the incorporation of schools, a quasi-labor organization (The Tailoresses' and Seamstresses' Benevolent Society in the City of New York), and other cultural and educational enterprises. Townsend, probably cautious after the widespread failures which followed in the wake of the devastating fire of 1835, consistently voted against incorporation of

---

[4] *The Mode of Protecting Domestic Industry, consistently with the desires Both of the South and the North, by operating on the Currency* (New York: McElrath and Bangs, 1833). As will appear later, Roosevelt ultimately succeeded in making these views a part of official Locofoco doctrine.

[5] Joseph Dorfman in his *Economic Mind in American Civilization* (New York: Viking Press, 1946), p. 652, has Roosevelt serving in the 1835 session. This is incorrect and results from confusion between Clinton Roosevelt, who served only in the 1837 legislature, and James J. Roosevelt, who was a member of the 1835 legislature. As a consequence, Dorfman's summary of Roosevelt's activities in the session is in error.

[6] *Journal of the Assembly of the State of New York, Sixtieth Session,* 1837, p. 41; Byrdsall, *History of the Loco-Foco . . . Party,* pp. 114–15.

[7] See *Journal, Sixtieth Session,* 1837, pp. 405–6, 734, 736, 754–55, 910–11, 912–13, 916, 919, 949, 955, for instances of such negative votes. One feature of the chartering of the bridge companies, for instance, which undoubtedly aroused opposition from Roosevelt and Townsend was the granting of monopoly privileges for one mile on either side of the bridge. Both men supported the incorporation of the Lenox Basin and Chenango Canal Turnpike Company, which involved no exclusive privilege provision and also provided that at the termination of the corporation the road was to revert to the public. Chap. 244, *Laws of the Assembly of the State of New York passed at the Sixtieth Session.*

fire insurance companies. Roosevelt, however, seems to have had no such scruples.[8]

This attitude on the part of the two Locofoco legislators is in accord with the general philosophy regarding corporations and "monopolies" usually associated with the "left wing" of the Jacksonian movement. William Leggett, sometimes taken as the spokesman of the Locofoco group in New York although he was never a member of the party, frequently wrote against the granting of exclusive privileges to corporations. As a matter of fact, in implementing his laissez-faire philosophy, he advocated the abolition of all legislatively imposed restrictions upon free entry into business.[9] William Gouge, another talented representative of the Jacksonian left wing, however, placed his emphasis more upon the menace of banks and paper money than upon the threat of monopolistic corporations.[10]

While in the Assembly Townsend and Roosevelt seem to have placed their emphasis where Gouge did, for their main concerns were banking and currency. A resolution instructing the banking committee to report unfavorably upon all applications for bank charters brought ready support from the two Locofocos,[11] but, after five days of argument, the resolution was defeated 70-50.[12] Actually, as the large number of supporters indicates, the measure did no more than question the wisdom of chartering additional banks during a highly speculative period. Neither the banking system nor paper money were in any way threatened. As a consequence,

---

[8] See *Journal, Sixtieth Session*, 1837, pp. 503, 538, 602, 810, 811, for instances of Townsend's solitary dissents from the Assembly on fire insurance companies' incorporations.

[9] See especially Richard Hofstadter, "William Leggett, Spokesman of Jacksonian Democracy," *Political Science Quarterly*, LVIII (December 1943), 581–94, and the *Collection of Political Writings* of Leggett, edited by his friend Theodore Sedgwick and published in 1840. Writers who stress the laissez-faire and even antilabor attitudes of Leggett when he opposed trade unions as characteristic of the Locofocos ignore the party's *Report and Constitution . . . of the Democratic Party* of 1836, in which the Locofocos specifically recognized unions as necessary for the protection of workingmen.

[10] William Gouge, *A Short History of Paper Money and Banking* (Philadelphia, 1833), Part I, p. 45.

[11] This was orthodox Democratic doctrine rather than extreme Locofocism. As early as 1834 Governor Marcy had called attention to the large number of banks being chartered by the legislature and counseled restraint in view of the times. Charles Z. Lincoln, ed., *Messages from the Governors* (Albany, 1909), III, 476.

[12] *Journal, Sixtieth Session*, 1837, pp. 80–81.

fired by a basic opposition to banks of issue, the two Locofocos now pushed for more drastic measures.

Toward the end of January, conscious that his original resolution calling for an investigation of the state banking system was not bearing fruit, Roosevelt moved for a new inquiry. This time the investigation was to examine the over-all economic situation, the constitutionality of paper money, the effect of paper money on trade, and, finally, the comparative merits of paper money and specie. The all-encompassing resolution evoked ridicule from the opposition for being comprehensive enough to include the whole field of economics. Undaunted, Roosevelt replied that such latitude was necessary in order to enable him to introduce his ideas on the subject.[13] The wide powers he asked for were not forthcoming, but a committee, with Roosevelt at its head, was authorized to inquire into the money situation.

On April 14 Roosevelt's committee reported its views on the currency and outlined the measures it thought "should be taken at the present session to reduce the amount of paper money in circulation." [14] The main purpose of the report was to show the evils resulting from a paper money system and the necessity of having only a specie currency. The sole way, the report concluded, in which the depreciation of the currency could be wholly checked was to have a medium of exchange with intrinsic value, such as gold or diamonds. In order to eliminate depreciated money, paper currency would have to be entirely withdrawn. Furthermore—and here Roosevelt echoed an argument reiterated by the hard-money men of the period—the "elasticity of a paper medium" was responsible for the "deep chasm of adversity" which followed each period of prosperity. Earlier William Gouge had called attention to the tendency of the banks to issue notes during speculative booms and to contract their loans and issues when the business tempo slackened, thereby further decelerating business activity. Now, Roosevelt and his committee, like other hard-money men, expressed their concern over the boom-and-bust character of the rocketing American economy.[15]

---

[13] *New York Times,* January 30, 1837.

[14] The report can be found in *Documents of the Assembly of the State of New York, 1837,* No. 302. Cited hereafter as *Report.*

[15] Roosevelt's ideas as put forth in this report are very close to Gouge's and represent a much more detailed analysis and condemnation of the banking system than those put forth earlier in his pamphlet of 1833. Harry E. Miller,

A metallic currency, the committee insisted, would act as a protection, not a hindrance, to American manufacturers. Working on the assumption of the quantity theory of money, the report contended that an excess of paper money inflated prices to the extent that foreign goods were able to circumvent our tariff and undersell the products of American labor.[16] Eliminate the paper currency, the report counseled, and manufactured goods will flow abroad instead of into the country.[17] Here was a convenient wedding of Whig tariff policy and extreme Democratic hard-money views.

Recognizing that paper money could not be abolished immediately, the report went on to recommend a gradual reduction in the amount in circulation. The legislature was urged to reduce the amount of currency in circulation by one third. But because such a contraction of the currency would work a hardship upon debtors, the report further recommended that debts should also be scaled down by one third in order to "correspond with the new value thus to be given the money." And finally, to ensure that the currency reduction would be meaningful, an effort was to be made to restrict the extension of bank credit in a like proportion.[18] The report, needless to say, was tabled.

This report was the major effort of the Locofocos in the Assembly,[19] and it was a concrete implementation of the principles of the party as a whole. In its 1836 Constitution, the Convention of the Locofocos had agreed to "unqualified and uncompromising hostility to bank notes and paper money as a circulating medium, because

---

Banking Theories in the United States Before 1860 (Cambridge: Harvard University Press, 1927), p. 8, observes that the new doctrines regarding banking prevalent in the early nineteenth century "stressed the fluctuations in the value of the monetary standards and bore fruit in discussion of the business cycle."

[16] *Report*, pp. 14–15. This had been the main thesis of Roosevelt's pamphlet of 1833. The doctrine regarding the tariff was rather widely accepted by the Locofocos. See *Democrat*, May 4, 1836, for resolution passed at a Locofoco meeting accepting the principle; *Union* (the Trades' Union's newspaper), June 8, 1836, for labor's acceptance; and *New York Evening Post*, August 18, 1836, for an article, "By a Loco Foco," setting forth the doctrine as a tenet of Locofocism.

[17] *Report*, p. 22.

[18] *Ibid.*, pp. 27–28.

[19] Townsend was in full accord with Roosevelt, for he moved that five times the usual number of copies of the report be printed. *Journal, Sixtieth Session*, 1837, p. 975.

gold and silver is the only safe and constitutional currency." [20] Certainly those who recommended such a drastic cut in the circulating medium and a cancellation of one third of the outstanding debts were friends of neither business nor creditors. Even Gouge, an ardent hard-money man, hesitated to advocate such a Draconian curtailment of paper money. "If the Bank medium," he wrote in his famous book on banking, "should be suddenly reduced only one fourth, the fall of prices would be at least twenty-five percent, and universal embarrassment would be the consequence." [21]

In the war over the Bank of the United States, businessmen had been on both sides of the struggle. Speculators and wildcat bankers had vociferously opposed the Bank because it successfully limited their inflationistic operations. More conservative businessmen and bankers, however, had recognized the advantages to be derived from a central bank of such power and efficiency and had strongly supported Nicholas Biddle's institution. Still other businessmen, like some in New York, had opposed the Bank because it rivaled their own state banking structure. But there were very few businessmen who opposed all banks as such. The drastically deflationary program of the Locofocos transcended the views of all factions of the business community and thereby constituted a threat to all of them. In this respect the Locofocos departed sharply from the expansionist pattern which modern writers have professed to find in the Jacksonian economic philosophy.

II

An analysis of the social composition of the party helps to explain how it was possible for the Locofocos to be at such variance with the prevailing business needs of the day. By means of a statistical analysis, the economic background of the party's supporters is made quite apparent. Generally, as Dixon Ryan Fox has demonstrated,[22] the poorer wards of New York City in the Jackson period voted Democratic. Since the Locofocos sprang from the Democratic ranks, little support for the party was to be expected in the wealthier

---

[20] Byrdsall, *History of the Loco-Foco . . . Party*, pp. 39–40.

[21] Gouge, *History of Paper Money and Banking*, p. 102.

[22] Dixon R. Fox, *The Decline of Aristocracy in the Politics of New York* (New York: Columbia University, 1919), pp. 409–49.

wards. As Table I shows, the strength of the party lay in the poorer wards.[23]

The election returns of 1835 and 1837 give striking evidence of the appeal the Locofocos had for the poor and the mistrust which the party engendered among the wealthy. The Locofocos gained their highest percentages in the election of 1837 in the seven poorest wards, with the exception of the Twelfth, which went Democratic by 69 per cent of the vote cast.[24] Furthermore, a rank-difference correlation of the 1835 vote and the wealthy wards is decidedly negative—over .50—all of which is to be expected when the economic implications of Locofoco doctrine are recognized.

Table I

Ward	Per Capita Personal Estate in 1835	Locofoco % of '35 Vote for Congressman	Locofoco % of '37 Vote for Mayor
1	$2,870	4	2
2	432	11	6
3	732	6	5
4	206	21	8
5	227	11	7
6	259	13	6
7	132	13	11
8	104	20	14
9	54	7	10
10	48	36	28
11	37	13	21
12	103	10	0.5
13	26	22	18
14	148	19	13
15	506	16	6

The apparent tendency of the wealthier wards to oppose Locofoco candidates should not leave the impression that the leadership was drawn from the labor movement. When, years ago, William

[23] Statistics of wealth and election percentages computed from Edwin Williams, *The New York Annual Register* . . . for 1836 and 1837. The statistics of personal wealth are also published in Thomas F. Gordon, *Gazetteer of the State of New York* (Philadelphia, 1836). The total for personal estate in Williams is the same as that given in the 1836 Comptroller's "Annual Report," Table K, Document No. 5, *Documents of the Assembly of the State of New York, 1836.*

[24] The exceptionally high percentage for the Locofocos in the Tenth Ward is partially attributable to the fact that Alexander Ming, Jr., the indefatigable politician of the Locofocos, lived there.

Trimble checked the names of Locofoco leaders against the index of Commons' *Documentary History of American Industrial Society,* he found only 23 names cited, and, of these, he says, only one half were of more than incidental importance in the labor movement of the time. Actually, only three—John Commerford, Levi Slamm, and Robert Townsend, Jr.—were prominent in both the Locofoco party and the trade unions.[25] There is no doubt that the party made appeals[26]—and genuine ones too—to labor, but that is an entirely different question.

An examination of the occupations of the known Locofoco leaders throws light on the social character of this group of Jacksonians. In Byrdsall's history of the party, 142 leaders' names are mentioned. Of these names 31 are not to be found in the directories. Ten additional names have no occupation listed for them, indicating either that no occupation was offered, or that the individual had retired. It is possible, however, to obtain occupational data for all the rest. The total breakdown appears as follows:

Not listed or not identifiable	31
No occupation listed	10
Artisans and mechanics	61
Physicians	9
Grocers	9
Lawyers	7
Government employees	4
Merchants	1
Manufacturers	1
Unclassified (includes 2 teachers, 2 druggists, a bathkeeper, 2 tobacconists, an architect, and an auctioneer)	9
	142

---

[25] William Trimble, "Diverging Tendencies in New York Democracy in the Period of the Loco-Focos," *American Historical Review,* XXIV (April 1919), 399 n.

[26] For example, in June 1836, when a large mass meeting was held in City Hall Park to protest a court decision heavily fining eleven tailors for striking against wage cuts, Locofoco leaders like Ming, Byrdsall, James Stratton, and William Boggs were elected to the Committee of Correspondence set up by the meeting. (*New York Evening Post,* June 14, 1836, and *New York Times,* June 14, 1836.) Out of that committee came the suggestion for a state convention to form a new party. Of the 26 delegates elected from New York City to that convention, 15 were active members of the Locofoco movement prior to the meeting in the Park and 4 more became active Locofocos after the convention. List appears in the *New York Evening Post,* August 19, 1836. The constitution which the convention adopted clearly recognized—and only a year after the Geneva Shoemakers' case—the right of union organization as a legitimate workingmen's demand.

If the identifiable group (101 individuals) is used as the total, it is significant that 60 per cent of the leaders of the Locofocos were artisans and mechanics. The merchants together with the grocers make up about 10 per cent, while the physicians bulk larger in numbers among the leaders than those staunch representatives of economic conservatism—the lawyers. These observations, of course, are not meant to suggest that the Locofocos were primarily proletarian in leadership. Considering the stage of economic development of America in the Jacksonian period, it is naïve and unhistorical to look among the Locofocos for signs of "nascent proletarianism." [27] Moreover, the directories do not distinguish among employed, employing and self-employed craftsmen. Consequently, it is entirely possible that many leaders counted as artisans and mechanics were actually employers or self-employed.[28] That the leaders were predominantly small craftsmen, shop-owners, and workers, rather than lawyers, manufacturers and merchants, seems, from the evidence, indisputable. These little men of business and labor did not identify themselves with the larger business and banking community; they were not concerned with the measures necessary to expand the American economy. They considered themselves essentially consumers who suffered from cheap money and high prices, and they saw no reason why an expanding currency which hurt the consumer, the worker, and the little shop-owner should be tolerated. Regardless of the undoubted constrictive effect upon the larger business community, these little men sought to control inflation by the drastic deflationary device of a metallic currency. It was for this precise reason that the Locofocos thought they saw champions in Andrew Jackson and his successor, Martin Van Buren.

III

The Locofoco defection from the ranks of the Democratic party in 1835 must be viewed as a part of the war upon the Bank of the United States, since the Locofocos were extreme Jacksonians, particularly so on matters of money and banking. Many leading Jacksonians on the national scene, like Jackson himself, Amos Kendall, Roger Taney, Thomas Benton, William Gouge, were committed

---

[27] Trimble, "Diverging Tendencies in New York Democracy . . . ," p. 401.

[28] The labor unions of the period, of course, often included employers in their ranks.

hard-money men. As Jackson admitted to Biddle, "I do not dislike your Bank any more than all Banks." [29] To such men the destruction of the Bank of the United States as a quasi-governmental institution was only a skirmish in a broader war upon the banking and currency system of the time. And for this reason the veto of the Bank bill was followed by a series of executive orders and Congressional acts which attempted to decrease the amount of paper money in circulation. Small notes, at first below five dollars, and then below ten dollars, were declared not receivable for payment of government dues, and government depositories were denied the right to issue notes below five dollars. [30] The climax in Jackson's personal attempt to establish a metallic currency was his Specie Circular of July 1836. [31] Jackson's successor, Van Buren, fully supported by the former President, tried to carry the hard-money policy another step when he suggested, in 1837, the divorce of state and banks under the Independent Treasury System. [32] The Jacksonian leaders on the national level, however, never ventured beyond such halfway measures. Their effort to reduce the amount of paper money and to make the circulating medium almost entirely specie was never even partially attained because the paper money issued by the increasing number of state banks more than filled the monetary void left by the Bank of the United States.

The Locofocos, though, were not satisfied with such mild ef-

---

[29] Quoted in Redlich, *Molding of American Banking*, p. 164. Other authorities like R. Catterall, *Second Bank of the United States* (Chicago: University of Chicago Press, 1903), p. 184, and M. Grace Madeleine, *Monetary and Banking Theories of Jacksonian Democracy* (Philadelphia, 1943), pp. 41–43, have accepted Jackson's position as an attack on the whole banking system and not just one directed against Biddle. In this connection it is important to call attention to the fact that in America, as Professor Redlich has observed, banking had note-issuing as its major form of credit extension (*Molding of American Banking*, pp. 10–13). Hence an attack on banks was an attack on paper money.

[30] A. M. Schlesinger, Jr., *Age of Jackson* (Boston: Little, Brown, 1945), p. 128. Margaret Myers in *New York Money Market* (New York: Columbia University Press, 1931), I, 16, called the prohibition a "logical outgrowth of his [Jackson's] growing hostility to the use of bank credit . . ."

[31] Earlier in 1836, Senator Thomas Benton, aroused by the host of new state banks, introduced a resolution making only specie acceptable for public-land purchases, but it failed of passage. W. G. Sumner, *Andrew Jackson* (Boston: Houghton Mifflin, 1910), p. 393.

[32] Jackson's so-called Farewell Address—to be found in J. D. Richardson, ed., *Messages and Papers of the Presidents* (n. p., 1909), III, 304–6—contained a strong and forthright statement of the hard-money views he had adopted by 1837.

forts, as we have seen. Their program boldly called for the total abolition of banks of issue, which they felt defrauded workers and consumers through depreciated currency[33] and brought about depressions by erratic currency expansion and contraction. The Locofocos here were carrying out faithfully the precepts of William Gouge and other hard-money antibank theoreticians of the Jacksonian left wing.

These monetary principles of the Locofocos and hard-money Jacksonians in general had serious consequences and implications for the future development of the American economy. Historians of early American banking have assured us that the "dearth of cash capital" in this country produced a scramble for capital because opportunities, ideas, and natural resources abounded, crying out for exploitation.[34] To help provide the much sought-after capital, Alexander Hamilton had enlisted the power and resources of the Federal government through the agency of financial devices like the Bank of the United States. As Hamilton had foreseen, industrial-commercial capitalism in the early decades of the Republic needed government aid and encouragement if it was to expand and develop rapidly. Conversely, those who opposed the metamorphosing of agrarian America into an industrial-commercial nation quite naturally turned to the doctrine of laissez faire as their intellectual weapon. Notable in this regard were agrarians like Thomas Jefferson and John Taylor of Carolina.

When Jackson destroyed the Bank of the United States he was following the agrarian demand for the severance of the connection Hamilton had established between the commercial community and the Federal government. Under the Jacksonians even use of the government deposits was denied the business community. Government aid to business enterprise was to cease, and a contraction of the currency was to be substituted for a much needed expansion.

---

[33] See Leggett's *Writings*, I, 43, 226–27 for editorials exposing the employers' practice of buying depreciated currency with which to pay their workmen. As late as 1850 payment of workers with such devalued money was a labor grievance, for in that year the Printers' Union cited it as an evil of the trade. *New York Evening Post*, May 23, 1850.

[34] Bray Hammond, "Long and Short Term Credit in Early American Banking," *Quarterly Journal of Economics*, XLIX (November 1934), 82. See also Miller, *Banking Theories . . .* , pp. 18–19. Carter Goodrich in "National Planning of Internal Improvements," *Political Science Quarterly*, LXIII (March 1948), points out that during the early nineteenth century the shortage of private capital required government to advance subsidies in order to open lines of transportation.

But the assault upon the Hamiltonian system made by the Jacksonians fell far short of completion, for in place of the defeated "monster" there arose scores of state banks to provide much cheap, if unstable, paper money. Unable to halt the drive toward the new economic order, the Jacksonians only impeded commercial and industrial development by substituting an inadequate financial system for one "as good as any the country ever possessed." [35] As Professor W. B. Smith has observed, they pushed American banking theory and practice from a place at the head of the Western nations to one at the rear.[36]

It was left to the Locofocos, however, to spell out and thereby reveal the essentially agrarian implications of the Jacksonian monetary ideas. In an America starved for capital and credit, the doctrines and utterances of the Locofocos could only be viewed with anger and alarm by the commercial community. The almost total absence of bankers, merchants, and lawyers among the Locofoco leadership underscores the serious threat the party's monetary principles offered to the business community.[37] It was the deflationary monetary principles of the Locofocos which seemed so dangerous to the Whig businessmen of the time, as President Van Buren found in August 1837 when he publicly advocated the severance of all connections between the banks and the Federal government. "The message of Mr. Van Buren," commented the *New York Courier and Enquirer,* "is the document that might have been expected . . . embodying in specious phrase and thin-veiled sophistry the most pernicious doctrines of Loco Focoism . . . The president in his message assumed all the positions of ultra Loco Focoism." [38]

Wedded to private property and profits as they were, the Locofocos were no socialistic opponents of capitalism like the Owenites or Brook Farmers. But by advocating deflationary doctrines in a society working to expand its businesses, industries, and enterprises,

---

[35] Bray Hammond, "Jackson, Biddle, and the Bank of the United States," THE JOURNAL OF ECONOMIC HISTORY, VII (May 1947), 20.

[36] W. B. Smith, *Economic Aspects of the Second Bank of the United States* (Cambridge: Harvard University Press, 1953), p. 263.

[37] For two examples of animosity toward the Locofocos because of their dangerous character, see the article signed "Vigilance" in *New York Times,* September 14, 1837, and the quotation from *Madisonians,* (the right-wing Democratic newspaper) in *New York Evening Post,* September 29, 1837. William Trimble, "The Social Philosophy of the Locofoco Democracy," *American Journal of Sociology,* XXVI (May 1921), 711–12, gives further examples.

[38] Quoted in *New York Evening Post,* September 7, 1837.

they threatened the economic way of life of their time. Their brand of hard money would help few businessmen and would open up precious few opportunities in a credit-hungry economy.

Bray Hammond pointed out a few years ago in THE JOURNAL OF ECONOMIC HISTORY[39] that the Western states, which he labeled "agrarian," were not as avid for banks and cheap money as has been commonly alleged. Their restrictions and prohibitions on banking and money, he said, signify their continuing connection with the old economic precepts of John Taylor and William Gouge. It might be further observed here that the West was not the only agrarian area in this respect: New York City in the era of Jackson and Van Buren also had "agrarians"—the Locofocos. A better term would be "opponents of industrialism." For, in the last analysis, all hard-money Jacksonians were knit together by a common principle. All of them opposed the developing commercial-industrial order that was fast displacing the simpler and supposedly more humane agrarian society which had been the America of the Declaration of Independence and Equal Rights.[40]

---

[39] Bray Hammond, "Banking in the Early West: Monopoly, Prohibition, and Laissez-Faire," THE JOURNAL OF ECONOMIC HISTORY, VIII (May 1948), 1–25.

[40] Cf. Walter Hugins, "Ely Moore: the Case History of a Jacksonian Labor Leader," *Political Science Quarterly*, LXV (March 1950), 105–25, who writes: "America's chief heritage from Jacksonian Democracy was not a growth of a militant labor movement, but the economic exploitation of a continent" (p. 125). One may agree with the first conclusion, but the second ignores the Locofocos, a group hardly nurturing capitalist expansion.

PART IV
PARTY CONTESTS AND ISSUES

SIDNEY H. ARONSON*

Jackson's Political Appointments

In all of the controversy that has raged over Jackson's "spoils system," it has been widely believed that the insiders he installed in office were plain if not highly talented men. Sidney H. Aronson shows that this was not the case for the several hundred most important appointive positions that made up what Aronson calls the civil service elite. The Jacksonian "appointments ideology" may have been egalitarian. The Jackson appointments practice was not. The significant Jacksonian legacy, according to Aronson, was less the policy of democratic appointments than the reputation the Jackson Administration had for making such appointments.

xxxxxxxxxxxxxxxxxxxxxxxxxxxxxxxxxxxxxxxxxxxxxxxxxxxxxxxxxxxxxxx

IT HAS BEEN suggested that Jackson was not genuinely committed to democratic goals; if so, this would help to account for the modest change in the social composition of Jackson's elite.[1] The

* Reprinted by permission of the publishers from Sidney H. Aronson, *Status and Kinship in the Higher Civil Service* (Cambridge, Mass.: Harvard University Press), pp. 192–199. Copyright, 1964, by the President and Fellows of Harvard College.

[1] Thomas P. Abernethy, *From Frontier to Plantation in Tennessee* (Chapel Hill, 1932), 248–249.

evidence dealing with appointments does not show that Jackson used democratic ideas for political purposes only. It was not yet the custom to campaign for election, and the promise to replace the old aristocracy of officeholders was presented in his first inaugural address.[2] Since he had originally planned to serve for only one term, such views were not aimed at re-election.[3] By the time he had decided to run again, he believed that the necessary reform of the civil service had been effected, and his interests switched to the dispute over the Second Bank of the United States. In addition, the desire to reform the civil service permeated much of Jackson's private correspondence during the period just before and after his election.[4] Indeed, the only motive for his serving seemed to be his desire to reform the government, whose liberties he felt had become endangered by the administration of John Quincy Adams.[5]

But reform meant several things to Jackson. First, it meant getting rid of the old aristocracy of officeholders. Second, it meant appointing men drawn from all strata in American society: "The road to office and preferment," he said, "is accessible alike to the rich and poor, the farmer and the printer." [6] Third, it meant appointing competent and honest men so that republican efficiency could be restored to the civil service. Honesty had become an indispensable requirement for officeholders, since Jackson believed that corruption had been common in the previous administration. "You will see from the public journals," he wrote, "we have begun reform, and that we are trying to clean the augean stables, and expose to view the corruption of some of the agents of the late administration." [7]

Although Jackson believed that honest and capable men could be found among average persons, circumstances made it difficult for him to locate such men in the crowd. He did not reckon on the unprecedented demand for office which followed his election.

---

[2] James, *Andrew Jackson*, 160; James O. Richardson, Comp., *A Compilation of the Messages and Papers of the Presidents* (Washington, D. C., 1908), II, 438.

[3] Bassett, *Andrew Jackson*, II, 541.

[4] See, for example, letters from Jackson to Rev. Hardy M. Cryer, May 16, 1829, and to Brigadier-General John Coffee, May 30, 1829, John S. Bassett, ed., *Correspondence of Andrew Jackson* (Washington, D. C., 1926–1935), IV, 33, 39.

[5] Jackson to Captain John Donelson, June 7, 1829, *ibid.*, IV, 42.

[6] Jackson to T. L. Miller, May 13, 1829, *ibid.*, IV, 32.

[7] Jackson to Coffee, May 30, 1829, *ibid.*, IV, 39.

He was hounded by hordes of job-seekers. "The most disagreeable duty I have to perform is the removals, and appointments to office," he wrote a few days after assuming the presidency.[8] "I have been crowded with thousands of applicants for office, and if I had a tit for every applicant to suck the Treasury pap, all would go away well satisfied, but as there are not office for more than one out of 500 who applies, many must go away dissatisfied." [9]

Significantly, Jackson ruled out any random selection from the mob of applicants. "These hungry expectants," he wrote, "are dangerous contestants over the public purse, unless possessed of the purest principles of integrity, and honesty." [10] Selection became all the more difficult because "any and every man can get recommendations of the strongest kind, it requires great circumspection to avoid imposition, and select honest men." [11] Because there did not seem to be any practical way of locating common men of talent and because of his determination to have an efficient and honest operation of the government, Jackson was forced to fall back on the same criteria his predecessors used—education, family reputation, previous positions of political leadership, eminence. Just as Jefferson before him must have come to realize, Jackson learned that the connections between high social status and high political roles were not so easily severed, after all.

What conclusions can be drawn about the influence of the appointment ideologies of Adams, Jefferson, and Jackson on the social-class backgrounds of the elite members? As far as Adams is concerned, the answer is fairly obvious. The President who believed that the country should be governed by the people who owned it was most likely to appoint the rich and wellborn to office. By most of the criteria used to measure social origins and social status Federalists ranked first. Of the thirteen indicators presented in Table 48, Federalists led on twelve. Furthermore, on the thirteenth —the proportions of positions filled by men who had high-ranking occupations prior to appointment—there was little difference between the elites. The relationship between ideas about appointments and the actual appointments is most evident in Adams' elite.

---

[8] *Ibid.*

[9] Jackson to Coffee, March 22, 1829, *ibid.*, IV, 14.

[10] Jackson to Coffee, May 30, 1829, *ibid.*, IV, 39.

[11] *Ibid.*

The degree of correspondence between the ideologies of Jefferson and Jackson and their appointment policies is not as great. Jefferson had called for an aristocracy of talent and education rather than one of wealth and lineage. However, at a time when less than two Americans out of a thousand went to college this insistence on college men seemed to imply that Jefferson was in effect looking for the old aristocracy. For this reason it could be predicted that in their social composition Jeffersonian elite members would not be different from Federalists.

Table 48. Summary of distributions of social-status characteristics.

Characteristic	Adams (N = 96) Per cent	Jefferson (N = 100) Per cent	Jackson (N = 127) Per cent
Father of high-ranking occupation	70	60	53
Father held political office	52	43	44
Father attended college	17	13	12
Class I social-class origins	62	58	51
High-ranking occupation	92	93	90
Political office prior to appointment	91	83	88
Class I social-class position	86	74	75
Member of voluntary association	50	41	39
Officer in military	52	39	32
Family in America in seventeenth century	55	48	48
Attended college	63	52	52
Professional training	69	74	81
Relative in appointive elite	40	34	34

But apparently there was a difference between the aristocracies of wealth and education. Not all the college men in Jefferson's elite were of high origins, nor, for that matter, were all the college men in Adams' elite from aristocratic families. But more important, it turned out that Jefferson was less insistent than Adams on a college education as a prerequisite to appointment, and fewer positions in his elite were filled by such men. Furthermore, there were several other status differences between Federalists and Jeffersonians. Of the thirteen indicators appearing in Table 48, Jeffersonians were nearer to or identical with the Jacksonians rather than the Federalists ten times; twice they were closer to the Federalists, and, as noted, in one instance there was virtually no difference between the elites. Seven times Jeffersonians and Jacksonians were either identical or there was only a 1 or 2 per cent difference between them; four times the differences between Jeffersonians and Jacksonians indicated higher status or training for the Jacksonians. Federalists and Jeffersonians were clearly not identical. But this in turn means that Jefferson's egalitarian appointment ideology was related to his appointment policy; by making a start toward taking men of merit wherever they were located in the social class order, Jefferson did make the elite somewhat more representative of American society than it had been.

Jefferson's record is all the more significant in view of the fact that in 1800 property qualifications for voting and office-holding were the rule in most of the states. Although the Constitution did not make ownership of property a condition of appointment to federal office, a President who wanted to appoint men who were politically experienced would have to turn to men of property. By 1829, however—thanks largely to Jeffersonian Democracy—property qualifications had been swept away, with the result that Jackson had complete freedom to bring his appointment policy in line with his democratic appointment ideology, which went well beyond Jeffersonianism because of Jackson's insistence on common men rather than men of education.[12]

And, in fact, Jackson's elite was somewhat more representative of the American population than that of Jefferson. Yet it is also evident from Table 48 that the radical change which is supposed to have followed his election did not occur at the elite level. At the time of appointment there was no important difference between Jacksonians and the members of the other two elites in the proportions of positions filled by men of high-ranking occupations. Furthermore, in seven cases no important differences separated Jacksonians from Jeffersonians; in the case of holding political office prior to appointment, Jacksonians were almost identical with the Federalists, and once—in professional training—they led the Federalists and Jeffersonians. Thus Jackson's attempt to democratize the elite fell far short of his goal; Jacksonian Democracy, it must be concluded, represented not a radical departure from Jeffersonianism, but rather a logical and moderate extension of the earlier political movement.

But Jefferson and Jackson did start a trend toward more representative elites, and their egalitarian ideas played a role in that

---

[12] John A. Krout and Dixon R. Fox, *The Completion of Independence* (New York, 1944), 133; Kirk H. Porter, *A History of Suffrage in the United States* (Chicago, 1918), 35, 54; Marvin Meyers, *The Jacksonian Persuasion* (Stanford, 1957), 182, 188–189; Chilton Williamson, *American Suffrage from Property to Democracy, 1760–1860* (Princeton, 1960), 138 ff.

process. Of course, the existence of ideological egalitarianism does not automatically guarantee that everyone will have an equal chance to get appointed to high government office. At no time did Jefferson or Jackson make an effort to find men of lowly origins or status to fill some office in the elite—nor can it be said that either one disqualified a man because he was a member of the aristocracy. Nor would it be accurate to say that Adams ruled out an otherwise qualified man because he was of lowly origins. Indeed, the egalitarian ideologies, by bringing forward armies of applicants in both Republican administrations, threw Jefferson and Jackson back on the same qualities Adams sought, qualities normally associated with high status. Jefferson and Jackson may have held different ideas about the role of social class in politics than Adams, but they shared with him ideas that stressed the absolute necessity of honesty and efficiency in government. It was for this reason that they were forced to use the same standard utilized by Adams, and by so doing they separated the upper classes from the common people.

The fact that both Jefferson and Jackson were leaders of opposition parties which had attracted much popular support seems to have played a role in bringing about the changes in the composition of the elites. In the first place, the appearance of an opposition party reduced somewhat the hereditary character of the elites. Members of the same family share the same values and some of these values deal with political ideas and political affiliations. By discriminating against the members of the parties that had been in power and by making appointments primarily from their own ranks, Jefferson and Jackson made government less of a family affair.

Perhaps as important is the fact that the Republican party tended to attract the have-nots in American society, men whose interests were neglected by the aristocratic Federalists and by the old Jeffersonian Republican party, which had lost its revolutionary enthusiasm by 1829. By limiting appointments to members of the new parties, Jefferson and Jackson increased the probability of appointing men of lower origins, since there was a larger proportion of such men in that party than in the other. By insisting on Republicans, for example, Jefferson seems to have increased the proportion of noncollege men in his elite. In Jackson's case, the higher proportion of people of lowly origins seems to have been the result of the fact that he made more appointments than any of his predecessors, and by making them primarily from the party which attracted the lower classes he increased the probability of getting men of lowly origins into his elite.

It may be that the most important consequence of the egalitarian ideologies was their influence on the development of democracy in later political generations. Jacksonian Democracy developed from Jeffersonian Democracy and extended it. Jeffersonianism removed the legal restrictions which had prevented the propertyless from voting and from holding office. Jacksonianism, by expending great effort in the area of education, succeeded in winning acceptance for free, tax-supported schools for all Americans, and thus made it possible for the newly enfranchised masses to pick up the training so essential for the performance of high political roles. The extension of democracy to the area of education apparently occurred too late to have been of much use to Jackson himself— although his college men were of lower origins than those in the other two elites—but it would be instrumental in furthering the political power of the average man when the practice became established of filling jobs by examination rather than by the traditional criteria which had always discriminated against the common people.

Jeffersonianism made the common man eligible for high office; Jacksonianism made it possible for him to receive the training required to run that office. But Jackson made one further contribution: although he did not succeed in democratizing the elite, everyone thought he had. Furthermore, Americans generally felt that Jackson's successors should do as he had done. If any of them achieved a moderate degree of success it was largely because they felt compelled to follow the lead of Andrew Jackson.

MARY E. YOUNG*†

Indian Removal and Jacksonian Justice

Perhaps the greatest gulf between Jacksonian preachment and per-
formance was to be found in its Indian policy. In this balanced and
judicious article, Professor Young exposes the illogic and the inconsis-
tencies that marked both the theory and the practice of Old Hickory's
Administration with regard to this issue. The Jacksonian policy was neither
corrupt nor inspired by an anti-Indian animus. From the viewpoint of the
Indians, Jackson's undeviating commitment to Indian removal west of the
Mississippi was even more dangerous than a less intransigent if more
venal policy would have been.

⊠⊠

BY THE YEAR 1830, the vanguard of the southern frontier had
crossed the Mississippi and was pressing through Louisiana, Ar-
kansas, and Missouri. But the line of settlement was by no means
as solid as frontier lines were classically supposed to be. East of the

---

*From Mary E. Young, "Indian Removal and Land Allotment: The
Civilized Tribes and Jacksonian Justice," *American Historical Review,* LXIV
(October, 1958), pp. 31–45.

† This article, in slightly different form, was delivered as a paper at the joint
meeting of the Southern Historical Association and the American Historical
Association in New York City, December 29, 1957.

Mississippi, white occupancy was limited by Indian tenure of northeastern Georgia, enclaves in western North Carolina and southern Tennessee, eastern Alabama, and the northern two thirds of Mississippi. In this twenty-five-million-acre domain lived nearly 60,000 Cherokees, Creeks, Choctaws, and Chickasaws.[1]

The Jackson administration sought to correct this anomaly by removing the tribes beyond the reach of white settlements, west of the Mississippi. As the President demanded of Congress in December, 1830: "What good man would prefer a country covered with forests and ranged by a few thousand savages to our extensive Republic, studded with cities, towns, and prosperous farms, embellished with all the improvements which art can devise or industry execute, occupied by more than 12,000,000 happy people, and filled with all the blessings of liberty, civilization, and religion?"[2]

The President's justification of Indian removal was the one usually applied to the displacement of the Indians by newer Americans—the superiority of a farming to a hunting culture, and of Anglo-American "liberty, civilization, and religion" to the strange and barbarous way of the red man. The superior capacity of the farmer to exploit the gifts of nature and of nature's God was one of the principal warranties of the triumph of westward-moving "civilization."[3]

Such a rationalization had one serious weakness as an instrument of policy. The farmer's right of eminent domain over the lands of the savage could be asserted consistently only so long as the tribes involved were "savage." The southeastern tribes, however, were agriculturists as well as hunters. For two or three generations prior to 1830, farmers among them fenced their plantations and "mixed their labor with the soil," making it their private property according to accepted definitions of natural law. White traders who settled among the Indians in the mid-eighteenth century gave original impetus to this imitation of Anglo-American agricultural methods. Later, agents of the United States encouraged the traders and

---

[1] Ellen C. Semple, *American History and Its Geographic Conditions* (Boston, Mass., 1933), p. 160; Charles C. Royce, "Indian Land Cessions in the United States," Bureau of American Ethnology, *Eighteenth Annual Report, 1896–1897* (2 vols., Washington, D. C., 1899), II, Plates 1, 2, 15, 48, 54–56.

[2] James Richardson, *A Compilation of the Messages and Papers of the Presidents of the United States* (New York, 1897), III, 1084.

[3] Roy H. Pearce, *The Savages of America: A Study of the Indian and the Idea of Civilization* (Baltimore, Md., 1953), p. 70; *House Report* 227, 21 Cong., 1 sess., pp. 4–5.

mechanics, their half-breed descendants, and their fullblood imitators who settled out from the tribal villages, fenced their farms, used the plow, and cultivated cotton and corn for the market. In the decade following the War of 1812, missionaries of various Protestant denominations worked among the Cherokees, Choctaws, and Chickasaws, training hundreds of Indian children in the agricultural, mechanical, and household arts and introducing both children and parents to the further blessings of literacy and Christianity.[4]

The "civilization" of a portion of these tribes embarrassed United States policy in more ways than one. Long-term contact between the southeastern tribes and white traders, missionaries, and government officials created and trained numerous half-breeds. The half-breed men acted as intermediaries between the less sophisticated Indians and the white Americans. Acquiring direct or indirect control of tribal politics, they often determined the outcome of treaty negotiations. Since they proved to be skillful bargainers, it became common practice to win their assistance by thinly veiled bribery. The rise of the half-breeds to power, the rewards they received, and their efforts on behalf of tribal reform gave rise to bitter opposition. By the mid-1820's, this opposition made it dangerous for them to sell tribal lands. Furthermore, many of the new leaders had valuable plantations, mills, and trading establishments on these lands. Particularly among the Cherokees and Choctaws, they took pride in their achievements and those of

---

[4] Moravian missionaries were in contact with the Cherokees as early as the 1750's. Henry T. Malone, *Cherokees of the Old South: A People in Transition* (Athens, Ga., 1956), p. 92. There is a voluminous literature on the "civilization" of the civilized tribes. Among secondary sources, the following contain especially useful information: Malone, *Cherokees;* Marion Starkey, *The Cherokee Nation* (New York, 1946); Angie Debo, *The Rise and Fall of the Choctaw Republic* (Norman, Okla., 1934) and *The Road to Disappearance* (Norman, Okla., 1941); Grant Foreman, *Indian Removal: The Emigration of the Five Civilized Tribes of Indians* (2d ed., Norman, Okla., 1953); Robert S. Cotterill, *The Southern Indians: The Story of the Civilized Tribes before Removal* (Norman, Okla., 1954); Merrit B. Pound, *Benjamin Hawkins, Indian Agent* (Athens, Ga., 1951). Among the richest source material for tracing the agricultural development of the tribes are the published writings of the Creek agent, Benjamin Hawkins: *Letters of Benjamin Hawkins, 1796–1806* in Georgia Historical Society *Collections, IX* (Savannah, 1916), and *Sketch of the Creek Country in the Years 1798 and 1799* in Georgia Historical Society *Publications,* III, (Americus, 1938). For the Choctaws and Cherokees, there is much information in the incoming correspondence of the American Board of Commissioners for Foreign Missions, Houghton Library, Harvard University. On the Chickasaws, see James Hull, "A Brief History of the Mississippi Territory," Mississippi Historical Society *Publications,* IX, (Jackson, 1906).

their people in assimilating the trappings of civilization. As "founding Fathers," they prized the political and territorial integrity of the newly organized Indian "nations." These interests and convictions gave birth to a fixed determination, embodied in tribal laws and intertribal agreements, that no more cessions of land should be made. The tribes must be permitted to develop their new way of life in what was left of their ancient domain.[5]

Today it is a commonplace of studies in culture contact that the assimilation of alien habits affects different individuals and social strata in different ways and that their levels of acculturation vary considerably. Among the American Indian tribes, it is most often the families with white or half-breed models who most readily adopt the Anglo-American way of life. It is not surprising that half-breeds and whites living among the Indians should use their position as go-betweens to improve their status and power among the natives. Their access to influence and their efforts toward reform combine with pressures from outside to disturb old life ways, old securities, and established prerogatives. Resistance to their leadership and to the cultural alternatives they espouse is a fertile source of intra-tribal factions.[6]

To Jacksonian officials, however, the tactics of the half-breeds and the struggles among tribal factions seemed to reflect a diabolical plot. Treaty negotiators saw the poverty and "depravity" of the common Indian, who suffered from the scarcity of game, the missionary attacks on his accustomed habits and ceremonies, and the ravages of "demon rum" and who failed to find solace in the values of Christian and commercial civilization. Not unreasonably, they concluded that it was to the interest of the tribesman to remove west of the Mississippi. There, sheltered from the intruder and the

---

[5] Paul W. Gates, "Introduction," *The John Tipton Papers* (3 vols., Indianapolis, Ind., 1942), I, 3–53; A. L. Kroeber, *Cultural and Natural Areas of Native North America* (Berkeley, Calif., 1939), pp. 62–63; John Terrell to General John Coffee, Sept. 15, 1829, Coffee Papers, Alabama Dept. of Archives and History; Campbell and Merriwether to Creek Chiefs, Dec. 9, 1824, *American State Papers: Indian Affairs*, II, 570; Clark, Hinds, and Coffee to James Barbour, Nov. 19, 1826, *ibid.*, p. 709.

[6] See for example, Edward M. Bruner, "Primary Group Experience and the Processes of Acculturation," *American Anthropologist*, LVIII (Aug., 1956), 605–23; SSRC Summer Seminar on Acculturation, "Acculturation: An Exploratory Formulation," *American Anthropologist*, LVI (Dec., 1954), esp. pp. 980–86; Alexander Spoehr, "Changing Kinship Systems: A Study in the Acculturation of the Creeks, Cherokee, and Choctaw," Field Museum of Natural History, *Anthropological Series*, XXXIII, no. 4, esp. pp. 216–26.

whisky merchant, he could lose his savagery while improving his nobility. Since this seemed so obviously to the Indian's interest, the negotiators conveniently concluded that it was also his desire. What, then, deterred emigration? Only the rapacity of the half-breeds, who were unwilling to give up their extensive properties and their exalted position.[7]

These observers recognized that the government's difficulties were in part of its own making. The United States had pursued an essentially contradictory policy toward the Indians, encouraging both segregation and assimilation. Since Jefferson's administration, the government had tried periodically to secure the emigration of the eastern tribes across the Mississippi. At the same time, it had paid agents and subsidized missionaries who encouraged the Indian to follow the white man's way. Thus it had helped create the class of tribesmen skilled in agriculture, pecuniary accumulation, and political leadership. Furthermore, by encouraging the southeastern Indians to become cultivators and Christians, the government had undermined its own moral claim to eminent domain over tribal lands. The people it now hoped to displace could by no stretch of dialectic be classed as mere wandering savages.[8]

By the time Jackson became President, then, the situation of the United States vis-à-vis the southeastern tribes was superficially that of irresistible force and immovable object. But the President, together with such close advisers as Secretary of War John H. Eaton and General John Coffee, viewed the problem in a more encouraging perspective. They believed that the government faced not the intent of whole tribes to remain near the bones of their ancestors but the selfish determination of a few quasi Indian leaders to retain their riches and their ill-used power. Besides, the moral right of the civilized tribes to their lands was a claim not on their whole domain but rather on the part cultivated by individuals. Both the Indian's natural right to his land and his political capacity for keeping it

[7] Wilson Lumpkin, *The Removal of the Cherokee Indians from Georgia* (2 vols., New York, 1907), I, 61–77; Thomas L. McKenney to James Barbour, Dec. 27, 1826, *House Doc.* 28, 19 Cong., 2 sess., pp. 5–13; Andrew Jackson to Colonel Robert Butler, June 21, 1817, *Correspondence of Andrew Jackson,* ed. John Spencer Bassett (6 vols., Washington, D. C., 1926–28), II, 299.

[8] For brief analyses of government policy, see Annie H. Abel, "The History of Events Resulting in Indian Consolidation West of the Mississippi," *Annual Report of the American Historical Association for the Year 1907* (2 vols., Washington, D. C., 1908), I, 233–450; George D. Harmon, *Sixty Years of Indian Affairs, 1789–1850* (Chapel Hill, N. Car., 1941).

were products of his imitation of white "civilization." Both might be eliminated by a rigorous application of the principle that to treat an Indian fairly was to treat him like a white man. Treaty negotiations by the tried methods of purchase and selective bribery had failed. The use of naked force without the form of voluntary agreement was forbidden by custom, by conscience, and by fear that the administration's opponents would exploit religious sentiment which cherished the rights of the red man. But within the confines of legality and the formulas of voluntarism it was still possible to acquire the much coveted domain of the civilized tribes.

The technique used to effect this object was simple: the entire population of the tribes was forced to deal with white men on terms familiar only to the most acculturated portion of them. If the Indian is civilized, he can behave like a white man. Then let him take for his own as much land as he can cultivate, become a citizen of the state where he lives, and accept the burdens which citizenship entails. If he is not capable of living like this, he should be liberated from the tyranny of his chiefs and allowed to follow his own best interest by emigrating beyond the farthest frontiers of white settlement. By the restriction of the civilized to the lands they cultivate and by the emigration of the savages millions of acres will be opened to white settlement.

The first step dictated by this line of reasoning was the extension of state laws over the Indian tribes. Beginning soon after Jackson's election, Georgia, Alabama, Mississippi, and Tennessee gradually brought the Indians inside their borders under their jurisdiction. Thus an Indian could be sued for trespass or debt, though only in Mississippi and Tennessee was his testimony invariably acceptable in a court of law. In Mississippi, the tribesmen were further harassed by subjection—or the threat of subjection—to such duties as mustering with the militia, working on roads, and paying taxes. State laws establishing county governments within the tribal domains and, in some cases, giving legal protection to purchasers of Indian improvements encouraged the intrusion of white settlers on Indian lands. The laws nullified the legal force of Indian customs, except those relating to marriage. They provided heavy penalties for anyone who might enact or enforce tribal law. Finally, they threatened punishment to any person who might attempt to deter another from signing a removal treaty or enrolling for emigration. The object of these laws was to destroy the tribal governments and to thrust upon individual Indians the uncongenial alternative of adjusting to the burdens of citizenship or removing beyond state jurisdiction.[9]

The alternative was not offered on the unenlightened supposition that the Indians generally were capable of managing their affairs unaided in a white man's world. Governor Gayle of Alabama, addressing the "former chiefs and headmen of the Creek Indians" in June of 1834 urged them to remove from the state on the grounds that

> you speak a different language from ours. You do not understand our laws and from your habits, cannot be brought to understand them. You are ignorant of the arts of civilized life. You have not like your white neighbors been raised in habits of industry and economy, the only means by which anyone can live, in settled countries, in even tolerable comfort. You know nothing of the skill of the white man in trading and making bargains, and cannot be guarded against the artful contrivances which dishonest men will resort to, to obtain your property under forms of contracts. In all these respects you are unequal to the white men, and if your people remain where they are, you will soon behold them in a miserable, degraded, and destitute condition.[10]

The intentions of federal officials who favored the extension of state laws are revealed in a letter written to Jackson by General Coffee. Referring to the Cherokees, Coffee remarked:

> Deprive the chiefs of the power they now possess, take from them their own code of laws, and reduce them to plain citizenship . . . and they will soon determine to move, and then there will be no difficulty in getting the poor Indians to give their consent. All this will be done by the State of Georgia if the U. States do not interfere with her law— . . . This will of course silence those in our country who constantly seek for causes to complain—It may indeed turn them loose upon Georgia, but that matters not, it is Georgia who clamors for the Indian lands, and she alone is entitled to the blame if any there be.[11]

Even before the laws were extended, the threat of state jurisdiction was used in confidential "talks" to the chiefs. After the

---

[9] Georgia, *Acts,* Dec. 12, 1828; Dec. 19, 1829; Alabama, *Acts,* Jan. 27, 1829; Dec. 31, 1831; Jan. 16, 1832; Dec. 18, 1832; Mississippi, *Acts,* Feb. 4, 1829; Jan. 19, 1830; Feb. 12, 1830; Dec. 9, 1831; Oct. 26, 1832; Tennessee, *Acts,* Nov. 8, 1833; George R. Gilmer to Augustus S. Clayton, June 7, 1830, Governor's Letterbook, 1829–31, p. 36, Georgia Dept. of Archives and History.

[10] Governor John Gayle to former chiefs and headmen of the Creek Indians, June 16, 1834, Miscellaneous Letters to and from Governor Gayle, Alabama Dept. of Archives and History.

[11] Feb. 3, 1830, Jackson Papers, Library of Congress.

states had acted, the secretary of war instructed each Indian agent to explain to his charges the meaning of state jurisdiction and to inform them that the President could not protect them against the enforcement of the laws.[12] Although the Supreme Court, in *Worcester* vs. *Georgia,* decided that the state had no right to extend its laws over the Cherokee nation, the Indian tribes being "domestic dependent nations" with limits defined by treaty, the President refused to enforce this decision.[13] There was only one means by which the government might have made "John Marshall's decision" effective—directing federal troops to exclude state officials and other intruders from the Indian domain. In January, 1832, the President informed an Alabama congressman that the United States government no longer assumed the right to remove citizens of Alabama from the Indian country. By this time, the soldiers who had protected the territory of the southeastern tribes against intruders had been withdrawn. In their unwearying efforts to pressure the Indians into ceding their lands, federal negotiators emphasized the terrors of state jurisdiction.[14]

Congress in May, 1830, complemented the efforts of the states by appropriating $500,000 and authorizing the President to negotiate removal treaties with all the tribes east of the Mississippi.[15] The vote on this bill was close in both houses. By skillful use of pamphlets, petitions, and lobbyists, missionary organizations had enlisted leading congressmen in their campaign against the administration's attempt to force the tribes to emigrate.[16] In the congressional debates, opponents of the bill agreed that savage tribes

---

[12] John H. Eaton to John Crowell, Mar. 27, 1829, Office of Indian Affairs, Letters Sent, V, 372–73, Records of the Bureau of Indian Affairs, National Archives; Middleton Mackey to John H. Eaton, Nov. 27, 1829, Choctaw Emigration File 111, *ibid.;* Andrew Jackson to Major David Haley, Oct. 10, 1829, Jackson Papers.

[13] 6 *Peters,* 515–97.

[14] Wiley Thompson to Messrs. Drew and Reese, Jan. 18, 1832, Indian Letters, 1782–1839, pp. 173–74, Georgia Dept. of Archives and History; John H. Eaton to Jackson, Feb. 21, 1831, *Sen. Doc.* 65, 21 Cong., 2 sess., p. 6; Cyrus Kingsbury to Jeremiah Evarts, Aug. 11, 1830, American Board of Commissioners for Foreign Missions Manuscripts; Tuskeneha to the President, May 21, 1831, Creek File 176, Records of the Bureau of Indian Affairs; Journal of the Commissioners for the Treaty of Dancing Rabbit Creek, *Sen. Doc.* 512, 23 Cong., 1 sess., p. 257.

[15] 4 *Statutes-at-Large,* 411–12.

[16] J. Orin Oliphant, ed., *Through the South and West with Jeremiah Evarts in 1826* (Lewisburg, Pa., 1956), pp. 47–61; Jeremiah Evarts to Rev. William Weisner, Nov. 27, 1829, American Board of Commissioners for Foreign Missions Manuscripts; *Sen. Docs.* 56, 59, 66, 73, 74, 76, 77, 92, 96, 21 Cong., 1 sess.

were duty-bound to relinquish their hunting grounds to the agriculturist, but they argued that the southeastern tribes were no longer savage. In any case, such relinquishment must be made in a freely contracted treaty. The extension of state laws over the Indian country was coercion; this made the negotiation of a free contract impossible. Both supporters and opponents of the bill agreed on one cardinal point—the Indian's moral right to keep his land depended on his actual cultivation of it.[17]

A logical corollary of vesting rights in land in proportion to cultivation was the reservation to individuals of as much land as they had improved at the time a treaty was signed. In 1816, Secretary of War William H. Crawford had proposed such reservations, or allotments, as a means of accommodating the removal policy to the program of assimilation. According to Crawford's plan, individual Indians who had demonstrated their capacity for civilization by establishing farms and who were willing to become citizens should be given the option of keeping their cultivated lands, by fee simple title, rather than emigrating. This offer was expected to reconcile the property-loving half-breeds to the policy of emigration. It also recognized their superior claim, as cultivators, on the regard and generosity of the government. The proposal was based on the assumption that few of the Indians were sufficiently civilized to want to become full-time farmers or state citizens.[18]

The Crawford policy was applied in the Cherokee treaties of 1817 and 1819 and the Choctaw treaty of 1820. These agreements offered fee simple allotments to heads of Indian families having improved lands within the areas ceded to the government. Only 311 Cherokees and eight Choctaws took advantage of the offer. This seemed to bear out the assumption that only a minority of the tribesmen would care to take allotments. Actually, these experiments were not reliable. In both cases, the tribes ceded only a fraction of their holdings. Comparatively few took allotments; but on the other hand, few emigrated. The majority simply remained within the diminished tribal territories east of the Mississippi.[19]

[17] Gales and Seaton, *Register of Debates in Congress*, VI, 311, 312, 320, 357, 361, 1022, 1024, 1039, 1061, 1110, 1135.

[18] *American State Papers: Indian Affairs*, II, 27. A general history of the allotment policy is Jay P. Kinney, *A Continent Lost—A Civilization Won: Indian Land Tenure in America* (Baltimore, Md., 1937).

[19] 7 *Statutes-at-Large*, 156–60, 195–200, 210–14; Cherokee Reservation Book, Records of the Bureau of Indian Affairs; Special Reserve Book A, *ibid.*; James Barbour to the Speaker of the House, Jan. 23, 1828, *American State Papers: Public Lands*, V, 396–97.

The offer of fee simple allotments was an important feature of the negotiations with the tribes in the 1820's. When the extension of state laws made removal of the tribes imperative, it was to be expected that allotments would comprise part of the consideration offered for the ceded lands. Both the ideology which rationalized the removal policy and the conclusions erroneously drawn from experience with the earlier allotment treaties led government negotiators to assume that a few hundred allotments at most would be required.

The Choctaws were the first to cede their eastern lands. The treaty of Dancing Rabbit Creek, signed in September, 1830, provided for several types of allotment. Special reservations were given to the chiefs and their numerous family connections; a possible 1,600 allotments of 80 to 480 acres, in proportion to the size of the beneficiary's farm, were offered others who intended to emigrate. These were intended for sale to private persons or to the government, so that the Indian might get the maximum price for his improvements. The fourteenth article of the treaty offered any head of an Indian family who did not plan to emigrate the right to take up a quantity of land proportional to the number of his dependents. At the end of five years' residence those who received these allotments were to have fee simple title to their lands and become citizens. It was expected that approximately two hundred persons would take land under this article.[20]

The Creeks refused to sign any agreements promising to emigrate, but their chiefs were persuaded that the only way to put an end to intrusions on their lands was to sign an allotment treaty.[21] In March, 1832, a Creek delegation in Washington signed a treaty calling for the allotment of 320 acres to each head of a family, the granting of certain supplementary lands to the chiefs and to orphans, and the cession of the remaining territory to the United States. If the Indian owners remained on their allotments for five years, they were to receive fee simple titles and become citizens.[22] Returning to Alabama, the chiefs informed their people that they had not

---

[20] 7 *Statutes-at-Large,* 334–41; manuscript records of negotiations are in Choctaw File 112, Records of the Bureau of Indian Affairs.

[21] John Crowell to Lewis Cass, Jan. 25, 1832, Creek File 178, Records of the Bureau of Indian Affairs.

[22] 7 *Statutes-at-Large,* 366–68.

actually sold the tribal lands but "had only made each individual their own guardian, that they might take care of their own possessions, and act as agents for themselves." [23]

Unlike the Creeks, the Chickasaws were willing to admit the inevitability of removal. But they needed land east of the Mississippi on which they might live until they acquired a home in the west. The Chickasaw treaty of May, 1832, therefore, provided generous allotments for heads of families, ranging from 640 to 3,200 acres, depending on the size of the family and the number of its slaves. These allotments were to be auctioned publicly when the tribe emigrated and the owners compensated for their improvements out of the proceeds.[24] Although the fullblood Chickasaws apparently approved of the plan for a collective sale of the allotments, the half-breeds, abetted by white traders and planters, persuaded the government to allow those who held allotments to sell them individually.[25] An amended treaty of 1834 complied with the half-breeds' proposals. It further stipulated that leading half-breeds and the old chiefs of the tribe comprise a committee to determine the competence of individual Chickasaws to manage their property. Since the committee itself disposed of the lands of the "incompetents," this gave both protection to the unsophisticated and additional advantage to the half-breeds.[26]

Widespread intrusion on Indian lands began with the extension of state laws over the tribal domains. In the treaties of cession, the government promised to remove intruders, but its policy in this respect was vacillating and ineffective. Indians whose allotments covered valuable plantations proved anxious to promote the sale of their property by allowing buyers to enter the ceded territory as soon as possible. Once this group of whites was admitted, it became difficult to discriminate against others. Thus a large number

---

[23] John Scott to Lewis Cass, Nov. 12, 1835, Creek File 193, Records of the Bureau of Indian Affairs.

[24] 7 *Statutes-at-Large*, 381–89.

[25] John Terrell to Henry Cook, Oct. 29, 1832 (copy), John D. Terrell Papers, Alabama Dept. of Archives and History; Benjamin Reynolds to John Coffee, Dec. 12, 1832, Chickasaw File 83, Records of the Bureau of Indian Affairs; Terrell to John Tyler, Feb. 26, 1841 (draft), Terrell Papers; G. W. Long to John Coffee, Dec. 15, 1832, Coffee Papers; Rev. T. C. Stuart to Daniel Green, Oct. 14, 1833, American Board of Commissioners for Foreign Missions Manuscripts.

[26] 7 *Statutes-at-Large*, 450–57.

of intruders settled among the Indians with the passive connivance of the War Department and the tribal leaders. The task of removing them was so formidable that after making a few gestures the government generally evaded its obligation. The misery of the common Indians, surrounded by intruders and confused by the disruption of tribal authority, was so acute that any method for securing their removal seemed worth trying. Furthermore, their emigration would serve the interest of white settlers, land speculators, and their representatives in Washington. The government therefore chose to facilitate the sale of allotments even before the Indians received fee simple title to them.[27]

The right to sell his allotment was useful to the sophisticated tribesman with a large plantation. Such men were accustomed to selling their crops and hiring labor. Through their experience in treaty negotiations, they had learned to bargain over the price of lands. Many of them received handsome payment for their allotments. Some kept part of their holdings and remained in Alabama and Mississippi as planters—like other planters, practicing as land speculators on the side.[28] Nearly all the Indians had some experience in trade, but to most of them the conception of land as a salable commodity was foreign. They had little notion of the exact meaning of an "acre" or the probable value of their allotments.[29] The govern-

---

[27] William Ward to Secretary of War, Oct. 22, 1831, Choctaw Reserve File 133; Mushulatubbee to Lewis Cass, Feb. 9, 1832, Choctaw File 113; W. S. Colquhoun to General George S. Gibson, Apr. 20, 1832, Choctaw Emigration File 121; A. Campbell to Secretary of War, Aug. 5, 1832, Choctaw File 113; John Kurtz to Benjamin Reynolds, Aug. 9, 1833, Office of Indian Affairs, Letters Sent, XI, 74; S. C. Barton to Elbert Herring, Nov. 11, 1833, Choctaw File 113; William M. Gwin to Lewis Cass, Apr. 8, 1834, Choctaw File 84, Records of the Bureau of Indian Affairs; Mary E. Young, "The Creek Frauds: A Study in Conscience and Corruption," *Mississippi Valley Historical Review*, XLVII (Dec., 1955), 415–19.

[28] Benjamin Reynolds to Lewis Cass, Dec. 9, 1832, Apr. 29, 1835, Chickasaw File 83, 85, Records of the Bureau of Indian Affairs; David Haley to Jackson, Apr. 15, 1831, *Sen. Doc.* 512, 23 Cong., 1 sess., p. 426; Elbert Herring to George W. Elliott, Jan. 23, 1833, Office of Indian Affairs, Letters Sent, IX, 516, Records of the Bureau of Indian Affairs; J. J. Abert to J. R. Poinsett, July 19, 1839, Creek File 220, *ibid*. See Special Reserve Books and Special Reserve Files A and C, and William Carroll's List of Certified Contracts for the Sale of Chickasaw Reservations, Special File, Chickasaw, Records of the Bureau of Indian Affairs, and compare Chickasaw Location Book, Records of the Bureau of Land Management, National Archives.

[29] George S. Snyderman, "Concepts of Land Ownership among the Iroquois and their Neighbors," in *Symposium on Local Variations in Iroquois Culture,*

ment confused them still further by parceling out the lands according to Anglo-American, rather than aboriginal notions of family structure and land ownership. Officials insisted, for example, that the "father" rather than the "mother" must be defined as head of the family and righteously refused to take cognizance of the fact that many of the "fathers" had "a plurality of wives." [30]

Under these conditions, it is not surprising that the common Indian's legal freedom of contract in selling his allotment did not necessarily lead him to make the best bargain possible in terms of his pecuniary interests. Nor did the proceeds of the sales transform each seller into an emigrant of large independent means. A right of property and freedom to contract for its sale did not automatically invest the Indian owner with the habits, values, and skills of a sober land speculator. His acquisition of property and freedom actually increased his dependence on those who traditionally mediated for him in contractual relations with white Americans.

Prominent among these mediators were white men with Indian wives who made their living as planters and traders in the Indian nations, men from nearby settlements who traded with the leading Indians or performed legal services for them, and interpreters. In the past, such individuals had been appropriately compensated for using their influence in favor of land cessions. It is likely that their speculative foresight was in part responsible for the allotment features in the treaties of the 1830's. When the process of allotting lands to individuals began, these speculative gentlemen made loans of whisky, muslin, horses, slaves, and other useful commodities to the new property-owner. They received in return the Indian's written promise to sell his allotment to them as soon as its boundaries were defined. Generally they were on hand to help him locate it on "desirable" lands. They, in turn, sold their "interest" in

---

ed. William N. Fenton, Bureau of American Ethnology *Bulletin 149* (Washington, D. C., 1951), pp. 16–26; Petition of Choctaw Chiefs and Headmen, Mar. 2, 1832, Choctaw Reserve File 133; James Colbert to Lewis Cass, June 5, 1835, Chickasaw File 84; Benjamin Reynolds to Elbert Herring, Mar. 11, 1835, Chickasaw File 85, Records of the Bureau of Indian Affairs.

[30] Memorial of Chickasaw Chiefs to the President, Nov. 25, 1835, Chickasaw File 84; Thomas J. Abbott and E. Parsons, Sept. 7, 1832, *Sen. Doc. 512*, 23 Cong., 1 sess., pp. 443–44; Elbert Herring to E. Parsons, B. S. Parsons, and John Crowell, Oct. 10, 1832, *ibid.*, p. 524; Leonard Tarrant to E. Herring, May 15, 1833, Creek File 202, Records of the Bureau of Indian Affairs; Alexander Spoehr, "Kinship Systems," pp. 201–31; John R. Swanton, *Indians of the Southeastern United States*, Bureau of American Ethnology *Bulletin 137* (Washington, D. C., 1946).

the lands to men of capital. Government agents encouraged the enterprising investor, since it was in the Indian's interest and the government's policy that the lands be sold and the tribes emigrate.[31] Unfortunately, the community of interest among the government, the speculator, and the Indian proved largely fictitious. The speculator's interest in Indian lands led to frauds which impoverished the Indians, soiled the reputation of the government, and retarded the emigration of the tribes.

An important factor in this series of complications was the government's fallacious assumption that most of the "real Indians" were anxious to emigrate. Under the Choctaw treaty, for example, registration for fee simple allotments was optional, the government expecting no more than two hundred registrants. When several hundred full-bloods applied for lands, the Choctaw agent assumed that they were being led astray by "designing men" and told them they must emigrate. Attorneys took up the Choctaw claims, located thousands of allotments in hopes that Congress would confirm them, and supported their clients in Mississippi for twelve to fifteen years while the government debated and acted on the validity of the claims. There was good reason for this delay. Settlers and rival speculators, opposing confirmation of the claims, advanced numerous depositions asserting that the attorneys, in their enterprising search for clients, had materially increased the number of claimants.[32] Among the Creeks, the Upper Towns, traditionally the conservative faction of the tribe, refused to sell their allotments. Since the Lower Towns proved more compliant, speculators hired willing Indians from the Lower Towns to impersonate the unwilling owners. They

[31] John Coffee to Andrew Jackson, July 10, 1830, Creek File 192, Records of the Bureau of Indian Affairs; John Crowell to John H. Eaton, Aug. 8, 1830, Creek File 175, ibid.; John H. Brodnax to Lewis Cass, Mar. 12, 1832, Sen. Doc. 512, 23 Cong., 1 sess., III, 258–59; John Terrell to General John Coffee, Sept. 15, 1829, Coffee Papers; J. J. Abert to [Lewis Cass], June 13, 1833, Creek File 202, Records of the Bureau of Indian Affairs; contract between Daniel Wright and Mingo Mushulatubbee, Oct. 7, 1830, American State Papers: Public Lands, VII, 19; W. S. Colquhoun to Lewis Cass, Sept. 20, 1833, ibid., p. 13; Chapman Levy to Joel R. Poinsett, June 19, 1837, Choctaw Reserve File 139, Records of the Bureau of Indian Affairs; James Colbert to Lewis Cass, June 5, 1835, Chickasaw File 84, ibid; Chancery Court, Northern District of Mississippi, Final Record A, 111, M, 235–37, Courthouse, Holly Springs, Mississippi.

[32] Mary E. Young, "Indian Land Allotments in Alabama and Mississippi, 1830–1860" (manuscript doctoral dissertation, Cornell University, 1955), pp. 70–82; Franklin L. Riley, "The Choctaw Land Claims," Mississippi Historical Society Publications, VIII (1904), 370–82; Harmon, Indian Affairs, pp. 226–59.

then bought the land from the impersonators. The government judiciously conducted several investigations of these frauds, but in the end the speculators outmaneuvered the investigators. Meanwhile, the speculators kept the Indians from emigrating until their contracts were approved. Only the outbreak of fighting between starving Creeks and their settler neighbors enabled the government, under pretext of a pacification, to remove the tribe.[33]

Besides embarrassing the government, the speculators contributed to the demoralization of the Indians. Universal complaint held that after paying the tribesman for his land they often borrowed back the money without serious intent of repaying it, or recovered it in return for overpriced goods, of which a popular article was whisky. Apprised of this situation, Secretary of War Lewis Cass replied that once the Indian had been paid for his land, the War Department had no authority to circumscribe his freedom to do what he wished with the proceeds.[34]

Nevertheless, within their conception of the proper role of government, officials who dealt with the tribes tried to be helpful. Although the Indian must be left free to contract for the sale of his lands, the United States sent agents to determine the validity of the contracts. These agents sometimes refused to approve a contract that did not specify a fair price for the land in question. They also refused official sanction when it could not be shown that the Indian owner had at some time been in possession of the sum stipulated.[35] This protective action on the part of the government, together with its several investigations into frauds in the sale of Indian lands, apparently did secure the payment of more money than the tribesmen might otherwise have had. But the effort was seriously hampered by the near impossibility of obtaining disinterested testimony.

In dealing with the Chickasaws, the government managed to avoid most of the vexing problems which had arisen in executing the allotment program among their southeastern neighbors. This

---

[33] Young, "Creek Frauds," pp. 411–37.

[34] Lewis Cass to Return J. Meigs, Oct. 31, 1834, *Sen. Doc.* 428, 24 Cong., 1 sess., p. 23.

[35] Lewis Cass, "Regulations," for certifying Creek contracts, Nov. 28, 1833, *Sen. Doc.* 276, 24 Cong., 1 sess., pp. 88–89; *id.*, "Regulations," Feb. 8, 1836, Chickasaw Letterbook A, 76–78, Records of the Bureau of Indian Affairs; Secretary of War to the President, June 27, 1836, Choctaw Reserve File 136, *ibid.* For adjudications based on the above regulations, see Special Reserve Files A and C and Choctaw, Creek, and Chickasaw Reserve Files, Records of the Bureau of Indian Affairs, *passim.*

was due in part to the improvement of administrative procedures, in part to the methods adopted by speculators in Chickasaw allotments, and probably most of all to the inflated value of cotton lands during the period in which the Chickasaw territory was sold. Both the government and the Chickasaws recognized that the lands granted individuals under the treaty were generally to be sold, not settled. They therefore concentrated on provisions for supervising sales and safeguarding the proceeds.[36] Speculators in Chickasaw lands, having abundant resources, paid an average price of $1.70 per acre. The Chickasaws thereby received a better return than the government did at its own auctions. The buyers' generosity may be attributed to their belief that the Chickasaw lands represented the last first-rate cotton country within what were then the boundaries of the public domain. In their pursuit of a secure title, untainted by fraud, the capitalists operating in the Chickasaw cession established a speculators' claim association which settled disputes among rival purchasers. Thus they avoided the plots, counterplots, and mutual recriminations which had hampered both speculators and government in their dealings with the Creeks and Choctaws.[37]

A superficially ironic consequence of the allotment policy as a method of acquiring land for white settlers was the fact that it facilitated the engrossment of land by speculators. With their superior command of capital and the influence it would buy, speculators acquired 80 to 90 per cent of the lands allotted to the southeastern tribesmen.[38]

For most of the Indian beneficiaries of the policy, its most important consequence was to leave them landless. After selling their allotment, or a claim to it, they might take to the swamp, live for a while on the bounty of a still hopeful speculator, or scavenge on their settler neighbors. But ultimately most of them faced the alternative of emigration or destitution, and chose to emigrate. The

---

[36] "Memorial of the Creek Nation . . . ," Jan. 29, 1883, *House Misc. Doc.* 18, 47 Cong., 2 sess.

[37] Average price paid for Chickasaw lands computed from William Carroll's List of Certified Contracts, Special Reserve File, Chickasaw, Records of the Bureau of Indian Affairs; Young, "Indian Allotments," 154–67.

[38] See calculations in Young, "Indian Allotments," 141–42, 163–64. No system of estimating percentages of land purchased for speculation from figures of sales is foolproof. The assumption used in this estimate was that all those who bought 2,000 acres or more might be defined as speculators. Compare James W. Silver, "Land Speculation Profits in the Chickasaw Cession," *Journal of Southern History,* X (Feb., 1944), 84–92.

machinations of the speculators and the hopes they nurtured that the Indians might somehow be able to keep a part of their allotted lands made the timing of removals less predictable than it might otherwise have been. This unpredictability compounded the evils inherent in a mass migration managed by a government committed to economy and unversed in the arts of economic planning. The result was the "Trail of Tears." [39]

The spectacular frauds committed among the Choctaws and Creeks, the administrative complications they created and the impression they gave that certain self-styled champions of the people were consorting with the avaricious speculator gave the allotment policy a bad reputation. The administration rejected it in dealing with the Cherokees,[40] and the policy was not revived on any considerable scale until 1854, when it was applied, with similar consequences, to the Indians of Kansas.[41] In the 1880's, when allotment in severalty became a basic feature of American Indian policy, the "civilized tribes," then in Oklahoma, strenuously resisted its application to them. They cited their memories of the 1830's as an important reason for their intransigence.[42]

The allotment treaties of the 1830's represent an attempt to apply Anglo-American notions of justice, which enshrined private property in land and freedom of contract as virtually absolute values, to Indian tribes whose tastes and traditions were otherwise. Their history illustrates the limitations of intercultural application of the Golden Rule. In a more practical sense, the treaties typified an effort to force on the Indians the alternative of complete as-

---

[39] For the story of emigration, see Foreman, *Indian Removal;* Debo, *Road to Disappearance,* pp. 103–107 and *Choctaw Republic,* pp. 55–57. Relations between speculation and emigration can be traced in the Creek, Choctaw, and Chickasaw Emigration and Reserve Files, Records of the Bureau of Indian Affairs.

[40] Hon. R. Chapman to Lewis Cass, Jan. 25, 1835, Cherokee File 7, Records of the Bureau of Indian Affairs; Lewis Cass to Commissioners Carroll and Schermerhorn, Apr. 2, 1835, Office of Indian Affairs, Letters Sent, XV, 261, *ibid.;* "Journal of the Proceedings at the Council held at New Echota . . . ," Cherokee File 7, *ibid.;* Joint Memorial of the Legislature of the State of Alabama . . . , Jan. 9, 1836, *ibid.;* William Gilmer to Andrew Jackson, Feb. 9, 1835, Jackson Papers; 7 *Statutes-at-Large,* 483–84, 488–89.

[41] Paul W. Gates, *Fifty Million Acres: Conflicts over Kansas Land Policy, 1854–1890* (Ithaca, N. Y., 1954), pp. 11–48.

[42] Memorial of the Creek Nation on the Subject of Lands in Severalty Among the Several Indian Tribes," Jan. 29, 1883, *House Misc. Doc.* 18, 47 Cong., 2 sess.

similation or complete segregation by placing individuals of varying levels of sophistication in situations where they must use the skills of businessmen or lose their means of livelihood. This policy secured tribal lands while preserving the forms of respect for property rights and freedom of contract, but it proved costly to both the government and the Indians.

How lightly that cost was reckoned, and how enduring the motives and rationalizations that gave rise to it, may be gathered from the subsequent experience of the southeastern tribes in Oklahoma. There, early in the twentieth century, the allotment policy was again enforced, with safeguards hardly more helpful to the unsophisticated than those of the 1830's. Once more, tribal land changed owners for the greater glory of liberty, civilization, and profit.[43]

---

[43] Compare Angie Debo, *The Five Civilized Tribes of Oklahoma: Report on Social and Economic Conditions* (Philadelphia, Pa., 1951) and Kinney, *Indian Land Tenure*, pp. 243–44.

JEAN ALEXANDER WILBURN[*]

Biddle's Not So Unpopular Bank

The Bank War has divided contemporary scholars as it once split voters and parties. One school of thought has praised Jackson's attack on the alleged monster of "rag money," while another scores a Jacksonian policy that in destroying the great bank, paved the way for precisely the unbridled speculation it had ostensibly sought to prevent. Almost all the experts, however, had assumed that Biddle's bank was unpopular with state banks. The latter allegedly resented the power of the Second Bank to curb expansion by requiring specie payment by the state banks for their paper notes that the BUS invariably accumulated in its role as government depository. Professor Wilburn shows that this was not so. The so-called monster was not regarded as such by its smaller rivals. Rather, they seemed to be very appreciative of the services performed by the government's bank.

⌘⌘⌘

NO EXPLANATION OF the influences working for the destruction of the second United States Bank has had wider acceptance

---

[*] Jean Alexander Wilburn, *Biddle's Bank: The Crucial Years* (New York: Columbia University Press, 1967), chapter 4: "State Bank Support of the Second Bank," pp. 31–45.

or a longer history than the theory of the state banks' hostility to the Bank. Jabez Hammond considered this hostility to be caused by the state banks' greed for the deposits of the United States government:

> The state banks believed, that if the United States Bank should be annihilated, these immense deposits would be made in their own vaults, and hence all the benefits arising from these deposits, and also the whole profits of the very great circulation of the United States Bank notes would be transferred from the United States to the state banks, without compelling them to increase their own capital to the amount of a single dollar. Was it in human nature, and especially, was it in *bank nature*, (if such an expression may be tolerated), to resist this prospect of adding to their gains? [1]

Catterall accepted the notion of the state banks' hostility, but explained it in these terms: "The opposition of state banks whose interests were involved arrayed a powerful party against the bank. It had forced many of them to restrict their business by compelling payment for their notes in specie, and it had been particularly active and particularly offensive in this in the South and West." [2] He went on to add that the profits of state banks were reduced because the Bank loaned at 6 per cent, being compelled to do so by its charter, whereas the state banks could have loaned at 7 per cent had they not been forced to loan at the lower rate "because the big bank did so."

Present day writers have accepted the existence of state banks' hostility as a very powerful force against the Bank and have used some combination of causes derived from the earlier writers to support their views. Govan is an exception to this generalization. Although his interest was not centered around the identification of the friends and enemies of the Bank, he noted that state banks ceased complaining against the Bank and he mentioned several state banks that were in favor of the Second Bank. [3]

In the face of almost universal consensus it might seem odd to be investigating support of the Bank in the area of the state banks.

---

[1] Jabez Delano Hammond, *The History of Political Parties in the State of New York* (2 vols., New York: H. and E. Phinney, 1846), II, 350.

[2] Ralph C. H. Catterall, *The Second Bank of the United States* (Chicago: University of Chicago Press, 1903), p. 166.

[3] Thomas Payne Govan, *Nicholas Biddle, Nationalist and Public Banker, 1786–1844* (Chicago: University of Chicago Press, 1959), pp. 85, 176.

However, Bassett, referring to the time, January 1832, when the Bank sent its memorial to Congress requesting renewal of its charter, remarked: "Petitions were secured in large numbers, the most notable being from banks and business organizations in favor of the bank."[4] One is compelled to ask why the most notable petitions should come from state banks if they were hostile? Nicholas Biddle, who was in a very good position to know, does not seem to have believed in the theory.

January 16, 1832

Jeremiah Mason, Esq.[5]
Portsmouth, N. H.
    . . . It would be very useful if your community and especially your banks would aid us, for we should then disarm the enemies of the institution of one of their most efficient weapons, the imaginary injury done to the State Banks, and the jealousy which they are presumed to feel toward the institution . . .[6]

February 27, 1832

Honble. H. Seymour[7]
Wash., D. C.
    . . . I do not care about this, the object being to multiply the proofs that the State Banks are in the main friendly to his institution.[8]

These letters show that Biddle was aware of the accusation that the state banks were hostile but that he disbelieved it. It appeared to him to be propaganda, resting on an imaginary base, spread by the Bank's enemies. Moreover, he was so sure of his convictions that he was willing to try to prove that "state banks are in the main friendly."

In attempting to locate support among the state banks, one naturally ought to begin by finding the areas in which Biddle hoped for support. In January of 1832 Biddle weighed two conflicting sets

---

[4] John Spencer Bassett, *The Life of Andrew Jackson* (2 vols., New York: Doubleday, Page & Co., 1911), II, 615.

[5] President of the United States branch bank at Portsmouth.

[6] Biddle to Mason, January 16, 1832, in the President's Letter Books (Manuscript Division, Library of Congress, Washington, D.C.). Cited hereafter as PLB.

[7] United States Senator from Vermont.

[8] PLB, February 27, 1832.

of advice: Members of Jackson's cabinet advised not petitioning for renewal of the charter that session of Congress; while Webster, Clay, and the Bank's lobbyists in Washington, Horace Binney and Thomas Cadwalader,[9] advised proceeding with the renewal request immediately. He decided in favor of the latter course. The petition was to be presented in the House of Representatives by George McDuffie of South Carolina and in the Senate by Dallas of Pennsylvania, both Democrats. Although Biddle had previously been informed of a pro-Bank majority in both Houses, he felt the need to rally the Bank's friends throughout the Union. As a result on January 16, 1832, he began a series of letters addressed mainly to officers of the branches of the Bank requesting that memorials be sent to Congress from citizens, from state banks, from state legislatures. To some areas he wrote only for memorials from citizens. To others, he wrote for state bank memorials and citizens' memorials. To still other areas he also asked for the state legislatures to pass resolutions and forward them to Congress. The extent of help asked for and the tone of the letters indicate the areas in which Biddle felt he had reason to hope for state bank support.

The answers he received reveal a great deal of information as to the attitudes of state banks in various sections of the country. Finally, the memorials of state banks actually recorded as presented in Congress provide the strongest and most clear-cut evidence of support.

Using these letters and memorials as basic materials, let us see what they reveal about the attitudes of state banks just prior to the 1832 Veto. Because these letters and memorials were so important, we will paraphrase them in the present tense and will try to be as faithful to the 1832 style of writing as we can.

Since the Bank is thought of as having been especially offensive to the state banks in the West and South, these sections will be examined first. To no one did Biddle write with greater confidence of success than to Samuel Jaudon, cashier of the New Orleans branch of the Bank. Though he recognizes that the New Orleans delegation to congress is pro-Bank, he asks that memorials from the citizens and the state banks be sent along.[10] On February 11, 1832, Jaudon answered that the memorial from the Louisiana State Bank has been adopted unanimously. He will furnish one for the Bank of

---

[9] Both were directors on the Philadelphia Board of the Bank.

[10] Biddle to Jaudon, January 16, 1832, PLB.

Orleans and it will be passed. During the week he hopes all banks will sign.[11] A few days later he wrote again to say the Bank of Orleans has sent a memorial and that the Canal Bank has appointed a committee to do the same. At the next meeting of the Bank of Louisiana, the question will be brought up there.

According to congressional records, memorials from the Louisiana State Bank,[12] the New Orleans Bank,[13] the New Orleans Canal and Banking Company,[14] and the Bank of Orleans[15] were presented in Congress. What proportion of the state banks in Louisiana did this represent?

Up to 1832 Knox referred to only two banks in Louisiana, the Louisiana State Bank and the Bank of Louisiana.[16] Jaudon wrote of "all" banks and specified three. Despite this discrepancy, it seems safe to conclude that the state banks of Louisiana were clearly pro-Bank. Their economic reasons for so feeling are contained in the memorials, and these, along with those from other states, will be examined later. The task for the moment will be to locate the areas of state bank support or hostility as the case may be.

Turning to Louisiana's neighbor to the east, Mississippi, there appears to be no evidence of antagonism there. In 1809 the Bank of Mississippi at Natchez was chartered as a private institution. In 1818 the Legislature extended its powers, and it became a state bank. This new charter was to continue until 1840, up to which time no other bank was to be chartered. This bank appears to have been successful and well managed, but the Legislature, disregarding its previous pledge, established in 1830 the Planter's Bank of Mississippi, and made it the state financial agent. "The managers of the Bank of the State of Mississippi, dreading the evils which they feared would result from speculation in negroes and wild land, then so prevalent, concluded to wind up that institution."[17] From this we deduce that in 1832 there were at most two state banks, the Planter's and the Bank of Mississippi.

---

[11] Jaudon to Biddle, February 11, 1832, NBP.

[12] House Journal, 22nd Congress, 1st Session, p. 450.

[13] Ibid., p. 534.

[14] Senate Documents, 22nd Congress, 1st Session, vol. II, doc. 108.

[15] Executive Documents, 22nd Congress, 1st Session, vol. IV, doc. 187.

[16] John J. Knox, A History of Banking in the United States (New York: B. Rhodes and Co., 1900), p. 611.

[17] Knox, p. 602.

Biddle wrote Wilkins, president of the branch in Natchez, for either citizens' memorials or state bank memorials. Both the Planter's Bank and the Bank of the State of Mississippi sent Congress memorials; Mississippi's state banks thus gave full support.[18]

Missouri's supposed state bank hostility can be quickly disposed of. Biddle in writing John O'Fallon, president of the United States branch in St. Louis, fails to ask for memorials from the state banks but requests an expression from the state legislature only.[19] This is not strange, since there were no state banks in Missouri at the time. "The disappearance of the two pioneer banks left the chief town in Missouri, now with a population of 4,500 and a growing trade, without any banking facilities, . . . and this condition of things lasted until 1829, when the United States Bank opened a branch at St. Louis . . ." The next bank to be chartered was in 1837.[20]

Illinois, lying between Missouri and Indiana, had no branch bank of the United States. Hence there is no correspondence in the Biddle Papers concerning the attitude of the state banks. Knox told us that Illinois had at most one bankrupt state bank; indeed, as late as 1835 there were only two banks in existence with a total circulation of $178,810.[21]

Similarly, Indiana had no branch of the Bank. But Knox pointed out "the collapse of the bank ended banking business in the State, so far as banks of issue were concerned, with the exception of the Farmers' and Mechanics' Bank, at Madison, which maintained its credit, and on the expiration of its charter was authorized by the Legislature to continue business until 1834, when the State Bank was chartered." [22] Indiana then need not concern us here any more than Illinois.

Biddle wrote Herman Cope, president of the Bank in Cincinnati, for an expression from its citizens and state banks.[23] Cope answered on February 4, 1832, that the Board of Directors of the Commercial Bank of Cincinnati will pass a favorable memorial. He went on to

---

[18] *House Journal*, 22nd Congress, 1st Session, p. 510.

[19] Biddle to O'Fallon, January 16, 1832, PLB.

[20] Knox, pp. 712–18.

[21] *Ibid.*, p. 729.

[22] *Ibid.*, p. 694.

[23] Biddle to Cope, January 16, 1832, PLB.

say that most, if not all, the state banks in Ohio will do the same.[24] As listed in the several records of Congress, memorials were received from the Commercial Bank of Cincinnati, the Bank of St. Clairsville, the Bank of Steubensville,[25] and the Farmers' and Mechanics' Bank of Steubensville.[26]

Just exactly how many banks existed in Ohio at the time is hard to tell. Judging from Knox one might hazard a guess of thirteen. However, it is clear from the memorial from the Commercial Bank of Cincinnati that outside of the Commercial Bank, whose capital was $500,000, the other banks were rather insignificant. Similarly a memorial from the citizens of Louisville, Kentucky, states that Kentucky, Indiana, Illinois, Missouri, and Tennessee have no banking institutions of their own and that Ohio and Alabama have none of extended credit.[27] Since the most important state bank, as well as three others, gave positive support to the Bank, it is fair to conclude that the Ohio state banks supported the institution. This will become even clearer when other memorials are examined.

There was a branch of the Bank at Louisville, Kentucky. Biddle asks John Tilford "will your fellow citizens aid?"[28] Why he asked for no help from the state banks is evident; none existed there.[29] According to Knox, "After the liquidation of the Bank of Kentucky and the Bank of the Commonwealth of Kentucky, the State had to depend for paper money on the notes of the branches of the Bank of the United States at Lexington and Louisville, and the bills of banks located outside its borders."[30] Not until 1833–1834 were any state banks chartered. Again, during this period, state bank hostility was obviously not to be found in Kentucky.

There is no correspondence from Nicholas Biddle to the branch in Nashville requesting supporting memorials. But as late as 1834 only one state bank was reported for Tennessee.[31] Since this was Andrew Jackson's home state, perhaps Biddle wisely hesitated from

---

[24] Cope to Biddle, February 4, 1832, NBP.

[25] *House Journal*, 22nd Congress, 1st Session, pp. 408, 413, 474.

[26] *Executive Documents*, 22nd Congress, 1st Session, vol. IV, doc. 167.

[27] *Ibid.*, vol. IV, doc. 111.

[28] Biddle to Tilford, January 16, 1832, PLB.

[29] We know from the previously mentioned memorial of the citizens of Louisville that this situation in Kentucky was also one of no existing state banks.

[30] Knox, pp. 634–35.

[31] *Ibid.*, p. 667.

asking legislative aid or memorials from citizens. Jackson, incidentally, was known to have kept his own banking account with the Nashville branch of the Bank. Had there been a state bank at the time, one would think—given Jackson's attitude toward the Bank—that his money would have been deposited with the state bank.

Turning to the southern states: Alabama is a particularly interesting refutation of the theory that the more "loosely run" state banks were the most hostile to the Bank, especially resenting its restraining hand. After two territorially chartered banks had failed, leaving only the Bank of Mobile, the state legislature enacted a law in 1820 to establish the Bank of the State of Alabama. This bank failed, but in 1823 the state legislature chartered another of the same name. Alabama was so short of gold and silver that the capital of the bank, on which no limit was imposed, was to be furnished by the credit of the state itself. The State General Assembly elected the president and directors. The bank issued all denominations of notes including shinplasters. The loans made were by law apportioned among the several counties. The way for constituents to get loans was through their legislator, and no director of the bank could hope to be reappointed unless he granted whatever loans the legislators requested. Two amusing stories are told to illustrate the situation. A member of the State House of Representatives died, and the other members, as was the custom, wore crepe on their sleeves for thirty days. This indicated to the bank directors the men to be wined and dined. A backwoodsman, observing this, put on a black crepe band and was royally feasted for several days before his identity became known.

The other story concerns a group of hotel keepers in Tuscaloosa and their relationship to banking. One hotel keeper, believing that if he were a director of the bank the popularity of his hotel would increase, had himself appointed to the post. At once his hotel was crowded. Perceiving this the other hotel keepers, in order to be competitive, also had themselves appointed as directors. One morning when John L. Tindall, president of the bank, was presiding at a meeting of the directors (most of whom were hotel keepers), a large number of bills were discounted. A small one was offered and no one knew the maker. It was about to be rejected when Tindall, looking at each of the hotel keepers in turn and getting no response from them, remarked quietly, "This man must have camped out last night." [32]

---

[32] Both these stories are in Knox, pp. 598–99.

Since times were prosperous between 1826 and 1836 and people had little difficulty in getting all the money they needed, we have, then, the typical agrarian community with the state bank over-extended and corrupt. It ought to have hated the Bank, but the very opposite was true, as the following correspondence shows.

On January 16, 1832, Biddle wrote two letters to Alabama re-questing help. One was to James Jackson of Tuscaloosa and the other to George Poe, cashier of the branch of the Bank in Mobile. He reminds the former of the good will manifested toward the Bank the previous winter by the Alabama state joint committee reporting on the Bank of Alabama and asks for just such an expression of good will by means of a private memorial or any communication of Jackson's own views to Alabama's delegation in Congress.[33] To the latter, George Poe, he wrote that probably Poe's community and perhaps the banks might be disposed to cooperate. He also asks that the legislature act by sending information to the delegates in Congress.[34]

In response, James Jackson wrote that he is sending Biddle two printed copies of the report of the joint committee of the state legislature on the state and condition of the Bank of the State of Alabama, because of the way in which that report spoke of the branch of the Bank at Mobile. It shows the change of opinion (from a hostile attitude to one of good will) in Alabama on the subject of the Bank.[35]

Poe answered and enclosed a copy of a letter he has written to Tindall, president of the state bank of Alabama. It reports that the Bank of Mobile has passed resolutions expressive of a wish to see the charter of the Bank renewed. Tindall had once said that his entire board felt the Bank was of great use to the state bank and that if renewal of the charter depended on his board, it would be renewed. If this is still so, an expression of that opinion in the form of a resolution or by information sent to Congress from the State will be very acceptable as testimony to the administration of the concerns of the Bank in that quarter. The state bank at Tuscaloosa has paid the Bank and the branches with which the state bank has had intercourse a handsome compliment. No state bank has derived more extensive and substantial benefits from the Bank than Mr. Tindall's. Will he please write and say so?[36]

---

[33] Biddle to Jackson, January 16, 1832, PLB.

[34] Biddle to Poe, January 16, 1832, PLB.

[35] Jackson to Biddle, January 30, 1832, NBP.

[36] Poe to Biddle, February 11, 1832, NBP.

Poe wrote again to Biddle on February 23rd and enclosed a memorial from the Bank of the State of Alabama. He reports that every member of the board of the state bank wants the Bank rechartered.[37] Besides this memorial, the congressional records show that the Bank of Mobile, chartered when Alabama was still a territory, also forwarded one.[38] We can conclude confidently from the above evidence that the banks of Alabama gave the Bank full support.

Strangely, Georgia, immediately to the east of Alabama, showed strong and long lasting state bank hostility. On January 16th Biddle wrote to John Cumming, president of the branch in Savannah, asking whether the community and state banks will cooperate. He is encouraged to think this because of the failure of the proscriptive measure in the state legislature the previous winter. (See p. 60 and footnote 32, p. 60 for a description of this measure.) It shows decreasing hostility. But he concludes that he will take any kind of help Cumming can get.[39] Cumming answered on January 27th that he and Mr. Hunter, cashier of the branch in Savannah, agree that a memorial will be bad because there are very few friends of the Bank there, and the political leaders are to a man opposed. If a memorial is started a counter-memorial to Congress will be started at once. Among the signers will be public men and stockholders and officers of the local banks. Feeling that he and Hunter might be wrong, they have consulted friends of the Bank, but the latter have all agreed with them.[40]

Thus Georgia is the one state where there is strong evidence of state bank hostility. Knox said that until 1810 only branches of the Bank existed there. Progress in the state was not particularly noticeable: While other states were building cities, promoting manufactures, and building roads and canals, Georgia made few material gains from 1800 to 1810. People consequently grew dissatisfied with the Bank and wanted their own state banks free of federal control.[41]

State banks and the Bank seem to have been in continual con-

[37] Poe to Biddle, February 23, 1832, NBP.

[38] *Senate Journal*, 22nd Congress, 1st Session, p. 143.

[39] Biddle to Cumming, January 16, 1832, PLB.

[40] Cumming to Biddle, January 27, 1832, NBP.

[41] Knox, p. 572.

flict in Georgia from 1817 on. The Bank tried to compel specie payment and the state banks resisted through any scheme available. Bills of the state banks were protested, but since the sentiment in Georgia was with the home banks the Bank was unable to retain counsel in Georgia to press its claims. The legislature passed an act in 1820 repealing enough of the law providing for resumption of specie payments so that the law would not apply to a refusal of specie to the Bank by the chartered banks of the state. Hostile legislation continued to be passed as late as 1826.[42] The hostility in 1832 against the Bank has been attributed primarily to loyalty to Jackson, whose Indian policy was universally popular in Georgia and to the fact that it meant political defeat to any politician who opposed Jackson.[43] The congressional records show no memorials as having been received from Georgia.

Neither do the congressional records show any state bank memorials received from South Carolina, but this should not necessarily be interpreted as hostility. Actually the correspondence indicates an awareness on the part of the state banks of the value of the Bank, but fear forces them not to act as a body. James Johnson, president of the Charleston branch, is asked by Biddle for both citizens' and state banks' memorials. He is urged to consult Mr. Alexander and Mr. Pringle, directors of the Charleston branch.[44] Johnson responds that the banks as such will not send memorials for fear of a counterattack but that the directors of the banks as individuals will sign. If George McDuffie will emphasize the economic advantages of the United States Bank, it will make things much easier.[45]

Biddle also wrote to his friend John Potter, formerly of South Carolina but then living in New Jersey, to write and stir up Hayne and some of his old friends in South Carolina.[46] Potter answered on January 25th and enclosed a letter from Mr. Alexander. He is against the Bank. This so mortified Potter that he exclaims, "To what lengths the democrats will go!" He asks what state has benefited more than South Carolina from the Bank. Alexander claims that there could be a memorial from the citizens, but they fear a countermove. Not one

[42] *Ibid.*, p. 576.

[43] Govan, p. 176.

[44] Biddle to Johnson, January 16, 1832, PLB.

[45] Johnson to Biddle, January 23, 1832, NBP.

[46] Biddle to Potter, January 16, 1832, PLB.

state bank has the courage—(here a phrase is illegible) even though they know the advantages of the United States Bank.[47]

Knox said that the Bank started in South Carolina at the same time the first bank was chartered:

> It did a profitable business in sterling and domestic exchange . . . At the close of the Branch Bank of the United States there arose the necessity of a bank with a large capital to take the place of the Branch Bank. The old banks in Charleston had not accustomed themselves to handling, to any extent foreign exchange; they were very conservative in their business. The great staples for Carolina of cotton and rice were chiefly sold for foreign exchange.[48]

It would appear from this that the function of the Bank and the state banks differed sufficiently as not to have caused friction. However, in the absence of any positive evidence either for support or hostility, South Carolina will have to remain an unknown.[49]

Apparently Biddle made a special effort to stabilize the currency in North Carolina. One would therefore expect the state banks there to have been especially hostile because of the restraining hand of the Bank which had to be used to bring the local note issues in line. Just the opposite was true. Here again Biddle's letter to John Huske, president of the Fayetteville branch, shows that *because* the Bank stabilized the currency, there should have been support of the Bank in North Carolina—just the opposite to the now prevalent theory.[50] Biddle asks for memorials from citizens, but more especially state bank memorials.

He also wrote Browne, a friend of the Bank in Raleigh, stating that there is a great diversity among the delegates in Congress. This he regrets. He has taken great trouble to try to bring a healthy condition to the currency in North Carolina. Could an expression from citizens, state banks, or the legislature be had?[51]

There were three state banks in the state at that time, the State

---

[47] Potter to Biddle, January 25, 1832, NBP.

[48] Knox, p. 566.

[49] In *The History of the Banking Institutions Organized in South Carolina Prior to 1860* (Columbia: State Co., 1922) by Washington Augustus Clark, there is no reference to any hostility on the part of state banks towards the United States Bank.

[50] Biddle to Huske, January 16, 1832, PLB.

[51] Biddle to Browne, February 27, 1832, PLB.

Bank, the Cape Fear Bank, and the Bank at Newbern.[52] The first and last mentioned sent petitions for renewal to Congress.[53] The contents definitely challenge the theory that those state banks disciplined by the Bank were the most hostile. An additional reason for not being hostile was that the Bank of Cape Fear and the State Bank both owned stock in the Bank. The State Bank claimed $214,000 of specie of which $140,000 was in stock of the Bank on which the state bank drew interest.

Information about the relation between the state banks and the Bank in Virginia, the last southern state to be considered, is limited. In 1832 there were four mother banks together with their branches scattered throughout Virginia and what later became West Virginia. Knox reported very favorably on the adequacy of this system of banking.[54]

There were two branches of the Bank in Virginia, one in Richmond and the other in Norfolk. Biddle in writing R. Anderson, president of the Richmond branch, says that the Bank of Virginia (one of the four mother banks) has in its public reports borne very kindly testimony in favor of the Bank and might be disposed to assist the Bank on this occasion.[55] It is clear from this letter that state bank support was the *only* sort of help Biddle thought possible from Virginia. He continues to Anderson, "I am not I confess sanguine, for between the ultra-constitutionalist, and those who are personally interested, there is a very small space for our friends." Again in writing to George Newton, president of the Norfolk branch, for aid, he says, "I am not sanguine of aid from Virginia, but if any could be obtained, . . ."[56]

Records show only one memorial sent to Congress, and that from another parent bank, the Northwestern Bank at Wheeling with branches at Wellsburg, Parkersburg, and Jeffersonville—all situated in the western part of Virginia.[57] This indicates that we might claim 50 per cent support, two out of four parent banks.

To sum up: In the whole South and West only one state,

---

[52] Knox, p. 550.

[53] *Executive Documents*, 22nd Congress, 1st Session, vol. IV, doc. 166.

[54] Knox, p. 550.

[55] Biddle to Anderson, January 16, 1832, PLB.

[56] Biddle to Newton, January 16, 1832, PLB.

[57] *House Journal*, 22nd Congress, 1st Session, p. 385.

Georgia, can be recognized as clearly evincing strong state bank hostility. On the other hand, the banks of Louisiana, Mississippi, Alabama, North Carolina, and Ohio were active supporters of the Bank, offering between two-thirds and 100 per cent state bank support. We conclude, then, that we must not think of the banks of the South and West as being especially hostile, but that among existing state banks of that era, a heavy majority gave the Bank active support.

RICHARD H. BROWN*

The Jacksonian Pro-Slavery Party

Richard H. Brown's thoughtful essay argues persuasively that there was more to Jacksonian politics than was dreamed of in accounts that featured the alleged struggles for egalitarianism and social justice waged by the Democracy. Edward Channing long ago noted the debt the Jackson party owed the slaveholding South. Brown argues the centrality of the slavery issue after 1820. One need not agree with all the particulars of his thesis to appreciate the significance of slavery and the high importance attached to its defense by the party of Andrew Jackson, slave-owner.

✕✕

FROM THE INAUGURATION of Washington until the Civil War the South was in the saddle of national politics. This is the central fact in American political history to 1860. To it there are no exceptions, not even in that period when the "common man" stormed the ramparts of government under the banner of Andrew Jackson. In Jackson's day the chief agent of Southern power was a

---

* From Richard H. Brown, "The Missouri Crisis, Slavery, and the Politics of Jacksonianism," *South Atlantic Quarterly*, LXV (Winter, 1966), pp. 55–72.

Northern man with Southern principles, Martin Van Buren of New York. It was he who put together the party coalition which Andrew Jackson led to power. That coalition had its wellsprings in the dramatic crisis over slavery in Missouri, the first great public airing of the slavery question in ante bellum America.

I

More than anything else, what made Southern dominance in national politics possible was a basic homogeneity in the Southern electorate. In the early nineteenth century, to be sure, the South was far from monolithic. In terms of economic interest and social classes it was scarcely more homogeneous than the North. But under the diversity of interests which characterized Southern life in most respects there ran one single compelling idea which virtually united all Southerners, and which governed their participation in national affairs. This was that the institution of slavery should not be dealt with from outside the South. Whatever the merits of the institution—and Southerners violently disagreed about this, never more than in the 1820's—the presence of the slave was a fact too critical, too sensitive, too perilous for all of Southern society to be dealt with by those not directly affected. Slavery must remain a Southern question. In the ante bellum period a Southern politician of whatever party forgot this at his peril. A Northern politician might perceive it to his profit. There had been, Martin Van Buren noted with satisfaction late in life, a "remarkable consistency in the political positions" of Southern public men. With characteristic insouciance the Little Magician attributed this consistency to the natural superiority of republican principles which led them to win out in a region relatively untainted by the monied interest. But his partisan friend Rufus King, Van Buren admitted, ascribed it to the "black strap" of Southern slavery.

The insistence that slavery was uniquely a Southern concern, not to be touched by outsiders, had been from the outset a *sine qua non* for Southern participation in national politics. It underlay the Constitution and its creation of a government of limited powers, without which Southern participation would have been unthinkable. And when in the 1790's Jefferson and Madison perceived that a constitution was only the first step in guaranteeing Southern security, because a constitution meant what those who governed under it said it meant, it led to the creation of the first national political party to protect that Constitution against change by interpretation. The party which they constructed converted a Southern minority into a national majority through alliance with congenial interests outside the South. Organically, it represented an alliance between New York and Virginia, pulling between them Pennsylvania, and after them North Carolina, Georgia, and (at first) Kentucky and Tennessee, all states strongly subject to Virginia's influence. At bottom it rested on the support of people who lived on that rich belt of fertile farmland which stretched from the Great Lakes across upstate New York and Pennsylvania, southward through the Southern piedmont into Georgia, entirely oblivious of the Mason-Dixon line. North as well as South it was an area of prosperous, well-settled small farms. More farmers than capitalists, its residents wanted little from government but to be let alone. Resting his party on them, Jefferson had found a formula for national politics which at the same time was a formula for Southern pre-eminence. It would hold good to the Civil War.

So long as the Federalists remained an effective opposition, Jefferson's party worked as a party should. It maintained its identity in relation to the opposition by a moderate and pragmatic advocacy of strict construction of the Constitution. Because it had competition, it could maintain discipline. It responded to its constituent elements because it depended on them for support. But eventually its very success was its undoing. After 1815, stirred by the nationalism of the postwar era, and with the Federalists in decline, the Republicans took up Federalist positions on a number of the great public issues of the day, sweeping all before them as they did. The Federalists gave up the ghost. In the Era of Good Feelings which followed, everybody began to call himself a Republican, and a new theory of party amalgamation preached the doctrine that party division was bad and that a one-party system best served the national interest. Only gradually did it become apparent that in victory the Republican party had lost its identity—and its usefulness. As the party of the whole nation it ceased to be responsive to any particular elements in its constituency. It ceased to be responsive to the South.

When it did, and because it did, it invited the Missouri crisis of 1819–1820, and that crisis in turn revealed the basis for a possible configuration of national parties which eventually would divide the nation free against slave. As John Quincy Adams put it, the crisis had revealed "the basis for a new organization of parties . . . here was a new party ready formed, . . . terrible to the whole Union, but portentously terrible to the South—threatening in its progress the emancipation of all their slaves, threatening in its immediate effect that Southern domination which has swayed the Union for the last twenty years." Because it did so, Jefferson, in equally famous phrase, "considered it at once as the knell of the Union."

Adams and Jefferson were not alone in perceiving the significance of what had happened. Scarcely a contemporary missed the point. Historians quote them by the dozens as prophets—but usually *only* as prophets. In fact the Missouri crisis gave rise not to prophecy alone, but to action. It led to an urgent and finally successful attempt to revive the old Jeffersonian party and with it the Jeffersonian formula for Southern pre-eminence. The resuscitation of that party would be the most important story in American politics in the decades which followed.

II

In Jefferson's day the tie between slavery, strict construction of the Constitution, and the Republican party was implicit, not explicit. After Missouri it was explicit, and commented upon time and again in both public and private discussion. Perceptive Southerners saw (1) that unless effective means were taken to quiet discussion of the question, slavery might be used at any time in the future to force the South into a permanent minority in the Union, endangering all its interests; and (2) that if the loose constitutional construction of the day were allowed to prevail, the time might come when the government would be held to have the power to deal with slavery. Vital to preventing both of these—to keeping the slavery question quiet and to gaining a reassertion of strict construction principles—was the re-establishment of conditions which would make the party in power responsive once again to the South.

Not only did the Missouri crisis make these matters clear, but it shaped the conditions which would govern what followed. In the South it gave marked impetus to a reaction against the nationalism and amalgamationism of postwar Republicanism and handed the offensive to a hardy band of Old Republican politicians who had been crying in the wilderness since 1816. In the early 1820's the struggle between Old Republicans and New would be the stuff of Southern politics, and on the strength of the new imperatives to which the Missouri conflict gave rise the Old Republicans would carry off the victory in state after Southern state, providing thereby a base of power on which a new strict construction party could be reared.

For precisely the same reason that it gave the offensive to the Old Republicans of the South—because it portrayed the tie between slavery and party in starkest form—the Missouri crisis put Northern Old Republicans on the defense. Doing so, it handed the keys to national party success thereafter to whatever Northern leader could surmount charges of being pro-Southern and command the necessary Northern votes to bring the party to power. For that reason Thomas Jefferson's formula for national politics would become, when resurrected, Martin Van Buren's formula for national politics. What has long been recognized as happening to the Democratic party in the forties and fifties happened in fact in 1820. After Missouri and down to the Civil War the revised formula for Southern pre-eminence would involve the elevation to the presidency of Southerners who were predominantly Westerners in the public eye, or of Northern men with Southern principles.

Because they shaped the context of what was to come, the reactions to the Missouri crisis in the two citadels of Old Republican power, Richmond and Albany, were significant. Each cast its light ahead. As the donnybrook mounted in Congress in the winter of 1820, the Virginia capital was reported to be as "agitated as if affected by all the Volcanic Eruptions of Vesuvius." At the heart of the clamor were the Old Republicans of the Richmond Junto, particularly Thomas Ritchie's famous *Enquirer,* which spoke for the Junto and had been for years the most influential newspaper in the South. Associates of Jefferson, architects of Southern power, the Old Republicans were not long in perceiving the political implications of the crisis. Conviction grew in their minds that the point of Northern agitation was not Missouri at all but to use slavery as an anvil on which to forge a new party which would carry either Rufus King or DeWitt Clinton of New York to the presidency and force the South from power forever. But what excited them even more was the enormity of the price of peace which alone seemed likely to avert the disaster. This was the so-called Thomas Proviso, amending the Missouri bill to draw the ill-fated 36°30′ line across the Louisiana Purchase, prohibiting slavery in the territory to the north, giving up the lion's share to freedom.

No sooner had the proviso been introduced in Congress than the temper of the Old Republicans boiled over, and with prescient glances to the future they leapt to the attack. Ritchie challenged the constitutionality of the proviso at once in the *Enquirer,* a quarter century before Calhoun would work out the subtle dialectic of a Southern legal position. Nathaniel Macon agreed. "To compromise is to acknowledge the right of Congress to interfere and to legislate on the subject," he wrote; "this would be acknowledging too much." Equally important was the fact that, by prohibiting slavery in most of the West, the proviso forecast a course of national development ultimately intolerable to the South because, as Spencer Roane put it to Monroe, Southerners could not consent to be "dammed up in a land of Slaves." As the debates thundered to their climax, Ritchie in two separate editorials predicted that if the proviso passed, the South must in due time have Texas. "If we are cooped up on the north," he wrote with grim prophecy, "we must have elbow room to the west."

When finally the Southern Old Republicans tacitly consented to the Missouri Compromise, it was therefore not so much a measure of illusion about what the South had given up, as of how desperately necessary they felt peace to be. They had yielded not so much in the spirit of a bargain as in the spirit of a man caught in a holdup, who yields his fortune rather than risk his life in the hope that he may live to see a better day and perhaps even to get his fortune back. As Ritchie summed it up when news of the settlement reached Richmond, "Instead of joy, we scarcely ever recollect to have tasted of a bitterer cup." That they tasted it at all was because of the manipulative genius of Henry Clay, who managed to bring up the separate parts of the compromise separately in the House, enabling the Old Republicans to provide him his margin of victory on the closely contested Missouri bill while they saved their pride by voting to the end against the Thomas Proviso. They had not bound themselves by their votes to the proviso, as Ritchie warned they should not. If it was cold comfort for the moment, it was potent with significance for the future.

In fact, the vote on the proviso illuminated an important division in Southern sentiment. Thirty-seven slave state congressmen opposed it, while thirty-nine voted for it. On the surface the line of division ran along the Appalachian crest and the Potomac, pointing out seemingly a distinction in interest between the South Atlantic states on the one hand and those in the Southwest and mid-Atlantic regions on the other—between those states most characteristically Southern and those which in 1820 were essentially more Western or Northern in outlook. More fundamental, within each section it divided Southerners between those who were more sensitive to the relationship of slavery to politics and those who were less so; between those who thought the party formula for Southern pre-eminence and defense important and those who thought parties outmoded; between particularists and postwar Republican nationalists; between the proponents of an old Republican polity and the proponents of a new one as defined in the years of postwar exuberance; between those closest to Jefferson, such as the Richmond Junto and Macon, and those closest to Monroe, such as Calhoun. It was a division which prefigured Southern political struggles of the twenties. When two years later 70 per cent of those congressmen from the South Atlantic states who had opposed the Thomas Proviso returned to the next Congress, compared to 39 per cent of those who had supported it, it was a measure of the resurgence of Old Republicanism. Two years after that, in the chaotic presidential election of 1824, the Southerners who had opposed the proviso were the Southerners who sought to sustain the party caucus as a method of nominating in a vain attempt to restore old party discipline. Four years after that they marched back to power at last under the banner of Andrew Jackson, restoring to effectiveness in so doing a political system intended to make future Missouri crises impossible, and committed in due time to rectify the Thomas Proviso.

Equally important to the reaction in Richmond was what went on in Albany. There command of the state's Old Republicans was in the hands of the Bucktails, a group of which State Senator Martin Van Buren, at thirty-eight, was already master spirit. Opposed to the Bucktails was Governor DeWitt Clinton, an erstwhile Republican who drew a good deal of his support from former Federalists. With the Bucktails committed to the old Virginia-New York alliance, the Missouri question offered Clinton a heaven-sent opportunity; indeed there were those who suspected the ambitious governor of playing God himself and helping to precipitate the crisis. Whether or not this was true, Clinton tried desperately while the storm was raging in Washington to get a commitment from the Bucktails which would stamp them as proslavery, but the Bucktails acted cautiously. When a large meeting was called in Albany to indorse the prohibition of slavery in Missouri, Van Buren found it convenient to be off on circuit. When the Clintonians whipped a resolution indorsing the restriction through the legislature, not a Bucktail raised a voice in dissent. But for all their caution against public commitment it was generally understood both in Washington and New York that the Bucktails were anxious for peace, and that they supported the corporal's guard of Northern Republicans in congress who, retreating finally from the Missouri prohibition, made peace possible. Several of the Bucktail newspapers said as much, and despite the lack of public commitment on the part of party leaders, more than one Clintonian newspaper would brand them the "Slave Ticket" in the legislative elections which followed.

In private, Van Buren left no doubt where he stood, or where he meant to go once the storm had passed. No sooner had the compromise been adopted in Washington than the Little Magician got off a letter to his friendly rival Rufus King, promising at "some future day" to give that veteran Federalist his own views on the expediency of making slavery a party question, and remarking meanwhile that notwithstanding the strong public interest in the Missouri question, "the excitement which exists in regard to it, or which is likely to arise from it, is not so great as you suppose." It was a singularly important assessment of Northern public opinion for a politician who had fallen heir to a tattered Southern alliance, and in it King apprehensively saw the panorama of forty years of national politics stretching before him:

> The inveteracy of party feelings in the Eastern States [he wrote a friend], the hopes of influence and distinction by taking part in favor of the slave States, which call themselves, and are spoken of by others as the truly republican States and the peculiar friends of liberty, will keep alive & sustain a body considerably numerous, and who will have sufficient influence, to preserve to the slave States their disproportionate, I might say exclusive, dominance over the Union.

Twenty months after that, in the late fall of 1821, Van Buren set off for Washington as a newly elected United States senator. With his party having taken the measure of Clinton in the meantime, he carried with him into the lion's den of presidential politics effective command of the thirty-six uncommitted electoral votes of New York. If he would be the most disinterested statesman in all the land, he could not avoid for long the responsibility that went with that power. It was an opportunity to be used for large purposes or small, as a man might choose, and the Little Magician lost no time in indicating his intended course. Within weeks of his arrival he was pulling the strings of the New York delegation in the House to bring about return of the speakership to the slave states, from whom it had been wrested by a straight sectional vote upon Clay's retirement the year before. The new speaker was P. P. Barbour of Virginia, a leader of the Old Republican reaction in the South. Three months after that Van Buren was on his way to Richmond to plan the resurrection of the Old Republican Party.

That he should do so was partly for reasons of personal ambition, partly because the Bucktails after years of frustrating struggle with Clinton had their own clear reasons for wanting to redraw party lines. Beyond this there would appear to be the simple fact that Van Buren believed implicitly in the whole system of republican polity as Thomas Jefferson had staked it out. Committed to the principle of the least possible government, the Republican party was the defender of that republican liberty which was the sole political concern of the disinterested agrarian constituency for which, through life, Van Buren saw himself as a spokesman, and which constituted the majority of Americans. That majority was strongest where it was purest, least subject to the corrupting power of money. That was in the South. Slavery was a lesser issue than republicanism. Nor was it by any means clear in 1820 that agitation was the best way to deal with it. For while some who were nominally Old Republicans, such as Senator William Smith of South Carolina, were beginning to argue that slavery was a positive good, it was generally true that no men in America were more honestly committed to the notion that the institution was wrong than those men of Jeffersonian conscience who were the Old Republicans of the South. Eleven years later, in 1831, some of them would mount in the Virginia legislature the last great effort south of the Mason-Dixon line to abolish slavery. It required no very extended rationalization to argue in 1820 that the whole perplexing question would be best left in their hands, even if in fact the North had the right to take it up. Particularly was this true when, as Van Buren put it, the motives of those in the North who sought to take it up were "rather [more] political than philanthropical." Because he believed as he did, Van Buren's efforts to revive party distinctions and restore the Old Republican Party were to be more than a mere matter of machinations with politicians, looking toward the making of the Democratic party. He looked to Southern power, and he would quiet the slavery question if he could. He was dealing with the root principle of the whole structure of ante bellum politics.

III

In the long history of the American presidency no election appears quite so formless as that of 1824. With no competing party to force unity on the Republicans, candidates who could not command the party nomination were free to defy it. They did so, charging that "King Caucus" was undemocratic. Eventually no fewer than four candidates competed down to the wire, each a Republican, every man for himself. Because they divided the electoral votes between them, none came close to a majority, and the election went to the House of Representatives. There, with the help of Henry Clay, John Quincy Adams outpolled the popular Andrew Jackson and the caucus nominee, William H. Crawford of Georgia, and carried off the prize.

Historians, viewing that election, look at King Caucus too much through the eyes of its opponents, who stated that the caucus represented an in-group of political officeholders attached to Crawford and anxious to preserve their own political power. In fact it was the Old Republicans who organized the caucus, not so much to sustain Crawford and preserve power as to revive the Virginia-New York party and regain power. They took up Crawford unenthusiastically because he came closest to the Old Republican pattern, and because he alone of all the candidates could hope to carry Virginia. They took up the caucus at the behest of Van Buren after two years of searching for a method of nominating which would command the support of all, because four years after Missouri the only hope of winning New York for a Southern candidate was to present him, however unpopularly, as the official party nominee.

Hidden in the currents and crosscurrents of that campaign was the reiterated issue of party versus amalgamation. Behind it, in turn, were repeated pleas by Old Republican presses, North and South alike, that unless genuine Republicans agreed on a method of choosing a candidate the division must be along sectional lines, in which case a Federalist or proto-Federalist might sneak into the White House. Behind it too was the repeated warning that party organization alone would make democracy work. Without it, the Old Republicans correctly prophesied, the election would end up in the House of Representatives, subject to the worst kind of political intrigue, and with the votes of the smallest states the equals of those of populous Virginia and New York.

When the caucus failed it was because amalgamation had destroyed the levers which made party discipline possible. Exhortation could not restore them. Meantime the issue of democracy had been turned against the advocates of party, because in key states like New York and North Carolina they tried to use the power of the party organizations for Crawford, bucking more popular candidates such as Jackson and Adams. It was a bogus issue. The real issue was whether a party was necessary to make democracy work, and because they were more nearly right than their opponents about this, and the election in the House shortly proved it, the Old Republicans would recover quickly after 1824, after Crawford and the caucus issue were politically dead. Let circumstances limit the number of candidates, and tie up party and democracy on the same side, and the results would be different another time.

In the campaign of 1824 and the years immediately following, the slavery issue was never far below the surface. The Denmark Vesey conspiracy for an insurrection in Charleston (now a subject of controversy among historians) was to contemporaries a grim reminder of the Missouri debates, and it was attributed publicly to Rufus King's speeches on the Missouri question. In 1823-1824 some Southerners suspected that an attempt by Secretary of State Adams to conclude a slave trade convention with Great Britain was an attempt to reap the benefit of Northern anti-slavery sentiment; and some, notably Representative John Floyd of Virginia, sought to turn the tables on Adams by attacking him for allegedly ceding Texas to Spain in the Florida treaty, thus ceding what Floyd called "two slaveholding states" and costing "the Southern interest" four Senators.

Old Republicans made no bones about their concern over the issue, or their fear that it might be turned against them. In the summer of 1823 an illuminating editorial debate broke out between the New York *American,* which spoke the thoughts of the old Federalists in New York, and the Richmond *Enquirer.* So vehemently had the *American* picked up a report of a plan to revise the Illinois constitution to admit slavery that Ritchie charged its editors with reviving the slave question to put New York into the lap of the "Universal Yankee Nation" and to put the South under the "ban of the Empire." "Call it the Missouri question, the Illinois question, what you please; it was the *Slave question,*" Ritchie shrilled, which the *American* was seeking to get up for political purposes. Shortly, the Albany *Argus* got into the argument. The *Argus,* which got its signals from Van Buren and spoke the thoughts of New York's Old Republicans, charged the *American* with trying to revive the slave question to "abrogate the old party distinctions" and "organize new ones, founded in the territorial prejudices of the people." "The more general question of the North and South," the *Argus* warned, "will be urged to the uttermost, by those who can never triumph when they meet the democracy of the country, openly, and with the hostility they bear towards it." Over and over the debate rang out the argument that the attempt to revive party distinctions was an attempt to allay sectional prejudices, and by the time the debate was over only the most obtuse citizen could have missed the point.

Nor was the election of Adams destined to calm Southern fears on issues having to do with slavery. A series of incidents early in 1825 suggested that the New Englander's election had made anti-slavery advocates more bold, and Southern tempers grew shorter in the summer of 1825 than they had been at any time since Missouri. One of the incidents was a reported argument before the Supreme Court in the case of the South Carolina Negro Seaman's Act by Attorney General William Wirt, stating that slavery was "inconsistent with the laws of God and nature." A second was a resolution offered in the Senate a scant nine days after Adams' election by Rufus King, proposing to turn the proceeds from the sale of western lands to the emancipation and export of slaves, through the agency of the American Colonization Society. In the same week the New Jersey legislature proposed a system of foreign colonization which "would, in due time, effect the entire emancipation of the slaves in our country." John Floyd enclosed a copy of the New Jersey resolution to Claiborne Gooch, Ritchie's silent partner on the *Enquirer,* with salient warning:

> Long before this manifestation I have believed, connected with the Missouri question, would come up the general question of slavery, upon the principles avowed by Rufus King in the Senate . . .
> If this indication is well received, who can tell, after the elevation of Mr. A. to the presidency—that he, of Missouri effort, or DeWitt C. or some such aspirant, may not, for the sake of that office, fan this flame—to array the non-slaveholding States against the Slaveholding states, and finally quiet our clamor or opposition, by the application of the slaves knife to our throats. Think of this much, and often.

Meantime, the New York *Commercial Advertiser* expressed publicly the hope that Adams' administration would introduce "a new era, when the northern, eastern, and non-slaveholding states, will assume an attitude in the Union, proportionate to their moral and physical power." Ritchie responded hotly in an editorial asking what the designs of such a combination would be against the "southern and *slave-holding* states." Soon in Georgia the Old Republican Governor George M. Troup, at the instigation of Senator John M. Berrien, put before the legislature a request for resolutions stating slavery to be exclusively within the control of the states and asking that the federal government "abstain from intermeddling." In May there was another violent editorial exchange between the New York *American* and the *Enquirer,* growing out of an *American* editorial which attacked the "slave press" and taunted the South with the comment that "the sceptre has departed from Judah, and those who have long ruled must be content to obey." Ritchie picked up the taunt as a challenge to the South, admitting that slavery was evil but insisting pointedly that the South had "too much at stake" to allow decisions on the matter by men ignorant of Southern "habits, manners, and forms of society." Ultimately, the Virginian concluded belligerently, Southern defense would be found in the traditional mechanisms of national politics: "Mr. John Adams the 2d is now upon his trial, [and] his friends consult as little his own interest as the public good, by conjuring up these prejudices against the *Slave people.* Should they persevere in their misguided policy, it will require no prophet to foretell that the son will share the fate of his father."

With the slavery issue thus drawn taut, the Old Republicans recovered quickly from the setback of 1824. Calhoun's inveterate foe William Smith was returned to the Senate from South Carolina, completing for the moment an Old Republican sweep of the South Atlantic states begun in 1821, a sweep which put Calhoun's political career in jeopardy and forced the Carolinian, now vice president, to break with Adams. For the Old Republicans, moreover, Adams made an infinitely better target than Monroe. The high-toned nationalism of the New Englander, combined with popular revulsion to the alleged bargain which secured his election, put the kiss of death on amalgamation as a political theory. The stage was set, under more favorable circumstances, for the Old Republicans to try again.

IV

For all the illuminating insights into Jacksonianism to which Americans have been treated in recent years, Jacksonian politics are still interpreted in Victorian terms, along classic lines descended from an early biographer of Jackson, James Parton, who recorded them one hundred years ago. To the Victorians, it is perhaps not too much to say, most of history could be ultimately attributed either to whores or to the unbridled pursuit of ambition. It was a simple view of history, and the Jacksonians got both barrels, one through the beguiling story of Peggy Eaton, the other through the notion of a sterile and essentially meaningless struggle for the succession between Van Buren and Calhoun. As Parton quaintly put it, "the political history of the United States, for the last thirty years, dates from the moment when the soft hand of Mr. Van Buren touched Mrs. Eaton's knocker."

When finally it rode to power, the Jacksonian party was made up of two clearly discernible and distinct wings. One comprised the original Jacksonians, those who had supported him in 1824 when he ran on his own, bereft, like all the rest, of party, and nearly of allies. As measured in that election this strength was predominantly in the West. It spilled over into a few states east of the mountains, most notably Pennsylvania, where the chaos of the existing political structure enabled Jackson as military hero to ride roughshod over all the rest. But this was all. The Western vote, especially when shared with Clay, amounted in electoral terms to little. Even with the votes of the Carolinas, thrown to him gratuitously by Calhoun and counting one-quarter of his total, he was far short of an electoral majority. To get even this much he had been formally before the public for two years, and all his considerable natural appeal as a Westerner and a hero had gone into the bargain.

After 1824 Jackson found himself the candidate of a combined opposition. The concrete measure of difference between defeat in 1824 and victory in 1828 was the Old Republican strength of the South Atlantic states and New York, brought to the Jackson camp carefully tended and carefully drilled by Van Buren. Nearly equal in size to the original Jackson following, they constituted a political faction far older, far more permanent, far more purposeful, far better led, and in the long run far more important. Their purposes were set forth by Van Buren in a notable letter to Ritchie in January, 1827, proposing support of the old hero. Such support, as the New Yorker put it, would be "the best and probably the only practicable mode of concentrating the entire vote of the opposition & of effecting what is of still greater importance, the substantial reorganization of the Old Republican Party." It would "restore a better state of things, by combining Genl Jackson's personal popularity with the portion of old party feeling yet remaining." It would aid Republicans of the

North and middle states "by substituting *party principle* for *personal preference* as one of the leading points in the contest. . . Instead of the question being between a northern and Southern man, it would be whether or not the ties, which have hitherto bound together a great political party should be severed." Most important, its effects would be highly salutary for the South:

> We must always have party distinctions and the old ones are the best of which the nature of the case admits. Political combinations between the inhabitants of the different states are unavoidable & the most natural & beneficial to the country is that between the planters of the South and the plain Republicans of the north. The country has once flourished under a party thus constituted & may again. It would take longer than our lives (even if it were practicable) to create new party feelings to keep those masses together. If the old ones are suppressed, geographical divisions founded on local interests or, what is worse prejudices between free and slave holding states will inevitably take their place. Party attachment in former times furnished a complete antidote for sectional prejudices by producing counteracting feelings. It was not until that defence had been broken down that the clamour agt. Southern Influence and African Slavery could be made effectual in the North . . . Formerly, attacks upon Southern Republicans were regarded by those of the north as assaults upon their political brethren & resented accordingly. This all powerful sympathy has been much weakened, if not, destroyed by the amalgamating policy . . . it can & ought to be revived.

Lastly, Van Buren noted, a Jackson administration brought to power by the "concerted effort of a political party, holding in the main, to certain tenets & opposed to certain prevailing principles" would be a far different thing from one brought to power by the popularity of a military hero alone. An administration brought to power by Old Republican votes would be governed by Old Republican principles. Van Buren would make himself the guarantor of that.

Because the Jacksonian party was what it was, Jacksonian policy was what it was, and Jacksonian politics as well. Because the administration rested on an Old Republican alliance which bridged the Mason-Dixon line and linked New York with the Old South, the two most important steps in the development of Jacksonian policy were the veto of the Maysville Road bill and the veto of the bill to recharter the Bank of the United States. Whatever the social and economic consequences of each, they were in their origins political measures, designed to solidify and hold together the Old Republican party; and they were predicated, each of them, on a strict construction of the Constitution. And, too, because its political base was what it was, the one great question of public policy which nearly brought the administration to disaster, one with which it could not deal and never did, was the tariff.

No less important, it was the structure of the Jackson party which gave meaning to—and dictated the course of—that struggle between Van Buren and Calhoun which bulks so large in the politics of the Jackson years. It was far more than an empty struggle for the succession. Its essence was competition between two conflicting ideas as to how best to protect Southern security in the Union, and thus, inferentially, how to preserve the Union itself. One of those ideas was the old Jeffersonian idea, resuscitated by Van Buren, sustained by the Jackson party and by the Democratic party until the Civil War. It was that Southern security rested ultimately on the maintenance in national office of a political party which would be responsive to the South because dependent on it for election. A political answer, not a doctrinaire one, it was product of the practical, pragmatic, and thoroughly political minds of Thomas Jefferson and Martin Van Buren. It depended for its success on the winning of national elections by a party which would maintain its identity in relation to the opposition as a states' rights—strict construction party, but which would at the same time be moderate, flexible, pragmatic in tone, able to win support in the North as well as the South if it would serve its purpose.

Counter to this was the proposition developed by John C. Calhoun. Last of the Southern nationalists, Calhoun had held to his position through 1824, long after the Old Republicans had routed Southern nationalism in every state but his own. In the mid-twenties, with his own political strength at rock bottom, his hold slipping even in South Carolina, Calhoun made his portentous switch from Nationalist to Sectionalist, squaring the two in his own mind with the development of a counter theory to that of the Jeffersonians. This was that Southern security was dependent in the last analysis on the maintenance of an effective Southern power to veto anything it didn't like—thus nullification—and that failing, on the right to secede. In contrast to the political and moderate remedy of the Old Republicans, this was a constitutional remedy, product of the brilliant legal, doctrinaire, and essentially nonpolitical mind of the great Carolinian.

That Van Buren won out over Calhoun in the Jackson years had nothing to do fundamentally with Mrs. Eaton or with a long chronicle of personal intrigue. It had everything to do with the fact that the Old Republican moderates controlled the South, all but South Carolina, almost that, in the twenties. While Calhoun brought only South Carolina and some personal support in Congress to the Jackson fold, Van Buren brought all the rest of the South, and New York as well. The fact was not lost on Jackson or his Tennessee friends, either before his election or after. Van Buren's triumph over Calhoun was won not on Washington backstairs after 1829 but on the Southern hustings in the early twenties. Two years before it came to power the Jackson party was already, in fact, a Jackson–Van Buren party.

V

There were postscripts, too, which harked back to the structure of the Jackson party, to the Missouri question, and to the political prophecies of Thomas Ritchie, woven into the very fabric of the party by the skilled political weaver from New York. First of these was that the Jackson party, the issue once raised, was committed to Texas. When in 1844 a new drumfire of antislavery sentiment in the North made it impossible for Van Buren to honor that commitment, Ritchie and Van Buren, after nearly a quarter century of fruitful political teamwork, would part company, and Van Buren would give up leadership of the party he had created. After 1844 the party of the Jeffersonian formula sustained itself in the face of the rising slavery issue by giving vent to its expansionist tendencies; and the Northern man with Southern principles who replaced Van Buren was in fact a Northwestern man with Southern principles, Stephen A. Douglas of Illinois. It was to be Douglas, governed by the irresistible logic of the party structure, who carried through Congress finally, in 1854, the repeal of the Missouri Compromise. And when three years after that the Supreme Court in the Dred Scott decision held the Thomas Proviso of the Missouri Compromise unconstitutional, as Ritchie and Nathaniel Macon had said it was thirty-seven years before, who were the judges who comprised the majority? Of six, one had been appointed in 1846 by "Young Hickory" James K. Polk, a second in 1853 by the next successful Democrat, Franklin Pierce. The four others were James M. Wayne of Georgia, coadjutor of Van Buren's Georgia lieutenant John Forsyth, appointed to the court by Jackson in 1835; Roger B. Taney of Maryland, appointed by Jackson in 1836; John Catron, Van Buren campaign manager in Tennessee, appointed by Jackson in 1837; and Peter V. Daniel of Virginia, long-time member of the Richmond Junto, confidante of Thomas Ritchie, appointed in 1841 by Van Buren.

A Bibliographical Note

One reason this note can be very brief is that a number of historiographical essays on the massive Jacksonian political literature have been published. Most useful is Alfred A. Cave, *Jacksonian Democracy and the Historians* (Gainesville, 1964), an entire book devoted to summarizing important interpretations printed prior to its publication. Also valuable are Edwin A. Miles, "The Jacksonian Era," in *Writing Southern History,* edited by Arthur S. Link and Rembert W. Patrick (Louisiana State, 1965); Charles G. Sellers, Jr., "Andrew Jackson versus the Historians," *Mississippi Valley Historical Review, XLIV* (March, 1958), pp. 615–634; and the bibliographical essays in Glyndon G. Van Deusen, *The Jacksonian Era, 1828–1848* (New York, 1959); Robert V. Remini, *Andrew Jackson and the Bank War* (New York, 1967), and Edward Pessen, *Jacksonian America: Society, Personality and Politics* (Homewood, 1969). For an original and provocative comparison of the interpretations of Arthur M. Schlesinger, Jr., and Lee Benson, see Gene Wise, "Political 'Reality,' in Recent American Scholarship: Progressives versus Symbolists," *American Quarterly, XIX* (Summer, 1967), pp. 303–328.

In view of the comprehensiveness of the above works, a bibliographer's most useful contribution is to cite a select number of important writings too recent to have been included in most of them. In addition to the writings reprinted here, I would recommend the following publications for their importance and originality: Alvin W. Kass, *Politics in New York State, 1800–1830* (Syracuse, 1965); Thomas B. Alexander, Kit C. Carter, Jack R. Lister, Jerry C. Old-shue, and Winfred G. Sandlin, "Who Were the Alabama Whigs?" *Alabama Review*, XVI (January, 1963), pp. 5–19; John Vollmer Mering, *The Whig Party in Missouri* (Columbia, 1967); Donald B. Cole, "The Presidential Election of 1832 in New Hampshire," *Historical New Hampshire*, XXI (Winter, 1966), pp. 32–50; Joel H. Silbey, *The Shrine of Party* (Pittsburgh, 1967); Peter J. Coleman, *The Transformation of Rhode Island, 1790–1860* (Providence, 1963); Robert V. Remini, *Andrew Jackson* (New York, 1966); Glyndon G. Van Deusen, *William Henry Seward* (New York, 1967); Kinley J. Brauer, *Cotton Versus Conscience: Massachusetts Whig Politics and Southwestern Expansion, 1843–1848* (Lexington, 1967); Edward Pessen, *Most Uncommon Jacksonians* (Albany, 1967); Richard P. McCormick, "New Perspectives on Jacksonian Politics," *American Historical Review*, LXV (January, 1960), pp. 288–301, and Mc-Cormick, "Suffrage Classes and Party Alignments: A Study in Voter Behavior," *Mississippi Valley Historical Review*, XLVI (December, 1959), pp. 397–410; Frank Otto Gatell, "Spoils of the Bank War: Political Bias in the Selection of Pet Banks," *American Historical Review*, LXX (October, 1964), pp. 35–58, and Gatell, "Sober Second Thoughts on Van Buren, the Albany Regency, and the Wall Street Conspiracy," *Journal of American History*, LIII (June, 1966), pp. 19–40; Lynn L. Marshall, "The Genesis of Grass-Roots Democracy in Kentucky," *Mid-America*, XLVII (October, 1965), pp. 269–287; William H. Freehling, *Prelude to Civil War: The Nullification Controversy in South Carolina* (New York, 1966); and Charles G. Sellers' continuing biography of James K. Polk (Princeton), two volumes of which have been completed. Whether they have been included elsewhere or not, every modern bibliographical account should list: John W. Ward, *Andrew Jackson, Symbol For an Age* (New York, 1955); Marvin Meyers, *The Jacksonian Persuasion* (Stanford, 1957); and, of course, Arthur M. Schlesinger, Jr., *The Age of Jackson* (Boston, 1945).